CONTENTS

THE PRESSURE OF THE SARS CRISIS ON THE REFORM
(in lieu of a preface) i

**NEW STAGE, NEW IDEAS AND NEW BREAK-
THROUGHS** 1
   New Stage, New Ideas and New Breakthroughs 3
   China: WTO Accession and the New Stage of Reform ... 14
   China: WTO Accession and New Breakthroughs in Reform ... 23
   Proposals for Actively and Steadily Pushing Forward Structural Reform ... 45
   Ten Major Issues Facing China's Reform of the Property Rights System ... 64

SHIFT IN GOVERNMENT FUNCTIONS AND THE DEVELOPMENT OF NGOS ... 79
   Government Reform in China's New Stage of Reform and Opening Up ... 81
   The Process of the Market-oriented Reform and the Development of NGOs in China ... 90

WTO ACCESSION AND THE NEW STAGE OF OPENING TO THE OUTSIDE WORLD ... 103
   The New Stage of China's Opening Up ... 105
   Promote Development by Opening Up and Make Chinese Economy More Internationalised in an All-round Way ... 117
   Promoting Reform by Opening Up, so as to Spur the Process of China's Economic Transition ... 134
   China's WTO Accession and Asian Regional Economic Cooperation ... 141

The Concept of a "China Free Trade Area"
— The prospects for economic and trade relations among China's Mainland, Hong Kong, Macao and Taiwan within the WTO framework 151

THOROUGH NATIONAL TREATMENT FOR FARMERS 167
Proposals on Giving Farmers National Treatment 169

Increasing Farmers' Income Needs New Ideas 177

Giving Land-use Right to Farmers 194

NEW TOPICS IN THE REFORM OF CHINA'S INFRASTRUCTURE AND PUBLIC UTILITIES SECTOR 201
New Topics in the Next-step Reform of China's Infrastructure and Public Utilities Sector 203

China's WTO Accession and New Breakthroughs in the Reform of the Infrastructure and Public Utilities Sector 210

Reform in the Infrastructure and Public Utilities Sector and China's Opening-up Drive 224

Break Monopoly and Introduce Competition to Establish an Adequate Market Competition Mechanism 238

Opening Markets and Accelerating Industrial Reorganization in the Infrastructure and Public Utilities Sector 252

Reconstructing the Government Regulatory and Supervisory System so that It Properly Matches an Open Economy 266

THE ENTREPRENEURSHIP SYSTEM AND ESOP IN THE NEW STAGE OF REFORM 281
China's WTO Accession and Innovations in the Enterprise System 283

Innovations in the Entrepreneurship System in the New Stage of China's Reform 292

Definition of the Value of China's Pioneering Entrepreneurs 304

The Practice of ESOP in China Needs to Be Standardized 314

CHINA: THE NEW STAGE OF REFORM

by Chi Fulin

Foreign Languages Press

First Edition   2004

Home Page:
  http://www.flp.com.cn
E-mail Addresses:
  info@flp.com.cn
  sales@flp.com.cn

ISBN 7-119-03484-7
© Foreign Languages Press, Beijing, China, 2004
Published by Foreign Languages Press
24 Baiwanzhuang Road, Beijing 100037, China
Distributed by China International Book Trading Corporation
35 Chegongzhuang Xilu, Beijing 100044, China
P.O. Box 399, Beijing, China
Printed in the People's Republic of China

THE PRESSURE OF THE SARS CRISIS ON THE REFORM

(in lieu of a preface)

My Two Preliminary Reflections

1. China is in a crucial period of economic and social transition, and an unexpected social event can have a bearing on the overall situation. If not well handled, it may lead to a certain degree of social crisis. This is determined by three sets of situations. First, in the process of economic and social transition, social contradictions and problems shoot up daily, and so do uncertainties that are likely to touch off economic risks and social crises. Second, in the course of economic transition, the traditional governance structure is in a process of all-round reform, while the new social governance structure and mechanism is still in a process of being established and improved, resulting in a weak ability of the government and the society as a whole to handle sudden disasters, and an imperfect management mechanism. This will often land the government and the entire society in a passive position at the onset of a disaster. Addressing the Special China-Asean (Association of Southeast Asian Nations) Leaders' Meeting on SARS, Premier Wen Jiabao gave an objective account of the real situation in China, as follows: "In face of the outbreak of this sudden epidemic, we lack experience for its

prevention and control. The crisis management mechanism and the work of certain localities and departments are not adequate. Due to these factors and, in particular, China's huge and highly mobile population, we are still faced with a serious situation despite a great deal of hard work." Third, against the general trend of globalization, China is faced with growing uncertainties as it strengthens economic and social ties with other countries and some unexpected social events are often of an international nature. Some unexpected international events will also quickly spill over to China, and vice versa. This is an important pattern of an unexpected event in terms of its outbreak and spreading in an open society. From this it can be seen that it is far from enough to assess only the impact of the SARS crisis on the Chinese economy; it will produce some inestimable effects not only on its economic development but also on its social stability and relations with other countries.

2. China faces a difficult choice in responding to and handling unexpected social events in this period of economic transition. For example, the government is in the midst of shifting from an omnipotent to a limited government, with its functions aiming primarily at economic development stronger than those aiming primarily at providing public products and effective public services. During economic transition, the government's role in economic development is very important. However, as the market economy has developed to a certain extent and social uncertainties have grown, the government should strengthen its functions in the sphere of social services. The inadequate crisis management mechanism and the work of some localities and departments in the early stage of the SARS epidemic were, as far as their objective side is concerned, a reflection of the difficult choice that the government functions face in the course of the country's transition. This shows that the SARS epidemic reflected and revealed some of our institutional flaws. If we have to speak about pressures, then this is where the greatest pressure comes from. A clear understanding of this point will help us to move faster with the reform by turning the pressures into a motive force.

The Pressure of the SARS Crisis on the Reform

I. Pressure on Government Reform

I once suggested that the government functions should shift from giving priority to economic objectives to giving priority to social objectives, so as to meet the needs of economic and social transition. The main reason is that with the reform and opening up approaching a new stage, the adjustment of various social interest relations and the solution to major social problems have become the main preconditions for realizing sustained economic growth. Therefore, the government should create a good social environment for sustained economic growth in terms of employment, social security, market order and other areas. The SARS crisis has once again shown that it is a very urgent and important matter for the government to redefine its functions as giving priority to addressing various major social problems. At the same time, fighting the SARS epidemic helped us to see clearly that the government has many tasks to tackle in its efforts to build a crisis management mechanism. For example, a) the building of a government crisis management mechanism; b) the building of a mechanism with regard to government credibility; c) the building of a government financial resources and social mobilization mechanism; d) the building of a government information release mechanism. To strengthen the building of a government emergency management mechanism on the basis of summing up the experience and lessons drawn from the anti-SARS work will speed up the government reform, and remarkably improve its ability and level of managing emergencies.

II. Pressure on Media Reform

It is the social responsibility of the government and media to provide truthful and reliable information to the society. Especially in the age of globalization, such information not only affects the health and personal safety of the citizens of the country in question, but also is directly related to the health and personal safety of nationals of other countries. Information should be made public, and, especially in the case of information about disasters that concern major public interests, it is all the more necessary to provide it to the public promptly and accurately. Both international and domestic experiences have proved that in handling emergencies, nothing is more important than a timely and objective disclosure of information. In contrast, any cover-up, failure to report or inadequate reporting will do inestimable harm. In an open society there are many channels for disseminating information, and people have an ever-stronger demand for information, especially about emergencies. It is necessary to seriously sum up the experiences and lessons from the SARS crisis, and speed up media reform, so as to keep pace with such an objective trend and actual needs. From an objective point of view, China's current media management system is seriously at odds with the requirements for building an open society. Social reality shows us that we should not place the disclosure of information about major social events and emergencies under the traditional scope of ideology, to say nothing of the fact that even the traditional ideology management system also needs reform. China Central Television (CCTV) televised the war on Iraq live on three of its channels. Then, why should not CCTV have opened a 24-hour special coverage of SARS, so that people across the country could have had prompt access to comprehensive, on-the-spot and detailed information on SARS prevention and control, and updates on the epidemic. This would have helped them do a better job in the epidemic prevention and control, and prevented the epidemic from getting out of control and causing people to panic for lack of information. Therefore, I suggest that during the fight against SARS, certain traditional controls in that area should be lifted to allow the relevant media to gather news, report and comment without any restrictions within the limits of the law during this period and in this area, and to exercise supervision over possible dereliction of duty, shirking of responsibility and embezzlement of relief funds in the fight against SARS and related fund-raising activities.

III. Pressure on Reform of Medical Care System

The outbreak of the SARS epidemic has revealed that our current medical care system is seriously flawed. If SARS had occurred mainly in the countryside, where medical facilities are poor, instead of in cities, the consequences would have been unthinkable. Now, it is extremely important to prevent such epidemics from spreading to the countryside. Under the pressure of the SARS crisis, we should seriously consider the reform of the current medical care system. For example, first, it is necessary to strengthen the building of the rural public medical care system; second, it is necessary to speed up the building of a public health pre-warning and emergency management system; third, it is necessary to build a public security mechanism for highly contagious diseases by which the central government openly undertakes to give free medical treatment to all SARS-infected patients and suspects within Chinese territory, with all expenses to be borne by the central treasury. I further suggest that we should lose no time in solving various major questions involved in the establishment and improvement of a comprehensive social security system, including reform of the medical care system. This is the most basic work for managing various types of unexpected social events.

IV. Pressure on Social Reform

In an open society, the handling of an emergency will depend largely on the degree of mobilization and participation of social forces, as the government has proved unequal to many tasks, and should have faith in social forces and expand the channels of social participation. A more developed civil society can form a good, harmonious and interactive relationship with the forces of the state. I suggest the following: First, an urban community self-management system be set up as soon as possible, with a view to enabling communities to perform their full social functions of sharing the anti-epidemic work. Second, various types of non-governmental organizations (NGOs) should be nurtured and developed so that they can play a major role in mobilizing and organizing the social forces to participate in the handling of emergencies. In the recent fight against the SARS, various professional societies and NGOs were encouraged to mobilize wide participation in society through various effective forms, and thus played their role in social stability. Third, relevant Chinese NGOs should be supported in carrying out cooperation with specialized international organizations in the fight against SARS. At present, few Chinese NGOs parallel specialized international organizations and international volunteer groups, and there are even fewer non-governmental foundations that are in a position to accept donations of various types. This situation should be changed as soon as possible.

V. Pressure on reform of the Cadre and Personnel System

During the SARS epidemic the actions and attitudes of relevant departments and local officials reflected certain drawbacks in the current cadre and personnel system. Therefore, I suggest that, first, since some officials attached excessive importance to the GDP among the indicators of performance appraisal, and treated the epidemic as a "major accident" in places under their jurisdiction lest they fail appraisal on just that score, such a system of cadre appraisal and appointment that holds cadres accountable only to the higher levels but not accountable for the lives and property of the people is in urgent need of reform. Second, the news media and democratic parties should exercise timely supervision over the government, and help it improve its decision-making. The government should admit mistakes and apologize to the victims and to the general public in good time if losses are caused by its ineffective measures. Third, government officials who are directly responsible for the spreading of the SARS epidemic, those who deserted their posts at a critical juncture and those who have been held responsible for other faults should be punished through fair and rigorous legal procedures, so as to assuage the public discontent. And fourth, in a special period, every move of the government should be placed under the close scrutiny of the public. To the government, the fight against the SARS epidemic was an opportunity to serve the people in a down-to-earth manner, improve its image and rebuild its credibility. The supreme principle it should follow can only be "life above everything else, people above everything else."

Chi Fulin

May 1, 2003
Haikou

NEW STAGE, NEW IDEAS AND NEW BREAKTHROUGHS

NEW STAGE, NEW IDEAS AND NEW BREAKTHROUGHS

— Some reflections on ways to bring about new breakthroughs in reform

(*November 2002*)

Since the advent of the new millennium, and especially in face of economic globalization and the country's accession to the World Trade Organization (WTO), China has entered a new stage in its reform. China has achieved significant and many-faceted breakthroughs and progress in its economic restructuring over the past two decades and more. Today, as economic and social interests have become increasingly more complex, the reform faces many new contradictions and problems. Compared with the tasks of the reform in the past, the future ones will be even more profound, complicated and pressing. Therefore, it is essential to make an in-depth analysis of some major contradictions and problems involved in the reform, in order to bring about new breakthroughs in the new stage. I believe that examining problems on three levels is prerequisite for achieving success in this new stage.

I. The reform has entered a new stage characterized by an all-out tackling of serious issues, with emphasis on adjusting interests in an all-round way.

How can we define the new stage of reform? Generally speaking, it is a new stage of reform in the circumstances of all-round opening to the outside world in the wake of the country's accession to the WTO, a new stage for pushing forward various reform tasks and adjusting interests in a comprehensive way. The problem is that we are faced with three outstanding problems now after more than two decades of reform. First, some reform tasks are not yet completed, because the reform of the property right system has faltered; second, the gap between the rich and the poor has gradually widened in the course of reform and development, with the root cause being the delayed reform of the income distribution system; and third, corruption of a group and institutional nature has become quite serious, which is an indication that political restructuring is behind schedule. How should we analyse these problems that have cropped up in the process of reform? Are they the outcome of the reform itself, or do they spring from the fact that the reform is not yet complete? There are two views on this. One view is that unemployment, the gap between the rich and the poor, and corruption are problems cropping up in the course of the reform, and are related to the reform. The other view is that many reform measures are not yet in place. In my own view, these problems are indeed directly related to the reform; not in the sense that something has gone wrong with it, but that it is not yet complete. Three points need to be clarified here: First, whether the direction of the reform is right or not. For example, some reforms are no more than readjustments in terms of methods or policies, and some such readjustments can be at odds with or run counter to the basic direction of the reform. Second, many reform measures are delayed. Many problems arising from income distribution and from the ownership adjustment are the results of failure to put the reforms into place, with some reforms being not thorough-going, some being untimely, and some being not truly implemented. And third, reforms are not rounded out. An outstanding aspect is that economic restructuring is placing ever-more direct and ever-stronger demands on the political restructuring.

The way to address the serious delays in these three areas of reform is to speed up the process of the market-oriented reform and to identify the real causes of the failures to forge a clear path for the reform, to put the reform in place and to round it out. In particular, whether with regard to attracting foreign investment, generating investment demand or creating consumer demand, major economic and social development demands are directly related to the reform in most cases. I made the following statement three years ago to sum up the situation: China's reform will decide its future. Our present investment demands come mainly from the reform, and there must be a shift in sources of investment. Nor can consumer demand be met without the reform, for example, with regard to expanding the rural markets. In such circumstances, we must have a sober-minded understanding of the fact that China has entered a new stage in its reform when analysing the current problems. My basic conclusion is that the reform has entered a new stage which calls for an all-out tackling of hard issues, with emphasis on the comprehensive adjustments of interests.

II. Issues concerning the basic approach to making breakthroughs in the reform

Every problem in the reform has something to do with the adjustment of major and basic interests. The reform of the property right system is a basic adjustment of interests, the reform in the system of income distribution aims at rationalising the relations of interests, and political restructuring touches on important interests even more. Now that the reform has entered the new stage of adjusting interests in an all-round way, what issues do we need to examine with regard to the basic approaches to the reform? I have been studying two basic issues:

1. The people's market economy. The demands of the socialist market economy are the product of a special background. The market economy is not divided into a socialist or capitalist one. At first we understood the socialist market economy to mean the public ownership plus the mechanism of market competition, which from today's perspective is an over-simplistic and superficial generalization that fails to bring out its most fundamental features. Within the framework of a socialist system, what are the most basic and most significant problems that the socialist market economy aims to solve? In face of the current outstanding economic and social contradictions we can see that the aim of the socialist market economy is precisely to organically combine the interests of the general public with the mechanism of market competition, wherein lies what is most vigorous and most vital in the essence of the market economy. I think that this is the angle from which to sum up and examine the reform efforts over the past two decades and more. Why did farmers' incomes register an ever-slower or even a negative growth in the late 1980s and in the 1990s? Why has the gap between the rich and the poor not tended toward a gradual narrowing in the process of reform but even showed a tendency to widen? The gap between the rich and the poor in China has aroused attention not only from people at home but also abroad. We have been successful in maintaining sustained economic growth in the course of exploring the market economy, but have not given enough thought to how to combine the interest of general public with the mechanism of market competition, or devised enough ways to do so, unaware that this combination is most fundamental and essential in the market economy. Now that the Communist Party of China (CPC) has called for representing the interests of the overwhelming majority of the people in the country, what is important is to combine the common people as the bearers of interests with the mechanism of market competition.

Therefore, the people's market economy as I understand means: First, socialization of the subjects of property rights. In my view, the most fundamental institutional deficiency of the orthodox planned economy was that the state served as the sole unitary property owner. The aim of our reform is precisely to shift from the situation in which the state was the unitary owner to one in which the masses of the people are subjects of property rights. The citizens' right to property must have strict legal protection in this process. Second, equity of social distribution. In primary distribution and micro-distribution we should pay more attention to efficiency, while in redistribution and social distribution we should pay more attention to fairness. Third, democratization of economic, social and political life. In economic life, the emphasis is placed on the mechanism of participation by broad masses of laborers; in social life, the emphasis is placed on the mechanism of supervision by the broad masses of the citizens; and in political life, the emphasis is placed on the mechanism of democratic elections. Not long ago, I attended a seminar on industry in China and Japan held in Suzhou, at which the chairman of the Board of Directors of Matsushita Electrical Industries of Japan cited an example to show that Japanese enterprises paid great attention to improving communications with the staff and workers, and emphasised the mechanism of participation. Earlier this year, I went with President Gao Shangquan of the China (Hainan) Institute for Reform and Development for a study tour of the Nordic countries, and was deeply impressed by what I saw. First, the basic achievement of common prosperity. Seventy to eighty percent of the population in Nordic countries are in the middle-income bracket. Second, social equity. For example, among the middle-income group, who make up 80 percent of the population, the lowest income generally is no less than 2,500 euros, while the highest income is no higher than 10,000 euros. Third, democracy and the legal system. The Nordic states belong to the people themselves; everything is transparent and there is basically no corruption. Affluence, equity, efficiency and absence of corruption — these are precisely the goals that the socialist market economy aims at. That study tour brought home to me the need to ponder over the path of reform oriented toward the people's market economy, and identify what factors are the most essential and the most vigorous in the socialist market economy.

  2. **Structural reforms.** Now that the reform has entered a new stage in which interests are to be adjusted in an all-round way, no separate reform alone can solve the problems. What is needed is to

push forward structural reforms. In my generalization, structural reforms cover three aspects: first, the adjustment of internal relationships within the economic restructuring. For example, the most outstanding relationship is that between the banks and enterprises. The Republic of Korea (ROK) has adopted many major reform and adjustment measures in the process of handling its financial crisis, and forcing a group of enterprises and financial institutions to go bankrupt one after another. The ROK has achieved initial success in solving the structural contradictions between its enterprises and banks only after having paid a heavy price. The Koizumi cabinet of Japan advanced a program of structural reform some time ago, but it has still not been implemented, because the problems are of long standing and very complicated. In a strict sense, the structural problems concerning enterprises and banks in China are also very serious. Second, social and political reforms of a structural nature in support of economic restructuring. Our political restructuring at present should place greater emphasis on meeting the need to adjust interests in an all-round way. It would be hard to solve certain problems in the absence of such structural reforms. The development of human resources we speak of is related to the issue of human capital in the course of economic restructuring, income distribution on a social level, and, even more so, the cadre and personnel system in the course of political restructuring. Third, the relationship between the reform and policy readjustments. Some policy readjustments have been at variance with the reforms. China is at a critical junction in the transition of its economic system, and the introduction of policies should conform to the direction of the reforms; some reforms need to go through policy readjustments to arrive at their goals and objectives. For example, how to make the pro-active fiscal policy help the shift in the subjects of investment is a very big policy issue. If the state had set aside a portion of the state bonds it has issued to the tune of hundreds of billions of Renminbi and used them for the purpose of policy readjustments by way of encouragement and subsidizing interest payments to non-governmental investment in infrastructure, it would have seen far greater results than the direct state investment has. Moreover, it concerns a major issue in the shift of market players in the course of China's economic transition. Another example is the policy statement: "He who invests owns." We all know that the 15th CPC National Congress in 1997 put forward the principle in clear-cut terms that "distribution according to work" be combined with "distribution according to the factors of production" and the 16th CPC National Congress in 2002 went a step further by establishing the principle that labor, capital, technology and management participate in the distribution. A series of major theoretical and practical issues remain to be resolved before the policy "He who invests owns" is combined with the basic direction of the reforms.

Practice has shown repeatedly that in order to adjust interests in an all-round way and move step by step toward a people's market economy, the issue of structural reforms should be raised in explicit terms. Against this background, the economic reforms can fall into place, political restructuring can advance steadily and appropriately, and some policies can take the direction of the reforms into consideration and be closely related to their goals.

III. Taking the all-round adjustment of interests as the focal point, and making new breakthroughs in reform

1. Ownership reform. The shift from developing a mixed economy to developing a mixed-ownership economy represents a leap in the development of the market economy. The mixed-ownership economy with the joint-stock system as its main body is estimated to make up about 40 percent of China's overall economy. It is estimated that the sector consisting of mixed ownership will make up about 80 percent of the total after five to ten years of further reforms. When that happens, the micro-foundation of the market economy in China will be fairly well established.

The proposal for a mixed-ownership economy is a very important issue. It signifies that the concept of unitary or orthodox "state-owned enterprises" and "private enterprises" will be changed to the concept of the mixed-ownership economy. By the mixed-ownership economy, it is meant, to put it simply, a blended state of capital and stock rights. Therefore, the fact that the direct use of the concept "developing the mixed-ownership economy" in the documents of the 16th CPC National Congress deserves close attention. The concepts of a pure "state-owned" enterprise and a pure "private" enterprise will become a thing of the past. The per-capita assets of China's top 500 enterprises are only 1.57 percent of that of the world's top 500 enterprises. Chinese enterprises can hardly match the world giants in terms of competitiveness and enterprise size unless the development of the mixed-ownership economy is speeded up.

The mixed-ownership economy with non-public capital as its main body is very important for the development of the non-public economy. For example, the way out for a further growth of the banking, public service and infrastructure sectors lies in the development of the mixed-ownership economy. The sounder its development and the more rational the structure of stock rights, the firmer the micro-foundation of the market economy.

2. Taking the development and nurturing of a middle-income group as the focal point, and making a breakthrough in the reform of the distribution system. First, the government should lift restrictions on the types of ownership and regulate the right of distribution. One of its main functions is social distribution, for an equitable social distribution is a major public product the government should provide. Second, rural reforms. China has set the goal of building a well-off society in an all-round way by the year 2020. However, if the middle-income group fails to make up about half of the population by then, it would be hard to say that an all-round well-off society had been achieved. What is fundamental to the achievement of this goal is a solution to the rural problems. There are different calculations, but the middle-income group in the cities roughly accounts for about 20 percent of the urban population. The problem lies in the countryside, for the income gap between the rural population and the urban residents has, over recent years, kept widening. The present income gap between town and country in China is enormously greater than the international level, and remarkably higher than the general level of developing countries. At the stage of "building a well-off society in an all-round way" in China, it will be extremely difficult to solve the problem of farmers' income by solely developing agriculture. The reason is the marked drop in the Engel's coefficient. During the last decade, the Engel's coefficient of urban residents has dropped by approximately 15 percentage points. The lower proportion of food expenditures in the increased income of urban residents makes it difficult to expand the market for agricultural produce, so that it will be more and more difficult for farmers to increase their incomes from agricultural work. Thus, there must be new ideas for increasing their incomes at the present stage. We should find a solution in the urban-rural structure and related systems, and seek a new breakthrough in the rural reform and development. First, it is essential to reform the fiscal and taxation systems for the rural areas, and gradually abolish irrational taxes levied on farmers, so as to conform to the needs of economic and social development in the rural areas. Second, it is essential to speed up the reform of land ownership in the rural areas. As conditions mature, farmers should be endowed with fairly complete ownership rights, including the right to mortgage their land. This will play a very important role in stabilizing the farmers' lives, stimulating their enthusiasm, making better use of the land and promoting the shift of redundant rural labor to cities. Third, it is essential to accelerate the democratic process at the grassroots level in the rural areas. A case in point is the institutional arrangement for the relationship between the farmers at the village level and the township and town governments. There are two options: to reduce township/town governments to township offices as agencies of the county governments, or to effect a transition from direct elections at the village level to direct elections at the township and town level. Another case in point is that the progress in the market-oriented rural reform is placing an objective demand for the establishment, from bottom to top, of farmers' associations as the representatives of their own interests. Fourth, it is vital to make breakthroughs in reforms at the county level. Although the county economy is markedly inferior to the economy of larger cities in scale, social capital, human resources and other factors, it is closely linked with the rural economy and, to a large extent, to develop the county economy is to develop the rural economy. Meanwhile, the county economy is where the urban and rural economies meet, and the development of the county economy will be of vital significance for easing the current employment pressure on farmers and reducing the burdens on them. It is necessary to deepen the discussions on reform and development at the county level with the aim of benefiting rural development, the farmers' efforts to increase their incomes and the shift of rural manpower.

3. Reform of the government is the focal point in the new stage of reform and opening up. Many examples demonstrate that the delay of the shift in government functions, with the government still taking care of many matters that it should not be responsible for and cannot possibly do well, is, of course, related to the legacy of the traditional planned economy system, but the basic reason lies in the fact that the self-interest of government departments is behind the expansion of administrative powers in some cases. It is not difficult to see from studies on the root cause of some sprawling corruption cases that the frequent occurrence of corruption cases is related to the imperfect mechanisms of conferral and use of administrative powers and to the lack of democratic supervision over and restraint on the use of administrative powers. At present, some public powers have evolved into tools in the hands of certain government departments and officials for seeking their self-interest, amid signs that institutional corruption and corruption of a bloc nature have evolved. This has turned the vested interests involved in the reforms into obstacles to the reforms. Against this interest-dominated background, it is very difficult for the government to shift its functions of its own accord. The way out is, in accordance with the requirements of the report to the 16th CPC National Congress, to take reform measures to strengthen the restricting, restraining and supervising power, so as to truly effect a substantial shift in government functions.

China has entered a new stage in its reform and opening up efforts. It is an arduous, long-term task to make new breakthroughs in the reforms. With a view to meeting the needs of the new stage, I hereby offer two specific suggestions: First, strengthen cultural building in the reforms. It is a fact that some traditional cultural notions are at odds with the reforms, and without a new cultural outlook reform will meet with obstacles to some extent. Second, enabling the departments in charge of reforms to fully play their roles. As far as certain specific reforms are concerned, localities and departments are in a position to push them forward. But when it comes to major issues concerning the reforms, they require investigation and study, and unified coordination. Especially with the entry into the new stage of structural reforms characterized by the overall tackling of hard issues, it is all the more necessary to attach importance to the role of the specialized departments in charge of reforms.

CHINA: WTO ACCESSION AND THE NEW STAGE OF REFORM

(*December 2002*)

Why has China's accession to the WTO aroused wide repercussions both at home and abroad? On the occasion of the first anniversary of the country's WTO accession, comments from all over the international community were positive. I think there are two reasons behind this: First, China is a developing country, a big country with a vast domestic market and sustained economic growth; and, second, China is also a big country characterized by a transition from a traditional planned economy to a market economy. As a big country putting into effect a transition of its economic system, China has been able to join the mainstream of the world market economy within a short period of time. This in itself is remarkable. Therefore, I call what is most profound, most substantial or most far-reaching in its WTO accession as China's second reform and opening up.

I. Opening up promotes reform — a salient feature of reform in its new stage

China's accession to the WTO signifies that it has entered a new stage in its opening-up program. The salient features of the new stage, as I see them, are: First, moving from policy-based opening up to institutionalised opening up; second, moving from partial opening up to all-round opening up; and third, moving from opening up in general competitive areas to opening up in all sectors, with emphasis on the service sector. What impact is the new stage of the opening up having on the on-going reform? Promoted by the opening up, the reform has made marked progress in a number of areas over the past two years. The following three areas are the most important of them:

1. The development of the mixed sector of the economy has proceeded at a much faster pace. The China Enterprise Federation released the list of China's top 500 enterprises not long ago. When compared with the top 500 enterprises of the world, they show a very big gap, and in some aspects this gap is astonishing. For example, the per-capita assets of the top 500 Chinese enterprises are only 1.57 percent of that of the world's top 500 enterprises. Against the background of China's WTO accession, Chinese enterprises will not only compete with foreign-funded enterprises in the home market but also must make a debut in the international arena, which requires the expansion of their scales and improvement of their key competitiveness. The way out lies in speeding up the development of the mixed-ownership economy. The 16th CPC National Congress called for vigorously developing this sector. We generally referred to it as the mixed economy in the past, while the present term is the mixed-ownership economy. The proportion of this sector in enterprises of all types has risen from only about 9 percent in 1990 to about 40 percent at present. According to my estimate, it will reach at least 60 percent in the next five years. When that happens, Chinese enterprises will show marked progress in terms of scale and competitiveness.

2. The reform of the state-owned and monopolistic sectors and service sector will be greatly accelerated. It can be said that up until a few years ago the reform in the telecommunications, civil aviation, railways, banking, insurance and other state-owned and monopolistic service sectors or infrastructure was very difficult. However, a very big breakthrough has been made in the past two years or so. Leaving aside whether the splitting of the telecommunications sector into two corporations (south and north) is in conformity with the principle of the market economy, the move represents a big step forward toward

the breaking of monopoly. In order to facilitate the reform in this respect, an anti-monopoly law is being formulated with vigorous efforts. I expect the reform in the infrastructure and services sectors, spurred on by China's WTO accession, to make fairly big progress in the next three years or so.

3. The reform of the government with focus on reducing administrative examination and approval will be greatly accelerated. Relevant statistics have already been published, and here I may well quote them. For example, the 60 departments under the State Council originally had 4,159 items that were subject to administrative examination and approval. The State Council published its first list of items earlier this year that no longer required administrative examination and approval (759), which indicated the intensity of the work to cut such items. It has also published a decision concerning the abolition of some administrative decrees and regulations in force before the end of year 2000, calling for a review of 756 administrative decrees and regulations in force issued from the early days of the People's Republic of China to the end of 2000. As things stand now, 442 such decrees and regulations have been nullified, and 34 documents issued in the name of the State Council or its General Office have ceased to be implemented.

In view of the above three aspects, the promotion of reform by opening up will be a salient feature of China's reform for a considerably long time to come. With the WTO accession as a motive force, China will continue to make breakthroughs in a number of areas in the new stage of the reform.

II. Government reform has become one of the focal points in the new stage of reform.

Over the past two decades, the reform in China has focused on enterprises. In view of the practice over the past year since China's accession to the WTO and trends forecast in the next few years, the government reform will be one of the focal points. This is to meet the needs of the process of China's market-oriented reform, of the WTO accession and even more so of the in-depth development of the reform. Such being the extent of China's market economy today, and especially following the WTO accession, China will have to act in accordance with the internationally accepted economic rules, and change the "rules of play" of the planned economy in terms of institutional innovations, the most important of which is a fundamental shift in the role of the government. For example, the government, first of all, must change its role as a certain kind of market player. So far as the state-owned monopolies and the state-owned economic sector are concerned, the government is still playing a partial role as a market player. Second, the government must change its functions. We have all along urged the government to fulfil its public functions. What are its public functions? Making and following rules are an important part of such functions. Third, given the extent of the economic transition in China, the need to change the government role, perform its functions and preserve the social stability all places the government reform on a more prominent position than enterprise reform. I envisage the government reform in the new stage as meeting three types of needs: those of the WTO accession, those of the process of China's market-oriented reform, and those arising from constantly deepening the reform as a whole.

We have been talking about government reform, especially the separation of government functions from enterprise management, ever since the beginning of the reform. Why has the shift in government functions been lagging behind all the time? This is definitely related to the traditional planned economy system. But the real reason is that the self-interest of government departments, which underlines the expansion of administrative powers in some respects. It is not difficult to see from studies on the root cause of some sprawling corruption cases that the frequent occurrence of corruption is related to the imperfect mechanisms of conferral and use of administrative powers, and to the lack of democratic supervision and of restraints on the administrative powers. This has turned certain vested interests of the reform into obstacles to further reforms, so the interest-dominated shift in the government functions is very difficult. Where is the way out? The political report to the 16th CPC National Congress has a very clear statement, that is, it is imperative to tighten restraints on and supervision over the use of powers and build a mechanism for the exercise of power featuring rational structure, scientific distribution, rigorous procedures and effective restraints, so as to strengthen supervision over the use of powers at the decision-making, implementation and other links and ensure that the powers entrusted by the people are used truly for their benefits.

Against the background of the WTO accession, the government reform in China will accomplish four major shifts in the next stage of reform:

1. A shift from the government-dominated economy to a market-dominated economy. A shift from the government-decreed economy to a government-dominated economy and then to a market-dominated economy — this is the entire process of China's market-oriented reform. Some East Asian countries, such as Japan and the ROK used to practice, to a large extent, a government-dominated market economy. The ROK has paid a heavy price for this, and the Koizumi cabinet in Japan has put forward the concept of structural reform. To keep in line with the requirements of the WTO, and on the basis of summing up the experience in practicing a government-dominated market economy, China should bring about a shift from the government-dominated market economy to a market-dominated economy as soon as possible.

2. A shift from economic goals as priority to social goals as priority. The key to whether the government can effectively play its role in the sustained economic growth, as shown clearly by present-day practice, is whether it can appropriately address such issues as unemployment, uneven income distribution and education, as well as social credit and market order. A successful resolution of these issues will provide a reliable social environment for economic development. Otherwise, sustained economic growth will be difficult to attain.

3. A shift from an economy based on administrative examinations and approvals to an economy based on (administrative) services. The government should further narrow the scope of administrative examinations and approvals by a big margin to allow the factors of production to flow, to rise or fall, and to form optimised combinations in the course of market competition. It is essential to correctly handle the relationship between the government and enterprises, between the government and the market, and between the government and social intermediaries, leaving to market players and intermediaries those matters which are beyond the reach of the government, or which the government is unable to handle well, or which the government should not meddle in. The main functions of the government are to improve legislation, promote the performance of government work according to law, standardize the relations of property, credit and contract in accordance with the market economy, maintain market order, ensure fair competition, establish and improve the social security system and social service system and other social public products and public services, and provide access to government affairs and government information through various channels.

4. A shift from a system of administrative control to an administrative system operating in accordance with the law. China's administrative system is characterised by vertical control. In keeping with the requirements of the WTO accession, it is essential to speed up the building of a legal system for the socialist market economy and carry out the administrative functions of the government strictly in accordance with the law. In order to ensure fair market competition, the government should strengthen legislation and law enforcement in a fair and strict way, standardize the various social roles in this respect and punish violations of the law.

The practice over the past year following the WTO accession has shown that the government has made great progress in reforming the administrative examination and approval system, thus playing a major role in creating an environment for fair competition. Continued efforts to take the government reform as one of the focal points in the new stage of the reform in accordance with the guidelines of the 16th CPC National Congress will play a major role in further promoting the process of China's market-oriented reform.

III. Structural reform is a major difficulty in the new stage of reform.

China's reform has entered a new critical stage, a stage at which all-out efforts must be made to tackle thorny problems, with the adjustment of interests as the main task. The government reform, a focal point of this stage, unavoidably and directly involves the issue of arrangements for the institutional structure as a whole. That is to say, China's accession to the WTO signifies its entry to the stage of structural reform. In view of the outstanding contradictions at present, China's structural reform faces four major tasks:

1. The relationship between economic restructuring and economic policies. One example is the relationship between the pro-active fiscal policy and the nurturing of non-public investors. So far, China has issued close to 600 billion yuan-worth of state bonds. Two years ago, I suggested that a portion of the state bonds, say one-third, be set aside for financing policy-related measures, such as subsidies on interest payment, to support and encourage non-public investment in infrastructure. If that had been done, the policy effects so generated would have been much better than now. Therefore, a major task of China's structural reform is to correctly handle the relationship between the economic restructuring and economic policies.

2. The relationship between the reform of the property system and policies concerning income distribution. In my view, in the new stage of reform and opening up, the government should lift its control over different types of ownership, and regulate income distribution. On the one hand, our current policies concerning income distribution rely on the means of redistribution, but the country is in a special period of economic transition right now, and a major or basic readjustment of interests will depend, to a great extent, on the actual progress of the reform of property ownership. For example, how to combine the policy that "He who invests owns" with the principle put forward at the 16th CPC National Congress that labor, capital, technology and management, as production factors, all participate in the distribution? In my view, the key to this combination is the reform of property right system. In other words, the readjustment of the policies related to income distribution during the period of economic transition in China has a highly intrinsic and ever-closer link with the reform of the property right system.

3. The relationship between a steady reform of the banking system and monetary policy. We describe the current state of banking as being lax at the macro level and tight at the micro level. Enterprises, especially non-public ones, find it difficult to get bank loans. Why? This is because the policies are at odds with the system. Who are responsible for the loans? Those handling loans may think that they have nothing to gain from a successful loan but will be held responsible for a bad loan. Therefore, the monetary policy does not fit well with the current banking system, under which no policy, no matter how good it is, can be implemented in real earnest. Another point is how to handle well the relationship between the enterprises and the banks, especially between state-owned enterprises (SOEs) and state-owned banks. The structural reforms of the ROK and Japan both face this serious problem. Whether China can solve these problems will depend, to a great extent, on when and how it pushes forward the structural reform.

4. The relationship between the urban and rural reforms. The great gap between urban and rural income distribution has already become a major problem for China's economic development and social stability. Conservative estimates put the actual gap in income at four to one, while some people put it at six to one. The real big difference between the western regions and eastern regions lies in the rural areas. Therefore, at the new stage of reform there should be some breakthroughs in the arrangements for the institutional structures of urban and rural areas. For example, is it possible to consider the abolition of the agricultural tax, agricultural special products tax and tax on slaughtering animals? In addition, is it necessary for township governments to maintain such elaborate offices? Is it possible to turn a township government into an agency of the county government out of consideration for lightening the burdens on the farmers? Furthermore, can the right to mortgage rural land be granted to farmers at an early date, so as to complete the reform task of capitalizing rural land? All these things are related to the question of arrangements for the institutional structures of urban and rural areas, and important issues to be resolved in the course of structural reform.

5. The relationship between economic restructuring and political restructuring. The reform of the cadre and personnel system, the performance of administrative duties in accordance with the law and the anti-corruption drive will be very difficult without economic and political restructuring supporting each other.

WTO accession has pushed China's reform to a new stage. I believe that China's market-oriented reform in the next few years will progress more rapidly than originally anticipated, thus playing a major role in promoting China's economic and social development.

CHINA: WTO ACCESSION AND NEW BREAKTHROUGHS IN REFORM

(*November 2002*)

China's accession to the WTO has ushered in a new stage in its reform and opening-up drive. Practice in the short period of one year has proved that WTO accession has not only provided the country with a new motive force for its reform as in the case of the major progress in the government reform with emphasis on the cutting the scope of administrative examination and approval, it has also brought about a new feature to the reform — opening up promoting the reform. Taking the all-round opening as a force for pushing forward the market-oriented reform and making energetic efforts to remove institutional obstacles to the development of the productive forces — these have become the main path for today's reform.

China is at a critical period of transition of its economic structure. Compared with the reform over the past two decades or so, the reform now is more profound, more complicated and more rigorous. The real significance of China's accession to the WTO is that it presents the country an opportunity to solve the deep-rooted contradictions and problems encountered in the transition of the economic structure by opening up the country's market. To keep abreast of the new situation arising from economic globalization and the WTO accession, the 16th CPC National Congress explicitly advanced the following important guideline, i.e., "promoting reform and development by opening up." We should act upon the requirements laid down at the 16th CPC National Congress and, continuing to take the WTO accession as a new motive force, make new breakthroughs.

I. Developing Mixed-ownership Economy and Making New Breakthroughs in Enterprise Reform

WTO accession means all-round market competition. This makes it all the more urgent for China to speed up the reform of its enterprises and improve their international competitiveness. Facts have shown that the call of the 16th CPC National Congress for "introducing the joint-stock system to develop the mixed-ownership economy" is the main way to make enterprises more competitive. Regarding the socialist market economy, the report to the CPC congress says, "All sectors of the economy may very well display their respective advantages in market competition and stimulate one another for common development." China's reform has, over the past two decades and more, gone through several stages — from acknowledging the non-public sector to developing mixed economy, and to encouraging and supporting the development of the mixed-ownership economy. Especially since the 15th CPC National Congress, held in 1997, China has seen a rapid shift from developing the mixed economy of multiple economic sectors to developing the mixed-ownership economy with the joint-stock system as the main form. By the end of 1999, the mixed-ownership economy accounted for 33 percent of all economic sectors, a very rapid increase from the 9.8 percent in 1990.

1. The mixed-ownership economy is the main form for realising forms of ownership that are in keeping with the requirement to develop the modern productive forces in China.

The concept of a "mixed economy" was introduced by the economist Paul A. Samuelson in the course of expounding the trends and origin of economic growth, and was later enriched by neo-institutional economists. When we borrow this term today, we have, in view of the conditions in China, given a special meaning to the economic growth and economic transition in the country. In fact, China's "basic economic system, with public ownership playing the dominant role and diverse forms of ownership developing side by side" is precisely a kind of mixed economy. The "mixed-ownership economy" here refers mainly to a mixed state of stock rights of enterprises, that is to say that diverse economic sectors can be blended into one entity to become the mixed-ownership economy with the joint-stock system as the main form.

The reason why the development of the mixed-ownership economy is expected to pick up speed in the next few years is that it suits the requirements for developing the modern productive forces in China better than other economic sectors. We should be bold in developing the mixed sector. What is important is to break away from the bondage of the traditional concept about ownership. In a given socio-economic system, a few more state-owned enterprises do not necessarily mean socialism while fewer SOEs do not necessarily mean capitalism either. The reason for developing the mixed-ownership sector in an all-round way is that it is beneficial not only to socio-economic development, but also to realizing the interests of the majority. If the mixed-ownership sector can make up 60 to 80 percent of the economy as a whole in the next five to ten years, China will have a very reliable micro-foundation for its economic development. It can be said that the development of the mixed-ownership economy will provide a durable motive force for China's sustained and rapid economic growth.

2. The development of the mixed-ownership sector is an important way to make breakthroughs in enterprise reform in the new stage of reform.

The development of the mixed sector of the economy is an important way to speed up the reform of SOEs. Not long ago, the China Enterprise Federation released a list of China's top 500 enterprises. Compared with the world's top 500, they show a considerable gap both in terms of scale and efficiency. Among them, the SOEs and the enterprises in which the state holds controlling shares, in particular, show a far lower efficiency level than foreign-funded and private enterprises do. An important way to make the SOEs stronger and bigger is to speed up the process of introducing the corporation system, with the joint-stock system as the main form. Both Shanghai and Shenzhen will soon release a list of SOEs available for merger and acquisition by Chinese and foreign investors. This is an indication that the merger and acquisition of SOEs by foreign and non-public investors will be a major trend in the future, and, in the course of enterprise merger and acquisition, SOEs will be headed towards the mixed-ownership economy. In particular, it was clearly stated in the report to the 16th CPC National Congress that, under a new state property management system, the central and local governments jointly perform the responsibilities of investor on behalf of the state, enjoying owner's equity. This points the direction for speeding up the reform of the state assets management system, and will be conducive to revitalizing state assets and speeding up the development of the mixed-ownership sector with the joint-stock system as the main form.

The development of the mixed-ownership sector is an important way to upgrade the development of non-public enterprises. The savings rate of social capital in China is very high, and non-public and private economic sectors are developing rapidly. However, taken as a whole, the non-public and private sectors are still small in their scale of development and are not strong as competitors. To meet the needs of the opening up and market competition, they should lose no time to expand their scale and raise their efficiency, and thus becoming more competitive. The way to do this is by mutual reorganization, merging and acquisition among enterprises of different types of ownership on the basis of the market economy. Thus, a batch of non-public and private enterprises will grow into enterprise groups of scale, strength and international competitiveness in the course of reorganization.

II. Making New Breakthroughs in Income Distribution System with Emphasis on Nurturing and Expanding Middle-income Group

Economic globalisation faces a serious problem — how to prevent the worldwide gap between the rich and the poor from widening further. China's WTO accession has ushered in a new stage of reform with emphasis on the all-round adjustment of interests. The report to the 16th CPC National Congress said, "Rationalising the relations of income distribution bears on the immediate interests of the general public and the display of their initiative." It also pointed out clearly: "Bearing in mind the objective of common prosperity, we should try to raise the proportion of the middle-income group and increase the income of the low-income group." This calls for a painstaking study of ways to establish an effective social security mechanism for the low-income group and an incentive mechanism for forming and expanding the middle-income group while protecting the high-income group who have become rich through lawful means, so as to gradually raise the proportion of the middle-income group in the whole society. Undoubtedly, this constitutes a major task in the course of building a well-off society in an all-round way in China, as well as a higher and more arduous goal than letting a part of the population get rich first.

1. Nurturing and expanding the middle-income group is a major objective of China's reform of its income distribution system.

As international experience shows, a more optimised social structure often depends on a rational income distribution structure. The middle-income group making up the majority of all social members is a hallmark of a more mature social structure. China has a large rural population, and the practice of separating town from country has a long history. Due to such special national conditions, China has a considerably large low-income group. It is estimated that by 1999 low-income households made up 31.79 percent of the urban residents throughout the country; lower-middle-income households, 32.36 percent; middle-income households, 19.67 percent; higher-middle-income households, 8.95 percent; and high-income households, 7.23 percent; with the lower-middle-income and low-income groups combining to make up 64 percent. In the light of Chinese conditions, nurturing and expanding the middle-income group and turning this group into the main body of society is a long-term and arduous task.

As China is in the midst of an economic transition period, "the middle-income group" is a dynamic concept, whose specific meaning varies at different stages of development. In the light of the current conditions in the country, the middle-income group may roughly include the middle-income group and higher-middle-income group who have fixed property and have an income higher than the per-capita average. This is a rough and ready classification, and is directly tied to the income and consumption levels in the current period in China. The use of the term "middle-income group" instead of "middle strata" here is aimed at emphasising the objective realities with regard to the changes in the income groups during the economic transition period. The various strata and interest groups in Chinese society are still in a period of change, since the country itself is at the stage of reform. In such a period, each interest group embraces a high-income group as well as middle-income and low-income groups. Classification into low-income, middle-income and high-income groups on the basis of income levels is a more realistic, dynamic generalization. In keeping with the basic national conditions in the country, the use of "middle-income group," as against the "middle class" or "middle strata" in the developed Western countries, has a Chinese characteristic. First, it is a classification of the income levels in present-day China, reflecting only the structure of groups with different income levels in the current period; second, it reflects the characteristics of continuous adjustments and changes in the group interest structure in the course of China's market-oriented reform.

2. The key to expanding the middle-income group in China's economic transition is the socialization of the owners of property rights.

As China is in an economic transition period, the effort to turn more workers into members of the middle-income group should take sustained and rapid economic growth as the prerequisite, and the socialization of owners of property rights through the market-oriented reform as an important condition. The report to the 16th CPC National Congress called for "establishing the principle that labor, capital, technology, managerial expertise and other production factors participate in the distribution of income in accordance with their respective contributions, thereby improving the system under which distribution according to work is dominant and a variety of modes of distribution coexist." This is an important basis for speeding up the reform of the income distribution system and nurturing and expanding the middle-income group. The traditional planned economy system rejected altogether the right of technology, capital, managerial expertise and other production factors to participate in distribution, and denies the workers the right to take part in residual distribution as owners of property rights of labor power. The traditional planned economy system acknowledged only one owner of property rights, that is, the state, and the institutional arrangement of a single owner of property rights was the root cause of the equalitarian distribution policy whereby all ate from the same big pot, as well as the deep-rooted institutional cause of the fact that workers remained members of the low-income group for a long time. Therefore, the reform of the income distribution system is an important task, involving a shift from a unitary owner of property rights to the socialization of owners of property rights. Under the stimulation of the property rights system, more and more people will turn from being members of the low-income group into members of the middle-income group.

3. The government should lift restrictions on ownership and regulate income distribution.

The development of the economy under various forms of ownership depends on a stable social environment and an equitable market competition mechanism. The main function of the government should be to create an economic and social environment for the development of enterprises rather than to run them. In the market economy, especially in the new stage of reform when the emphasis is on an all-round adjustment of interests, the government should give priority to realising social development objectives. It is important for the government to play a correct and effective role in regulating the income distribution of the whole society through taxation, fiscal and banking means — the so-called "visible hand." This is an important condition for nurturing and expanding the middle-income group. Since the country is at a critical juncture in its economic transition, the present conditions with regard to the adjustment of income distribution and major relations of interests in the society are much more complicated and difficult than in the early period of the reform. In such circumstances the government's role is very important.

III. Bearing in Mind the Objective of Increasing Farmers' Income, and Making a New Breakthrough in Rural Reform

The impact of the WTO accession on China's agriculture shows that the main contradiction has not been one of demand and supply of agricultural produce, but one of farmers' employment and income. The report to the 16th CPC National Congress pointed out clearly that "a major task for building a well-off society in an all-round way is to make overall planning for urban and rural economic and social development, build modern agriculture, develop the rural economy and increase the income of farmers." At present, the rural economy and farmers' income are outstanding problems. The main manifestations are: First, the farmers' real income since 1997 has not only been slow in its increase but also shown a tendency to lose ground. Second, it has become increasingly more difficult to transfer the surplus rural labor force in recent years, and the situation is grim. Reduction of the rural population by transferring rural labor is a fundamental way to raise their income. By 2001, the number of people employed in agriculture exclusively amounted to 325 million, showing an increase of 40 million over 1978. Third, the income gap between the rural population and urban residents has been widening year by year. It approaches a ratio of one to three at present. When some benefits that urban residents enjoy are taken into calculation, then, according to some estimates, the ratio is as high as one to six. The current income gap between town and country in China is much bigger than the international level and also remarkably bigger than the general level in the developing countries.

At the present stage of building a well-off society in an all-round way in China, it is extremely difficult to solve the problem of farmers' income solely through agricultural development, for the reason that the Engel's coefficient has dropped markedly. In the past decade, the Engel's coefficient of the urban residents has dropped by about 15 percentage points, and the proportion of their food expenditure in their increased income has dropped, making it difficult to expand the farm produce market. Thus, farmers have found it more and more difficult to increase their incomes from farming. This shows that we need to look for new ways to increase their income at the present stage, and find new ways to examine the urban-rural structure and related systems, in an effort to seek new breakthroughs in rural reform and development.

1. It is necessary to reform the rural fiscal and taxation systems, and gradually abolish irrational taxes levied on the farmers, as an answer to the requirements of rural economic and social development at the present stage.

At the moment, the taxes that farmers pay directly are mainly the agricultural tax, the agricultural special product tax and the tax on slaughtering animals, which add up to less than 40 billion yuan, only about 2 percent of the total national tax revenues. However, this figure is already a heavy burden on the farmers. If the extra burden of 60 billion yuan that the farmers bear annually to support rural compulsory education and some irrational fees imposed on them are taken into calculation, their real burden is considerably heavier. They have contributed tremendously to accumulation for the country's industrialization for five decades. Statistics show that the price scissors (between industrial goods and farm produce) during the days of the planned economy cost them 600-800 billion yuan, and since the reform and opening-up program was introduced they have suffered a loss of at least 2,000 billion yuan from the under-priced requisitioning of land. And now, when the industrial and commercial sectors account for about 85 percent of the total GDP, it is tremendously difficult for the agricultural sector, which accounts for 15 percent of the GDP, to support half of the total working population. Against this background, if the farmers are made to continue to bear the irrational taxes and levies for a long time to come, they can hardly increase their income, nor can their enthusiasm be brought into further play.

Therefore, reform of the rural taxation system should be speeded up. The tax burdens on the farmers should be gradually phased out when the conditions are ripe. The following options are offered for consideration: First, a step-by-step approach by which the tax on slaughtering animals and the agricultural special product tax are abolished first, and the agricultural tax abolished later; second, all kinds of agricultural taxes should be abolished first in the backward rural areas in the western region in view of the fairly backward conditions prevalent in the western rural areas and the basic policies of the central government on large-scale development of the western region. If breakthroughs in the rural taxation system can be made within the next year or two, this will greatly mobilise the farmers' enthusiasm and create important conditions for increasing their incomes. Meanwhile, the state should bear the expenditures of rural compulsory education and take measures to greatly downsize the governments at the township and town level, so as to create conditions for increasing the farmers' income.

2. It is necessary to speed up the reform of the property right over rural land.

The Law of the People's Republic of China on Rural Land Contracts promulgated recently is a very good law which, for the first time, defines some of the rights of the farmers related to the property rights over land. Regrettably, farmer households' right to mortgage land has not been confirmed by that law. Only when complete property rights of farm households are explicitly established, can the farmers enjoy permanent right to the use of land, so as to stabilise the land relations in the countryside and prevent encroachments on their right to the use of land under the pretext of "operations of scale." Only thus can a solid foundation be laid for market transactions of rural land and the formation of rural shareholding cooperatives. When conditions are ripe in the future, the farmers should be granted fairly complete property rights, including the right to mortgage land. This will play a very important role in stabilising the farmers' lives, mobilising their enthusiasm, making good use of land and facilitating the transfer of rural labor power.

3. It is necessary to speed up the democratic process at the grassroots level in the countryside.

In the actual work of promoting democracy at the grassroots level in the countryside, the question of how to achieve a harmonious development of economic and political democracy is faced with contradictions and problems that require thoroughgoing solutions:

First, while direct elections at the village level have obviously strengthened democracy and encouraged democratic participation at the grassroots level in the countryside, the present contradiction is the relationship between villages and township/town governments. The latter are the main providers of rural "public products." How should the villages and cooperatives as well as the farmers deal with the township/town governments? And how can the latter correctly reflect the interests and demands of the former? Problems of various kinds have often cropped up in this respect. This has something to do with the institutional arrangements for the relationship between the villages, cooperatives and farmers on the one hand and the township/town governments on the other. There are two options for solving this problem: the township/town governments can be changed into township offices as agencies of the county governments; or, the transition from the direct elections at the village level to those at the township/town level can be completed at the earliest possible date.

Second, the broad masses of farmers need representatives of their interests to transmit and express their demands, as negotiators on their behalf and spokesmen for their demands in the course of rural market-oriented reform. Although relevant organizations at the levels of villages and townships may play a certain role in this respect, for their interests and demands to be reflected directly and widely a farmers' organization that can truly represent their interests is called for. The progress in the rural market-oriented reform has raised an objective demand for establishing, from bottom to top, farmers' associations purely as representatives of their interests.

Third, along with the development of the rural market-oriented reform and the rural economy, cases of disputes involving farmers' interests are snowballing. A considerable number of them are directly or indirectly related to the farmers' right to the use of land, while others are economic disputes between rural organizations or between farmers and rural organizations. As things stand now, farmers are often at a disadvantage in such disputes. They are not yet in a position to file a lawsuit or enter into consultations or negotiations with relevant economic and administrative organizations. This shows that how to protect farmers' interests and how to provide legal assistance to them in dealing with various rural economic disputes have become practical issues of considerable urgency.

4. It is vital to make new breakthroughs in the reform at the county level.

As about 100 million rural laborers are expected to leave the countryside for cities in the next 10 to 20 years, rapid urbanization has become an issue of strategic importance. The way to push forward the urbanization process is to expand the large cities and speed up the building of medium-sized and small cities as well as central towns with the emphasis on county towns. Although the county economy is obviously inferior to that of big and medium-sized cities in terms of industrial scale, social capital, human resources and other factors, it is very closely linked with the rural economy and, to a considerable extent, to develop the county economy is to develop the rural economy. Meanwhile, as it is where the urban and rural economies meet, its development will be of extremely important significance in addressing the current rural employment pressure and lightening the farmers' burdens. It is necessary to discuss the reform and development at the county level in a deep-going way with a view to benefiting rural development, increasing farmers' incomes and transferring rural labor power.

First, how can the "stagnant" situation in the reform and development at the county level be solved? From the mid-1980s the reform at the county level became quite lively, creating important conditions for the rural reforms. However, in recent years, the voice of reform at the county level has become more and more muted, and, correspondingly, the county economy has met with increasingly greater difficulties. For the benefit of the overall situation of China's rural reform and development, it is necessary to treat the reform and development at the county level as an important development strategy. Only when a new breakthrough in the county-level reform is made will the rural reform and development have a bright future.

Second, out of the need to promote rural development and stability, it is necessary to grant the county-level governments certain powers of economic and social development, so as to mobilize the initiative at the county level for developing the local economy. China is a big country with a dual structure of cities and countryside, so its urbanization level is low, and the countryside makes up a considerable proportion. Therefore, it is very important that the county-level governments display the initiative for economic development. It is not right to take away, in the name of preventing the overlapping of power on the part of the localities, from the county-level governments certain functions and powers that they should have. Take the arrangements for the banking system as an example. The support that the county-level governments get from the banking sector has been diminishing. Such a deficiency in the banking system has put restraints on county-level economic development and, as a consequence, on the farming and non-farming economies in the rural areas. It should be said that the current institutional arrangements in the banking sector are the main reason for the shortage of funds in rural areas.

Third, proceeding from China's actual conditions and on the basis of the practical experience gained over the past few years, the strategic focus in the development of small cities and towns in China should be quickly shifted to the building of central cities and towns with emphasis on developing the county seats, and take necessary supporting measures and practice relevant incentive policies.

IV. It Is Essential to Make New Breakthroughs in the Reform of the Service Sector Focusing on Banking.

China's most important commitment to the WTO is to open the service markets in the banking, insurance, telecommunications, electrical power and aviation sectors. These are very attractive to foreign investors. Due to the fact that China has been relatively slow in the reform of its service sector, the state monopoly has not yet entirely been broken and the service sector has developed tardily and shown fairly poor economic returns. "To promote reform and development by opening up" — this will be the general trend of the service sector in the next few years.

1. Making substantial breakthroughs in reform of state commercial banks in the course of addressing their loan problem in an all-round way

Preventing banking risks is a major task of China's reform in the new stage. At present, bad loans still make up about 23 percent of the total. Moreover, the country's banking system is weighed down with serious structural contradictions and problems. About two-thirds of the loans from the state-owned commercial banks have found their way into SOEs, whose low efficiency is a major reason behind the structural deficiencies of the state-owned commercial banks. Such structural problems between enterprises and banks are a major factor touching off possible financial risks. How is it that the Japanese economy has not been able to rise from the trough after more than a decade has passed, and that the Korean economy was hit by a financial crisis when it was in the midst of rapid growth? A major reason in both cases was the mishandling of the relations between enterprises and banks. When enterprise groups and banks are inextricably mixed together, the entire banking system will collapse once enterprises go wrong.

Learning a lesson from the ROK and Japan, China should carry out a structural reform in which bold moves should be made to push forward the reform featuring the introduction of the joint-stock system into the state-owned banks in the course of speeding up the reform of SOEs, so as to thoroughly break through the limitations of the self-reform of the state-owned commercial banks. On the one hand, ways should be found to dispose of undesirable creditors' rights once and for all. For example, a package settlement can be made in the form of wholesale trusteeship of debts by which the government undertakes to establish authoritative and transitional debt trusteeship organizations from the central to the local levels. As a package deal, such organizations are responsible for operating, managing and disposing of the undesirable assets of the present state-owned commercial banks, and proceeding to push forward the reorganization of state assets. The assets management corporations of the four major banks, whose main line of operations is to dispose of undesirable assets, may be arranged along the lines of non-state-run enterprises, so as to allow non-public capital to enter the assets management corporations in a form of paid-in capital. The undesirable assets of one solely state-owned bank may be sold to multiple assets management corporations, and on the basis of strict supervision the non-public assets management corporations may be given a fairly big business scope and enjoy appropriate preferential policies. On the other hand, the reform involving the introduction of the joint-stock system into the state-owned commercial banks should be carried out in an all-round way. An important feature of the equity arrangements or structure of the joint-stock system is the effective separation of the ownership from the property rights of the legal person and of the "residual claim" of the investor from the direct capital disposal right and the enterprise management right, thus the enterprises have acquired independent form of property rights and the status as a legal person. From this flow the decision-making and governance structures of the commercial banks, from shareholders to the board of directors, and then to the manager and the staff, which in turn gives rise to a motivation mechanism for seeking maximum profits. On this basis, and to meet the requirements of the WTO accession, efforts should be made to speed up legislation concerning banking, establish a strict and effective regulatory system for the banking sector, and introduce at the right time a regime that allows markets to set interest rates and improve the building of the capital market.

2. Against the WTO background, the reform in the area of infrastructure should be speeded up.

China has made important headway in reform in the area of infrastructure. There are four main tasks in the next step of this reform: (1) Speeding up the establishment and improvement of the corporation governance structure in this area. While important progress has been made in separating the government and enterprise in this respect, one problem now is that reform aimed at adopting the corporation system is not fully in place in a number of respects. It is imperative to act upon the stipulations of the Company Law, and adopt a strict corporation governance structure as soon as possible. (2) The state should come up with policies in support of and encouraging non-public and other non-governmental investment in infrastructure as soon as possible. These policies may cover, for example, subsidized interests, subsidies and entrusted management, in order to create conditions for the entry of non-governmental capital into the area of infrastructure. The state should take a variety of measures to bring the initiative of the non-public sector and various other sectors of society into full play, and allow non-public capital to gradually enter the field of infrastructure on a large scale, so as to speed up the pace of changing the backward state of infrastructure and lay a foundation for long-term stable economic development. (3) It is necessary to build a scientific, effective regulatory system in the area of infrastructure. Effective government regulation is the precondition and foundation for protecting effective competition in the natural monopolies. At present, China's regulatory departments do not apply sufficient regulation to the monopolies, and their forms of regulation are not soundly based on laws and rules and regulations. The objective of the government reform with regard to rules and regulations should be to "abolish market access barriers and protect fair competition." (4) Anti-monopoly in the area of infrastructure and legislation. The area of infrastructure is faced with a heavy anti-monopoly task. China will soon publicise the Anti-Monopoly Law, following its

WTO accession. Meanwhile, it should intensify the work of formulating or revising the laws on telecommunications, aviation, electricity and railways.

V. Making New Breakthroughs in Government Reform with Emphasis on Tightening Restraint on and Supervision Over the Use of Administrative Power

China's WTO accession poses a challenge to government reform. As practice over the past year shows, the country is in a stage of all-round opening up, and to focus the all-round reform on government reform is an objective requirement of China's accession to the WTO. The report to the 16th CPC National Congress called for "tightening the restraint on and supervision over the use of power. We should establish a mechanism for the exercise of power featuring rational structure, scientific distribution, rigorous procedures and effective restraint, so as to strengthen supervision over power in terms of decision-making, execution and other links, and ensure that the power entrusted to us by the people is truly exercised in their interests." Many examples show that the delay of the shift in government functions, with the government still taking care of many functions that it should not do and cannot possibly do well, is of course related to the legacy of the traditional planned economy system. But the real reason lies in the fact that the self-interest of government departments is hidden behind the expansion of certain administrative powers. It will not be difficult to find from the studies on some sprawling corruption cases that the frequent occurrence of corruption is related to the imperfect mechanisms of conferral and use of administrative powers, and to the lack of democratic supervision over and restraint of the use of administrative powers. Some public powers have evolved into mere tools for some government departments and officials to seek their self-interest amid signs that they have evolved into nests of institutional corruption and corruption of a bloc nature. This has turned some vested interest groups of the reform into obstacles to further reform. Against this interest-dominated background, it would be very difficult for the government to shift its functions of its own accord. The way out lies in reform measures to be taken in accordance with the report to the 16th CPC National Congress and, with a view to keeping abreast with the new situation following the WTO accession, in measures designed to restrict, restrain and supervise power, so as to truly bring about a substantial shift in government functions.

First, the shift from a government-dominated economy to a market-dominated economy. From a government-decreed economy to a government-dominated one to a market-dominated one — this roughly traces the process that China's economic transition has undergone. The examples of Japan and the ROK have shown that a government-dominated economy is not a successful model. China's experience in its reform has also shown that a fundamental shift in government functions and its means of management in accordance with the requirements of the market economy is the most substantial issue in the economic transition as well as one that makes a thorough solution difficult. From the very onset of the reform, China set the clear objective of shifting government functions and separating government and enterprise functions. But even today, many reforms concerning government departments are still not in place, and there has not been a fundamental shift in government functions. As a result, instances of mixing up the functions of government and investors or enterprises still exist. Non-performance and displacement of government functions, and overstepping of authority exist side by side, without a substantial change in the modes of economic management on the part of the government. The WTO accession requires the government to intensify its self-reform to bring about a real shift in its functions and improve its efficiency in providing services.

Second, a shift from giving priority to economic goals to giving priority to social goals. The process of China's market-oriented reform and the realities and problems have clearly shown that the key to whether the government is able to play an effective role in sustained economic growth lies in whether it is able to successfully address the problems of unemployment, income gap and education, as well as of social credit and market order. With a good solution to these problems will come a reliable social environment for economic development. Otherwise, if the government is unable to effectively solve these social problems, sustained economic growth will be very difficult. In order to adapt to the new situation in China's economic and social development, government functions should focus on achieving social development goals.

Third, a shift from an economy subject to (government) examination and approval to one based on (government provision of) services. The establishment of a "unified, open, competitive and orderly big market" was a major institutional guarantee for China's WTO accession and its participation in economic globalization. It is necessary to complete as soon as possible a review of all categories of government administrative examination and approval, and reduce them by a big margin and break sectoral monopolies. This will provide a good environment for competition among enterprises of various types, promote the flow of the factors of production, and make it possible for enterprises and the factors of production to rise or fall in the course of market competition and form optimized combinations. It is necessary to reconstruct the relations between the government and enterprises, between the government and the market, and between the government and social intermediaries, leaving those matters that the government is unable to take good care of to the market players and intermediaries. The main roles of the government in the future are to improve legislation, put government work on a legal basis, standardize the relations of property, credit and contract in the market economy, maintain the market order, ensure fair competition, and establish and improve the social security and social service systems, as well as other social public products and public services.

Fourth, a shift from an administration-dominated system to a system that carries out its administrative duties according to law. China's administrative system is characterised by vertical control. In order to adapt to the needs of the new stage of reform, China should accelerate the building of a legal system for the socialist market economy, and carry out administrative duties strictly according to law. The government should strengthen the legislation in this respect and make its enforcement just and rigorous, standardize the operations of various social roles, and punish violations of the law, so as to ensure the efficiency and equity of market competition.

Fifth, a shift from a power-based society to an ability-based society by weakening the decisive role of power while strengthening the basic role of the market mechanism in resource allocation. In the course of developing the socialist market economy, the state aims at enabling workers to have access to resources on account of their own abilities within the limits of laws and policies, and to be able to improve and develop themselves.

Sixth, a gradual shift from an administrative system featuring one-way control to a management mechanism featuring consultations and cooperation. This calls for improving the hierarchy and, more importantly, establishing a grid-type organization.

Seventh, a gradual shift from a state society to a citizen society. This calls for changing the outdated notions about "government departments," "enterprises and public institutions," "cadres" and "job assignments" that were ossified in people's minds under the planned economy system, carrying out community self-management and sectoral self-regulation, encouraging people to find jobs on their own or become self-employed, and fostering the citizens' independent identity characterized by self-respect, self-reliance and self-improvement.

I stated two years ago that the WTO accession would mean a second reform for China. Facts have shown that it has pushed our country's reform and opening up to a new stage. Acting in accordance with the requirements of the 16th CPC National Congress, adapting to the new situation as a result of economic globalization and the WTO accession, and pushing forward economic and political restructuring in the new period under the guidance of the important idea of the "Three Represents,"[1] China will certainly be able to build a new system of socialist market economy based on democracy and a legal system, and full of vitality and efficiency.

---

[1] The "Three Represents" is a short form of the statement that the Chinese Communist Party represents the requirement to develop the advanced productive forces, the orientation of the development of advanced culture and the fundamental interests of the overwhelming majority of the Chinese people.

PROPOSALS FOR ACTIVELY AND STEADILY PUSHING FORWARD STRUCTURAL REFORM

(*December 2002*)

Structural reform is an inevitable requirement of the reform when it has developed to a certain stage, emphasizing the reform of the institutional framework and changes in the rules of economic regulation, with the main aim of providing a good institutional environment and an environment in terms of rules and regulations for enterprise innovation and development. After more than two decades of market-oriented reform, China's economic transition is facing with many new contradictions and challenges: (1) The gradual approach to the reform that we have adopted has made historic achievements, but at the same time the deep-rooted problems and contradictions of a structural nature that have accumulated in the course of the reform and are left over from history have increasingly come to the fore in a concentrated way, and are putting constraints on the reform process and economic and social stability and development. (2) Whether at the macro level or at the micro level, structural readjustments and structural reform are intertwined, with structural readjustment depending, to a great extent, on structural reform, which in turn injects new motivation and vigor into structural readjustment. This is an important feature of China's economic transition period. (3) The acceleration of economic globalization and China's accession to the WTO have raised from outside new requirements on the goals and schedule of China's structural reform, bringing new motivation and pressures to the country.

In the light of the actual course of China's economic reform and development, the key to addressing the deep-rooted contradictions and institutional obstacles to economic development and social stability lies in actively and steadily pushing forward structural reform focusing on the adjustment of major interests and on institutional innovation in accordance with the requirement to put into practice the idea of the "Three Represents."

I. Structural Problems of an Institutional Nature Are Increasingly Becoming Outstanding Contradictions Hampering China's Reform Process, and Affecting Its Economic and Social Stability.

The internal and external environment and conditions of the present stage of reform have seen major changes as compared with the early period of reform. There has been a major shift in the main contradictions and problems of economic and social life. Adapting to the new situation, the reform needs to address many new focal points and tasks.

1. We should take the effective coordination of major social interests as a major task of structural reform, and proceed to bring the economic structure into harmony with the socio-political structure.

In a certain sense, the economic reform is a change in and readjustment of economic interests from which some people are bound to benefit while others will suffer losses. The key to the problem is that the economic reform will be able to take the interests of various parties into consideration, and provide rational compensation and assistance through corresponding social reforms to those who suffer losses in the reform and the disadvantaged social groups. The course of the reform and opening up has been accompanied by major changes in the country's original social interest mechanism, interest patterns and corresponding social structure. The new stage of reform calls for urgent efforts to readjust with initiative and vigor the major social relations of interests. This constitutes an outstanding contradiction in China's reform at present.

China's social reform has lagged behind its economic restructuring, resulting in a series of social contradictions and problems. Their outstanding manifestations are, first, that the social security system is not yet in place, seriously hampering economic restructuring, and, second, that the employment mechanism has not worked smoothly, resulting in a grim employment situation. Statistics show that laid-off and unemployed workers total 14.6 million. In the next five years, in addition to 12 million newly added job seekers annually, another 16 million jobs will be needed every year. Among those seeking jobs, the disadvantaged group has kept expanding. With the WTO accession, the trend of labor power supply outstripping the demand will continue to grow, further aggravating the employment situation. Third, the development of human resources can hardly keep abreast with the actual progress of the reform and opening up. On the one hand, China has a large reserve of labor power, but at a low level; on the other hand, it suffers a shortage of professionals well versed in the WTO rules and trained for the service sector, and faces a crisis resulting from a brain drain. Fourth, the income gap between various strata has widened to the extent that the conflict of social interest is quite pronounced. At present, widening gaps exist not only between town and country and between regions, but also between different industries and among urban residents. An outstanding problem is that the urban population living below the poverty line is showing a steadily growing tendency.

As economic restructuring deepens, economic and social contradictions and problems cropping up in practice have gone beyond the limits of the economic restructuring itself. Pushing forward the political restructuring appropriately and steadily has become an important condition for deepening economic restructuring. One of the most outstanding contradictions is the fact that the shift in the government management system and government functions have lagged behind the actual process of economic restructuring. Second, there is the lack of effective supervision over government power, social supervision in particular. This has led to the tendency of some government departments becoming interest groups, aggravating institutional corruption and weakening their public service functions. Meanwhile, it has also led to serious encroachments by competent authorities administering trades and local governments on the rights of enterprises, adding to their business costs. In addition, the building of a legal system in keeping with the process of economic restructuring has been weak.

2. The progress of the market-oriented reform varies from area to area, and the practice of reform and development has raised more urgent demands on the complementarity and harmonization of the institutional structure.

The uneven progress of the market-oriented reform is manifested on various levels. For example, in the building of a market system, the building of the products market is progressing faster, and shows a higher degree of marketization than the building of the production factors market covering capital and labor power. On the level of enterprises, the reform of non-state-owned enterprises in an effort to adapt to market competition is progressing faster, while the state-owned ones, as the central link and hard nut of economic restructuring, have remained the focus of the reform in the next step. And, as against a diversified market structure on a micro-level, the reform of the management system on a macro-level has progressed slowly. Such uneven progress on different levels has created a series of institutional frictions and conflicts of interest.

The practice of excessive government intervention in and control over the economic field is far from suiting the present changed market structure in the country and seriously dampens the enthusiasm of players in the micro market for further innovation. For example, the imperfections in the resources distribution mechanism have become a "bottleneck" for the reorganization of the assets of state-owned enterprises and the expansion of the non-state-owned economy. First of all, the distribution in the non-state-owned sector of banking resources, which are the most important factor for the organization of modern production, is extremely out of proportion to that sector's share of the national economy. Close to 80 percent of the resources in the credit market is monopolized by the state-owned banks, and flows mainly to the state-owned sector of the economy through banking subsidies and credit support. Second, the government has not yet lifted restrictions on the entry of non-public capital into the banking sector, so that the non-state-owned banking institutions and non-public capital market are undeveloped. More importantly, due to a lack of competition and efficiency, the potential risks that have accumulated in the banking sector pose an extremely great threat to the market environment.

Without an effective state assets management system, SOEs lack the precondition for constructing and standardizing corporate governance, and establishing a modern enterprise system. As facts in recent years show, more and more SOEs have found themselves in a state of work stoppage or semi-stoppage, or have even closed down, resulting in many workers being laid off. The development potential of SOEs has further diminished. The deep-rooted reason for this situation is the fact that a state assets management system adapted to the market economy has not come into being, and the mixing up of government and enterprise functions and of the government's and investors' functions is still an outstanding problem troubling the reform process of SOEs.

In fact, the irrational institutional structure is the cause of many contradictions in the economic structure. The structural contradictions on the economic level are intertwined with the structural problems on the institutional level. Structural problems exist not only on an economic level, but also on the level of institutions and systems. In a certain sense, the structural contradictions of the systems are the root cause of all problems of economic structures. To speed up the market-oriented reform and solve the deep-rooted structural problems of the systems is even more fundamental for effectively promoting the readjustment of the economic structures, and economic and social development.

3. Faced with the pressures and new challenges from the external environment in the new period, no single reform measure can fundamentally solve the problems of the institutional structure. We must find a long-term way through seeking new motivation and forms.

In the new stage of reform, no single reform measure or arrangement in terms of macro-economic policies can promote adjustment and development in other areas and departments. In the light of reality over the past few years, the government has adopted a series of macro-control measures focusing on expanding the domestic market, in an effort to promote a steady growth of the national economy. Additional issuance of state bonds, greater government expenditures and a pro-active fiscal policy are important measures for expanding the domestic market at the present stage. In the course of this, non-public investment has not been activated in real earnest for several successive years, falling far short of the anticipated policy objectives. Another outstanding contradiction is that while we tried to expand the domestic market by increasing government investment, the total tax revenues have grown by a big margin over several years, showing a faster rate of growth than that of the GDP. The most rapid growth has come from value-added tax (VAT) and income tax. Facts show that the effects of such measures as intensifying some macro-economic policies and making institutional arrangements in some areas are short-term and limited, and as a result we will miss a good opportunity to push forward institutional reform, and the difficulties and costs of the reform will be augmented. At present, the many-faceted practical contradictions in the country's economic restructuring all demand that we take the initiative in making adjustments to the reform approaches of recent years, so that the reform will once again gain a new motive force and progress, and release to the full its potential energy.

II. Grasping the Deep-rooted Contradictions of the Reform in the New Period and Their Main Features, We Should Vigorously Promote Structural Reform Focusing on the Adjustment of Major Interests and Institutional Innovation.

The economic transition is a long process. It is not only the supersession of one operating mechanism by another, but in essence a process of institutional innovations and a continuous accumulation of structural elements for a new system. Moreover, the transition is bound to be a process in which the economic, social and political structures are organically combined and transformed as a whole. To gradually push forward and realise such a structural readjustment and reform in compliance with the needs of efficiency and development is of the most significance to countries in the course of economic transition. In fact, against the background of economic globalization and the profound changes in the development environment, to push forward structural reform to find a way for a sustained and steady economic growth is an objective that many developing and developed countries are working together to attain.

As a large developing country in the course of economic transition, China shows both a similarity with other countries and a peculiarity in pushing forward the structural reform. At present, we should not only address the economic structural contradictions that are putting constraints on economic development, such as the town-country, industrial and employment structures, but, more importantly, pay attention to the fundamental role of optimising the institutional structure of economic development and social stability in this particular period of economic transition.

1. The reform process in the new period should give ever-greater prominence to the need for taking the people's interests as its fundamental starting point and ultimate end-result.

An important factor behind the success of China's economic restructuring over the past two decades and more was ensuring that the reform brought practical benefits to the people. The ultimate aim of the reform is to achieve common prosperity for all in China. As the reform goes deeper step by step, the original pattern of interests has undergone major changes. In real life, the phenomena of going against the interests of the people have become more and more prominent, greatly lowering people's expectations of the reform, and dampening their enthusiasm for understanding, supporting and participating in the reform process. Such problems are manifested conspicuously in the irrational widening of the income gap; obvious tendencies of government departments to turn into interest groups and non-public institutions and spreading corruption; a growing population of laid-off and unemployed workers and urban poor as a result of the structural readjustment and deepening reform of SOEs; and the slowdown in the increase in farmers' income, as well as the various resultant structural contradictions and problems.

In a complex external environment and amid ever-increasing uncertainties, it is all the more necessary for our reform to get the understanding and support of the general public, which is the key to further promoting the reform and maintaining social stability. In order to carry out and push forward structural reform, we should assess the foundation and conditions of the reform objectively, with special attention to identifying and grasping the main motive force of the reform. To promote structural reform in the new period, we should place special emphasis on the role of the general public in it, and attach greater importance to the extent of their support for it and their enthusiasm for participating in it. Placing the fundamental interests of the people above everything else in accordance with the requirements of the "Three Represents" should always be the fundamental starting point of the reform.

The advantages of the market economy lie in its diverse social and cultural differences, and adaptability. In essence, China's socialist market economy is a people's market economy, a market economy with the general public as its main beneficiaries. Therefore, its fundamental advantages lie in the wide participation of the general public on the basis of their constant access to benefits. Defining the objectives of the structural reform, increasing its transparency by informing the general public of its process and content, and enabling the majority to benefit from it — these have always been and will continue to be the important principles we should persist in for the smooth operation of structural reform.

2. We should accelerate the reform of the property rights system, and lay an institutionalised and socialised foundation for the effective operation of the new system.

A breakthrough in the reform of the property rights system is crucial to the new stage of reform. A shortage of products was a salient feature and manifestation of the planned economy system. But as far as its institutional deficiencies are concerned, the most burdensome one was a shortage of subjects of property rights, as primarily shown in the unitary subject of property rights. That was the institutional reason for the absence of competition and economic vigor. After more than two decades of reform, China's reform of the property rights system has made some headway in certain areas, resulting in the basic pattern of public ownership playing a dominant role in the national economy and diverse economic sectors developing side by side. But it should also be noted that this reform is far from being completed in China. An outstanding problem is that the proportion of the state-owned sector in the national economy is still too big, and it is still too much over-extended. By the end of 2000, the SOEs and the enterprises in which the state holds controlling shares (not including banking ones) throughout the country numbered 191,000 (as against 238,000 by the end of 1998). According to relevant statistics, the SOEs whose debts exceeded their assets and the so-called "hollow-shell enterprises" (whose registered losses exceeded the owners' rights) totalled 85,000, or 44.5 percent of the total SOEs.

As the market economy unfolds in width and depth, socialization of the subjects of property rights becomes an inevitable demand and trend. In the light of the actual progress of the country's economic restructuring, one of its major tasks in the new period is to realise the value of the entrepreneurs, especially those of the pioneering type, through a variety of channels, and to standardize and push forward a Chinese-style system of workers holding shares, so as to effectively build a community in which enterprises and workers share interests. We should then proceed to push forward the shift from a unitary to multiple and socialised subjects of property rights and build a micro-institutional foundation for the socialist market economy. In addition, we should grant and protect the property rights of rural land in legal terms to the farmers, creating a fundamental institutional condition for their effort to increase incomes.

Two questions of a policy nature need early clarification if the reform of the property rights system is to be accelerated. One is that, in the light of the actual process of the reform of the SOEs, there should be an analytical approach to the quantification of state assets, using different approaches to different sets of situations. When a portion of the additional value of net state assets is set aside for realising the value of the entrepreneurs and financing the workers' shareholding system on the basis of an objective assessment, and strictly in accordance with the correct procedure, it should not be considered a drain on state assets, but rather as a reward that the entrepreneurs and workers deserve in recognition of their contributions. It will be beneficial for stimulating the enthusiasm of entrepreneurs and workers, for the stability of enterprises and society in general, and even more so for keeping and increasing the value of state assets. The other requirement is that the principle of "He who invests owns" should be given a new and comprehensive interpretation. In the course of property rights reform, emphasizing only the control right and residual claim of the investors in material capital without recognising the usufruct of the investors in human capital does not conform to the general principle that technology, managerial expertise and other factors of production should participate in the distribution of income.

3. In order to push forward the structural reform, we should take the optimization of the institutional structure and the effective combination of macro-economic policies and market-oriented reform as the two major objectives.

The structural reform not only sets store by a new institutional arrangement, it pays even greater attention to the rationality of the institutional structure. For every institution in a given period has its structural nature, and is supplemented by other institutional arrangements. The complementarity and rationality of a new institution is the basis and precondition for its full effectiveness. As shown by practice in China, the aim of carrying out and pushing forward structural reform is precisely to address the structural contradictions between the new and old systems, speed up the development of elements of the new system, and further adjust and optimise its institutional structure, so as to improve and fully release the potential efficiency of the market mechanism and give full play to the basic role of institutional innovations and changes in economic growth and social development. Therefore, supporting reforms and an overall tackling of difficult issues following the establishment of the basic framework of the socialist market economy are of considerable urgency. The structural reform calls for both the matching of the reform measures in the economic restructuring and a close coordination of the economic restructuring with social reforms and political restructuring. The contradictions and problems accompanying economic restructuring have gone beyond economics itself. A comprehensive supporting reform has increasingly become a general trend.

It should be emphasised that the macro-economic policies aimed at solving economic structural contradictions must be effectively combined with measures for economic restructuring. In a certain sense, the role of institutional innovations in promoting structural readjustment and economic and social development in the period of economic transition are even more fundamental. On the whole, China has been quite successful in adopting macro-economic policies and promoting sustained and steady economic growth out of the need to stabilise the macro-economics, overcome the aftermath of the Asian financial crisis and address deflation, but has been relatively inadequate in making substantial progress in advancing institutional innovations, which lessened the effects of the macro-economic policies. Therefore, to promote the reform in the new period we must effectively combine the macro-economic policies and the reform measures by keeping the policy objectives consistent with those of the market-oriented reform, and making the reform measures meet the needs of macro-economic development, and try to remove the institutional obstacles to the development of the productive forces.

4. While maintaining a general approach of gradualism, we should make timely breakthroughs in the current stage of economic restructuring, and substantial breakthroughs in reforms in specific fields.

Practice shows that in its transition from the planned economy to the market economy, China has been successful in adopting a gradual approach to the reform in order to avoid social upheavals. However, such is the extent of the reform that the marked change in its environment and background forces us to speed it up. For one reason, the deep-rooted contradictions and problems that have been accumulated in the reform process can no longer be bypassed, nor can this present situation continue. Therefore, China should speed up the reform in the unfulfilled areas and weak links, and try as far as possible to avoid too long a continuation of the old, irrational system because of inadequate reforms or an institutional vacuum, so that the overall effects of the reform will not be harmed. In the course of this, we should, making a good judgment of the situation and seizing opportunities, achieve breakthroughs in the current stage of the reform, as well as substantial breakthroughs in reforms of specific fields. This is our inevitable choice. For another reason, competition in the international market under even more open conditions is, in the final analysis, competition concerning institutions and mechanisms. To a certain extent, the key to winning a competitive edge is to win an institutional edge. The WTO accession has pushed China's reform and opening to a new stage. In order to adapt to the WTO rules, China will have to roughly fulfil the main aspects of the restructuring and bring it into line with international market practices in the five-year transitional period. In this sense, the WTO accession represents China's second round of reform and opening up, with more clearly defined objectives and an even stronger binding force than in the past.

III. The Main Task of Advancing the Structural Reform Is to Strive for Institutional Innovation in the New Period.

At the present stage, the basic objective and main tasks of speeding up the structural reform are to concentrate on resolving the institutional structural contradictions that hamper the development of the productive forces and social stability, make the socialist market economy more mature and sounder, and achieve institutional innovation in the new period through structural reform.

1. We should speed up the macro-economic reform with emphasis on relaxing control and creating a market environment favorable for business and innovation by players of the micro market.

First, we should deepen the reform of the banking system, with the objective of bringing into being an efficient mechanism for distributing banking resources and a safeguard mechanism that is capable of effectively managing banking risks and maintaining banking stability, and improve the international competitiveness of Chinese banking institutions. Therefore, it is essential to bring about a fundamental change in the operating mechanism of the state-owned commercial banks through an all-round settlement of the undesirable creditors' rights and introduce the joint-stock system; make vigorous efforts to develop medium-sized and small banking institutions to solve the difficulties of medium-sized and small enterprises and the county economy in raising funds and expanding their operations; provide non-public capital with access to the banking and service sectors under the precondition of strict supervision; improve the money market system, and push forward in good time the reform to allow the market to set interest rates; and improve and standardise the building of a capital market to enable it to fully play its role in optimizing resources distribution and improving the efficiency of assets operations.

Second, we should ensure the effective management and improve the operating mechanism of state assets as soon as possible. There are two main reform measures in this respect: (1) Changing the ownership of state assets from a unitary one into one at various levels with the aim of mobilizing the enthusiasm of various quarters for investment; and (2) Improving the mechanism for entrusted operations of state assets so as to realise the market-oriented management of the state assets. In keeping with the strategic adjustment of state assets and the introduction of the standardized corporate system and the joint-stock system into the large and medium-sized SOEs, it is essential to realise as soon as possible the separation of the functions of the government as a public administrator and a state assets owner, and institute new-type state-asset management, operating and supervisory systems, so as to ensure that investors in state assets and their supervisors are well placed to exercise their rights as owners in accordance with the law. In this process, although strengthening supervision by sending in a supervisory board from outside is, of course, very important, reform in many enterprises has shown that authorized operations under which entrepreneurs become representatives operating state assets under authorization are beneficial to mobilizing the enthusiasm of enterprises, and to maintaining and increasing the value of state assets. In addition, it is necessary to speed up the work of improving the competitive mechanism of incentives and controls covering the managers and key technical personnel of SOEs that is suited to the market economy and embraces the system of incentives in the form of property rights, so as to ensure the accumulation of human capital in the state sector and bring their enthusiasm into full play.

Third, we should improve the institutional and legal environment for the development of the non-state-owned sector of economy. In the present circumstances in which the world economy is experiencing recession on a wide scale and the expansion of domestic demand has become China's basic policy objective, the building and improvement of a system of protecting private property, removal of institutional obstacles to market access of the non-state-owned economy, granting national treatment to it, expansion of its scope for investment, increased access to bank loans, and permission for non-public capital to participate in banking reform — all these are the objective requirements for developing the non-state-owned sector of economy and bringing about institutional innovation. Against the background of gradually opening the market to foreign funds during the limited period of transition following the WTO accession, giving priority to internal opening and speeding up the development of the non-state-owned sector are of even greater urgency.

Fourth, we should further promote reform in the fiscal and taxation system, in order to activate non-public capital. We should shift the situation from the government being the sole source of public investment to the government mainly playing leverage and guiding role through fiscal and taxation means, standardize the system with regard to the issuance and use of state bonds, and experiment with the issuance of local government bonds and local municipal special-purpose bonds. At the same time, it is necessary to bring about a reshaping of the pro-active fiscal policy, shifting the operation of state bonds from the current direct investment mode to state bonds supporting structural tax reduction and the reform of the taxation system.

2. We should speed up rural reform, with emphasis on the reform of the rural land-use system.

First, more rapid urbanization is of strategic significance. In the next 10 to 20 years, 100 million to 200 million surplus rural inhabitants will move to cities. This is not only one of the basic tasks for the deepening of rural reform but, more importantly, one of the strategic objectives of the effort to promote China's urban reform and economic restructuring as a whole. The realization of this strategic objective will be beneficial to promoting the optimization of China's economic structure and to laying a solid foundation for sustained economic and social development. To this end, we must have a sufficient and correct understanding of the issue, and begin reform of the household registration system as soon as possible, with the aim of basically opening an avenue between town and country with regard to the household registration system, so as to create the necessary conditions for the urbanization process.

Second, we should, as soon as possible, define the farmers' permanent and secure property rights over rural land. The key to speeding up innovation of the rural land system lies in a permanent, capitalized and market-oriented right to use rural land by granting to the farmers the permanent right to use land and dispose of the land they have contracted, including transfer, mortgage and land shares. With the precondition of ensuring them the right to land use, vigorous efforts should be made to encourage the building of a market for the flow of rural land, and provide legal protection for the farmers' various land rights and interests.

Third, we should speed up the institutional innovation of the rural production and operation organizations. Farmers should be encouraged to pool their land as shares, and vigorous efforts should be made to develop agricultural organizations for industrialized operations linking corporations and farm households, combining production and institutions of learning and research, and integrating production, processing and marketing. Organizations such as agricultural production and service cooperatives, as well as agricultural associations, should be developed to provide commercialized services for the production and operations of farm households. It is necessary to reshape the governments at the township level and the self-management organizations at the village level, and bring into play the function of the collective economy as an organizer, so as to provide a good environment for the operations of farm households.

3. We should speed up social reforms with emphasis on creating an equitable and stable social environment.

First, substantial progress should be made in reforming the income distribution system, and standardizing the social distribution order. It is essential to gain a new understanding of the theories of labor and labor value, with a view to promoting a combination of distribution according to work and distribution according to production factors. The reform of the property rights system should be accompanied by an effort to establish a workers' shareholding system with Chinese characteristics, defining ways for capital, technology, managerial expertise, labor power and other factors of production to participate in income distribution, shape an effective state mechanism for regulating the relations of income distribution, standardize the distribution order, and strive to work out rational relations of property distribution in the course of the structural reform, so as to create further scope for people to ensure their interests.

Second, it is necessary to speed up the improvement of the social security system and build a solid social safety net. Continued efforts should be made to extend the social security coverage in the areas of old-age pension and medical and unemployment insurance in accordance with the law, and gradually raise the level of socially pooled funds. A number of ways should be employed to enrich the social security fund through the reduction of state shares, taxes on the interest, issuance of state bonds and increasing the proportion of expenditures on social security in the fiscal expenditures, so that a timely and full issuance of social security funds will be ensured. Greater attention should be paid to disadvantaged social groups by establishing a general system for ensuring subsistence allowances for urban residents and gradually raising the level of social security. In addition, it is necessary to increase the outlay for poverty alleviation, and disaster and social relief, in order to ensure the basic standards of living for farmers and rural stability.

Third, we should intensify the development of human resources. To search for a market-oriented way of developing and distributing human resources, establish an effective property-rights-based incentive system and shape a rational personnel system — these are all effective ways to promote the development of human resources through institutional innovations in the new situation. The improvement of the quality of the labor power throughout society should be taken as an essential task in the development of human resources. There are acute contradictions and a grim situation in employment in China at present, and the proportion of older-age, unskilled and female workers among the laid-off workers is increasing. In such circumstances, reemployment training for these disadvantaged groups is an important task for the development of human resources at the current stage.

4. We should steadily push forward political restructuring with emphasis on shifting the government's functions and governing in accordance with the law.

First, speeding up government reform is crucial. Following its WTO accession, China is participating in international competition in even more open conditions in what is a test of government efficiency. To adapt to the WTO accession and the requirements of structural reform, the government should effect a thorough shift in the scope and modes of its activities and functions. It should review its administrative procedures of examination and approval, and reduce them drastically; further define and divide between the central and local governments the limits of legislative and administrative powers with a view to strengthening the authority of the central government; strengthen its public functions, standardize its actions, foster and enhance its credit and promote a shift in the government administrative system from one of control to one of supervision.

Second, it is essential to strengthen the building of the legal system. In accordance with the WTO rules and China's commitments, we should review the laws, decrees and regulations currently in force to identify those stipulations in them that are at odds with the WTO rules and China's commitments, and complete the work of revising or nullifying them in due time while speeding up new legislation. It is essential to emphasize the supremacy of the Constitution of the People's Republic of China, and see to it that the government carries out its administrative functions in accordance with the law. It is essential to enforce the laws strictly, take effective measures to prevent the recurrence of the practice in which the rule by man prevails over the rule of law, and resolutely root out corruption in the judicial departments.

Third, it is essential to strengthen democracy and democratic participation and supervision over the use of administrative powers. On the one hand, supervision of administrative powers and actions should be strengthened through stricter law enforcement, and on the other, it is necessary to increase the extent of social involvement in government actions, and enhance the extent of democracy and transparency through developing social intermediaries, public welfare organizations, trade associations and other non-governmental organizations. It is necessary to further improve the related institutions, such as public hearing, announcements and administrative assistance, in order to provide an institutional guarantee for promoting democracy and democratic participation and supervision of the administration.

TEN MAJOR ISSUES FACING CHINA'S REFORM OF THE PROPERTY RIGHTS SYSTEM

(October 2001)

- Shortage was a salient feature and economic manifestation of the planned economy. But as far as institutional deficiencies are concerned, the greatest deficiency in the traditional planned economy system was its shortage of subjects of property rights, as primarily shown in the unitary subject of property rights. That was the institutional reason why the traditional planned economy system was void of competition and lacked economic vitality.
- What is most significant in the transition from the planned economy system to the socialist market economy system is to push forward the transformation from a unitary subject of property rights to the socialization of subjects of property rights, which is the institutional foundation for the socialist market economy.
- As China has already entered a new stage in its economic restructuring, substantial breakthroughs in the reform of the property rights system are critical to speeding up economic restructuring. The reform of the property rights system has made some breakthroughs in certain areas, but its tasks are far from being complete. The delay has resulted in a series of new contradictions and problems. Pushing forward the reform in this area will be of most substantial significance in the institutional innovations during the new period.

I. Making New Breakthroughs in SOE Reform Through Socialising Property Rights

To establish a community of interest between an enterprise and its staff and workers on the basis of the actual ownership of the property rights is the fundamental measure to mobilise the enthusiasm of the workers; and to turn the workers, technical personnel, managerial staff and entrepreneurs gradually into owners of the property rights of their enterprises is the key to making breakthroughs in the reform of SOEs.

1. Speeding up the reform of the property rights system is the precondition for establishing an effective corporate governance structure in SOEs.

— Socialising the subjects of property rights is the basis and precondition for separating the functions of the government and enterprises and establishing a modern enterprise system.

— An effective corporate governance structure is possible only with the socialization of the subjects of property rights and clearly defined ownership.

— Socialization of the subjects of property rights is beneficial to shaping an awareness of risks and responsibilities on the part of diverse subjects of interests and strengthening the self-regulating mechanism of the enterprises.

2. Property rights reform is the foundation for a community of interests between an enterprise and its staff and workers.

— The close combination of an enterprise and its staff and workers on the basis of a modern market economy is an important universal objective in a modern market economy. Turning the staff and workers of an enterprise into actual owners of the enterprise's property is an institutional basis for the wide participation by workers in enterprise management and shaping a corporate culture.

— It is necessary to introduce the system of staff and workers holding shares, and maintain a rational differentiation under the prerequisite of fully recognising and realising the different roles and contributions among workers, managers and technical personnel, and proceed to bring the enthusiasm of various types of human resources into fuller play.

— It is necessary to achieve a long-term, rational unity of the interests of workers with those of the enterprises and the state on the basis of recognising and establishing the property rights of labor power, and gradually establish a community of interests among the state, the collective and individuals.

3. It is essential to speed up the property rights system reform of large enterprises, focusing on introducing the joint-stock system.

— We should push forward the introduction of the joint-stock system in large SOEs step by step and in groups, based on sectoral classifications.

4. Various forms should be employed to promote reform in the property rights system of the medium-sized and small SOEs.

At this crucial period in China's economic transition, promoting the development of medium-sized and small SOEs will be of far-reaching significance in promoting economic development and social stability. At present, we should further emancipate our minds, sum up experiences and intensify our efforts to relax control on and revitalize such enterprises. Under the precondition of gradual standardization, raising the proportion of stocks to be held by staff and workers and those to be bought by management in the course of introducing the shareholding system is an important choice for medium-sized and small SOEs in speeding up their reform.

5. Speeding up the search for an effective form of state assets

management is an important condition for SOE institutional innovation.

The establishment of an effective state assets management system in keeping with the requirements of the socialist market economy is vital for deepening the reform of SOEs. It is essential to correctly appraise and understand the positions and roles of the SOEs and state assets in the course of establishing and improving the socialist market economy system. It is essential to increase the extent to which state assets are operated in a market-oriented way while a rational size and proportion of the state-owned economy is retained, so as to bring about a shift from state assets to state capital, and establish a scientific management and operating mechanism.

II. Using the Generalization of Subjects of Property Rights to Promote Further Development of Non-public Sector

A differential holding of the enterprise's shares by its investors, managers and technical personnel is the key to high growth of non-public enterprises, especially hi-tech ones, in a modern market economy.

1. The generalization of the subjects of property rights is the most important measure to break the bottlenecks of the non-public sector in its development in terms of professionals and technologies.

— Incompleteness with regard to the subjects of property rights also exists in the property rights system of the non-public sector to a certain extent.

— The role of human capital in the operations of non-public enterprises is becoming more and more evident, to the extent that whether or not an enterprise is able to retain the core members of its managerial and technical staff will decide its very survival and development. To readdress the imbalances in the supply of and demand for competent personnel in the non-public sector, such as a lack of sense of achievement and obstacles to innovation, the establishment of a property-rights-based incentive system under which such personnel become actual owners of non-public enterprises is essential.

2. The generalization of the subjects of property rights is an inevitable choice of the non-public sector after reaching a certain stage of development.

— Removal of restraints as a result of family ownership is an important experience in furthering the development of the non-public sector.

— The generalization of the subjects of property rights is the precondition for non-public enterprises to become corporations.

III. Using Diversification of Investors to Promote Infrastructure Reform

1. The unitary state investor is the key factor behind low efficiency and delayed development of infrastructure.

— The government is the main investor in infrastructural construction while the scope and channels for investment by non-public capital have not yet been opened.

— The unitary state investment system is the root cause of the difficulty in breaking the administrative monopoly of the infrastructure.

2. Increasing investment in infrastructure must go hand by hand with the reform to diversify sources of investment in infrastructure.

— The government cannot become, in the long run, sole investor in infrastructure; the real investors should be enterprises, especially those in the non-public sector.

— Only when the sources of investment are diversified can the efficiency of the government investment be raised.

3. It is essential to break the administrative monopoly, and lift restrictions on market access so as to create the conditions for non-public capital to enter infrastructure.

— We should give priority to internal opening in the wake of the WTO accession, and allow non-public capital to step in ahead of the schedule.

— We should promote the entry of non-public capital into the infrastructure step by step and through a variety of forms.

4. It is essential to reform the management system and the investment and financial system of the government concerning the infrastructure.

We should open the market, and combine the industrial reorganization with the reorganization of property rights so as to bring about a shift in the subjects of investment in the infrastructure. We should promote the reform related to infrastructure to bring about an appropriate separation of the areas where competition is possible and those where competition is not possible, and break the monopoly by placing equal emphasis on introducing competition and on bringing non-public investment into the infrastructure. It is essential to review and revise discriminatory policies currently in force against the non-public sectors so as to create a fair policy-related environment for competition. Related supporting policies should be adopted to facilitate direct and indirect financing by the non-state-owned sector. The government should use fiscal subsidies for interest payment and set up an investment guarantee fund to facilitate the financing of non-state-owned enterprises for the purpose of investing in infrastructure.

IV. Speeding Up the Introduction of Joint-stock System in State-owned Commercial Banks Under the Precondition of Clearly Established Ownership

1. The introduction of the joint-stock system into state-owned commercial banks is extremely urgent. With the WTO accession, the state-owned commercial banks have come under tremendous pressure. The core of the reform in these banks is to speed up ownership reform under the prerequisite of separating bad assets from them, and establish an effective governing structure.

2. It is necessary to find a way to more thoroughly dispose of undesirable creditor's rights to create conditions for the introduction of the joint-stock system into state-owned commercial banks. Excessive bad assets are what makes it difficult for these banks to practice the joint-stock system, and where enormous banking risks are concentrated. A more thoroughgoing way is needed to fundamentally dispose of bad assets that have been accumulated over a long period of time. It may be advisable to work out a comprehensive debt trusteeship package, allow non-public capital to buy shares in state assets management corporations and, on the basis of strict supervision, grant a fairly big share of the business and appropriately preferential policies to the non-public assets management corporations.

3. We should speed up banking legislation, and establish an effective banking regulation system. To meet the principles and requirements of the WTO accession, we should, in reference to international practice, step up the work of formulating and improving China's banking regulations and rules covering bank assets, trust and investment corporations and the supervisory regulations of the central bank, gradually improve the country's system of regulation of the banking sector, and gradually shift from sector-wide regulation to mixed-sector regulation, while paying greater attention to risk prevention in the course of opening up.

4. We should promote in good time a regime allowing the market

to set interest rates, and improve the building of the capital market. An imperfect capital market and a low degree of the responsiveness of banking assets prices to the market are outstanding manifestations of the fact that China's banking reform has not yet met the requirements of the socialist market economy. During the Tenth Five-Year Plan period (2001-2005), we should promote the process of forming a regime allowing the market to set interest rates in good time, and, in combination with the reform, to introduce the joint-stock system into the state owned commercial banks. We should also optimise the allocation of resources, and improve the operating efficiency and returns of the assets.

V. Using Property-rights-based Incentive Mechanism as Foundation for Making Early Substantial Breakthroughs in Reform of Income Distribution System

A rational property-rights-based incentive is most effective, and is the key to the development of human resources. Therefore, the reform of the income distribution system should match the reform of the property rights system.

1. The reform of the property rights system is the key to reform of the income distribution system.

— Under the precondition of establishing the property rights of labor power, encouraging labor, managerial expertise, technology and other factors of production to participate in income distribution is a manifestation of combining the principle of distribution according to work and the principle of distribution according to production factors in the new period.

— A property-rights-based incentive is an effective breakthrough in the reform of the income distribution system.

2. A property-rights-based incentive is an institutional basis for promoting the rational allocation of human resources.

— Human capital was not recognised under the planned economy system, and the allocation of human resources was extremely irrational.

— The practice of property-rights-based incentives in forms of stock rights and options is of importance in promoting a rational allocation of human resources.

— That entrepreneurs own property is an inevitable requirement of their role in enterprises in the modern market economy. Practice proves that partial ownership by the entrepreneurs is an effective way as they become the actual controllers and residual claimants of their enterprises; this is a concrete indication of the increasingly rising role of human capital in modern enterprise governance, and a reflection of a new feature and trend of the governance structure of modern enterprises.

3. We should look for multiple effective forms of a rational property-rights-based incentive by proceeding from reality and making active explorations.

— It is necessary to adopt different forms of property-rights-based incentives to suit different types of human capital.

— It is necessary to make bold explorations in search of an effective property-rights-based incentive mechanism on the basis of the current reality with regard to the stock rights and options system, and the system of workers holding shares.

VI. Introducing a Science and Technology System Focusing on Converting Managerial Expertise, Technology and Other Production Factors into Shares

The core of the effort to introduce such a science and technology system is to shape an institutional environment enabling scientific and technological personnel to play their roles to the full. To recognise their intellectual power and convert it into shares is of decisive significance for innovation in the science and technology system.

1. In a knowledge-based economy, managerial expertise, technology and other factors of production focusing on manpower are playing an ever more obvious role.

— Knowledge and management are special labor, distinct from general labor, and, in a knowledge-based economy, become an important factor contributing to the creation of value.

2. It is necessary to make breakthroughs in the innovation of the science and technology system focusing on converting production factors into shares and socializing such factors.

— The establishment of the property rights of labor power through workers holding shares and other forms will effectively renovate the science and technology system.

— Workers and technological personnel are not only salary earners in the traditional sense but also beneficiaries of a new system combining the principle of distributing income according to the factors of production and the principle of distributing income according to work.

— The practice of allowing technological factors to take part in the distribution of profits through technology for shares and other experimental forms is a built-in motive force for science and technology system innovation.

3. It is necessary to increase the proportion of the property-rights-based incentive, and establish an effective incentive mechanism.

The development of human resources requires a scientific incentive mechanism. We should establish the income distribution principle that gives priority to efficiency with due consideration to fairness, and gives incentives to the strong while protecting the weak; establish a property-rights-based incentive mechanism, and bring into the fullest play the enthusiasm of those who have started hi-tech businesses and have management talent.

VII. Deepening Rural Reform, Taking as Its Core the Conversion of Land-use Right into Real Right

To grant to the farmers long-term and secure land-use right is to recognise their rights to their land. At present, the problems that require the most urgent solution is to clearly establish the farmers' property rights to land in legal terms, speed up the innovation of the rural land system, and bring about a long-term, capitalised and market-oriented rural-land-use right.

1. Farmers should be granted a long-term right to land use as well as disposal right over the land they have contracted, including transfer, mortgage and putting up land for shares.

2. It is necessary to speed up the development of the rural land exchange market.

The government should make vigorous efforts to develop the market for rural land transfer under the prerequisite that the farmers' land-use right is ensured, formulating explicit stipulations on market access, exchange procedure, rights and obligations, and format of contracts.

3. The state should provide legal protection for the farmers' various land rights and interests.

The state should establish a legal protection system for the farmers' land-use right as soon as possible, and, except in cases where the law provides otherwise, no government or organization at any level should be allowed to violate their land rights and interests or interfere with the exercise of their various rights in accordance with the law.

VIII. Speeding Up Shift of Government Functions, with Standardization and Retention of Subjects of Property Rights as Basic Task

1. The key reason for the overstepping, misplacing and absence of government functions is the absence of a clearly established property rights foundation.

— Due to the blurring of property rights and a mistaken definition of the government role, in the past the government has meddled in affairs outside its jurisdiction while failing to do a good job of affairs in its own domain, resulting in misplacing, overstepping and neglect of its public functions.

2. An important task in the shift of government functions is to protect property rights.

— If the government is excessive in direct interference in the economy while not doing enough to protect property rights, then the vitality of the non-public sector will be stifled.

— The government should, centring on the protection of property rights, relax control, encourage competition and truly revitalize the economy.

IX. Building Property Rights Exchange Markets of Various Forms

It is necessary to gradually build and improve a multi-tier, multiform property rights exchange market to serve as a market environment for the reform of the property rights system.

1. A sound property rights exchange market is the precondition for an overall reform of the property rights system.

— Exchange of property rights requires a standardized market for that purpose.

— The development of a standardized property rights exchange market is the precondition for promoting reform in the property rights system.

2. It is necessary to build and improve a multi-tier, multiform property rights exchange market by moving gradually and in an orderly way.

— It is necessary to constantly improve the property rights exchange market on the basis of long-term practice.

— It is necessary to actively innovate and gradually build a property rights exchange market system covering both physical and non-physical markets, diverse sellers and buyers, multi-layer varieties of property rights exchange, and multiple forms of exchange.

X. Speeding Up Property Rights System Reform Should Be Combined with Legislation on Relations of Property Rights, Personnel System Reform, and Promotion of Democracy and Democratic Participation at the Grassroots.

1. Speeding up legislation related to property rights is of important significance in the course of China's economic transition. The country's Constitution should provide explicitly for the protection of private property and the independent ownership of private property.

2. The reform of the property rights system should be used as an opportunity to promote democracy and democratic participation at the grassroots.

— It is necessary to promote the villagers' self-management system by reforming the property rights system.

— It is necessary to speed up the process of democratic elections at the grassroots in cities by reforming the property rights system.

SHIFT IN GOVERNMENT FUNCTIONS AND THE DEVELOPMENT OF NGOS

SHIFT IN GOVERNMENT FUNCTIONS AND THE DEVELOPMENT OF NGOS

GOVERNMENT REFORM IN CHINA'S NEW STAGE OF REFORM AND OPENING UP

(*May 2003*)

I. The Focus of Reform in the New Stage Is Government Reform

China's WTO accession marked the beginning of a new stage in its reform and opening up. As practice over the past year and more and forecasts for the coming few years show, government reform will be one of the focal points of the reform. This is the requirement of China's market-oriented reform process, its WTO accession and, even more so, the requirement to deepen the reform. We should follow the internationally accepted economic rules and, in terms of institutional arrangements, change the "rules of play" of the planned economy. What is most important is a fundamental shift in the role of the government. For example, first, the government should change its role as a kind of market player. So far, it is still playing a partial role as a market player in the case of the state monopolies and the state-owned sector. Second, the government should shift its functions. We have been talking about the need of the government to perform its public functions. What are meant by public functions? Drawing up plans and implementing them are among its main public functions. Third, given the extent of China's economic transition, the need to change the government role, perform its public functions and maintain social stability places government reform in a more prominent position than enterprise reform. In this connection, I term the necessity of government reform as meeting the needs in the following three areas: China's obligations to the WTO, the country's market-oriented reform process, and the constant deepening of the reform.

We have taken a gradual approach to reform, and achieved enormous successes, leaving, however, quite a few problems behind. The special features of gradual reform are: (1) proceeding from the outside (extra-institutional) to the inside (intra-institutional), leaving the core part of the traditional system virtually intact. (2) Proceeding from the easy to the difficult. "Crossing a river by feeling for the stepping-stones" — this phrase, used at the early stage of the reform, applied to the shallow water area, while the restructuring has entered the deep water area now. What remain are all tough tasks focusing on adjusting major interests, especially the reform of SOEs and government reform. (3) Proceeding from the top to the bottom. The past course of the reform was dominated by the government, and aimed at delegating decision-making powers to enterprises and allowing them to keep more of their profits. Now the government needs self-reform. In that case, what should be the main force pushing forward this reform? (4) Economics before politics. It is an objective fact that the political restructuring in the country has been lagging behind. A further delay would affect both development and stability.

Along with the deepening of the market-oriented reform, rise of the non-public sector, formation and growth of the middle-income group, development of the labor power market, various types of market exchanges, free migration and resultant expansion of organizations suited to the needs of the market economy and social organizations, various social groups hope that the government will abandon artificial restrictions and controls in certain areas on the one hand and provide them with the public services they need badly on the other. This is the inevitable logic of the reform.

II. Separation of Government and Enterprise Functions Has Become an Increasingly More Urgent and Complex Task.

We have been calling for the separation of government and enterprise functions ever since the beginning of the reform. Why has the shift in government functions been lagging behind all along? This, of course, has something to do with the traditional planned economy system and the stunted development of industrial associations and other social organizations. But the deep-rooted reason lies in the fact that the self-interest of government departments is hidden behind the expansion of some administrative powers. It is not difficult to find out from the studies on some sprawling corruption cases that the frequent occurrence of such cases is related to the imperfect mechanisms of conferral and use of administrative powers, as well as to the lack of democratic supervision over and restraints on them. This has turned some vested interest groups of the reform into obstacles to further reform.

Here is the problem: It is an indisputable fact that to a certain extent state power has turned into departmental power, which in turn has turned into interest groups. Institutional corruption has kept spreading, the social income gap has widened and problems accumulated over the past decade concerning agriculture and the rural areas defy an easy solution. We are faced with increasingly greater and more complex economic and social problems, and the reform is faced with increasingly greater demands and increasingly higher expectations.

What is the way out? The report to the 16th CPC National Congress pointed out with particular clarity the need to tighten restraints on and supervision over the use of power, establish a mechanism for the exercise of power featuring a rational structure, scientific distribution, rigorous procedures and effective restraint, and strengthened supervision over the use of power at decision-making, execution and other links, so as to ensure that the power entrusted by the people is truly used for their benefit.

III. The Role and Functions of the Government

Last year, the fifth edition of *Comparison of Socio-economic Systems* carried an article by Qian Yingyi titled, "Government and the Rule of Law." In the article he stated that to enable the market, the "invisible hand," to play its role, it is necessary to restrain the economic man. And this role is played by the government in a modern market economy. Such restraint is manifested in three ways: intellectual property rights protection, implementation of contracts, and appropriate regulation. At the same time, another major problem that the market economy needs to solve is that the government which restrains the economic man itself needs to be restrained. What is in a position to restrain the government? The rule of law, the citizen society and democracy. Qian Yingyi placed particular emphasis on the point that the rule of law restrains the government by making it limited and effective. We often see in real life that either there are too many laws restricting the scope of economic man's activity or there are too few laws restricting the arbitrary power of the government. The result is that the rule of law fails to restrain the government, which has not yet become a truly limited government.

Qian Yingyi's article can help us to understand the functions and role of the government as well as their boundaries under the conditions of market economy. I am not going to list excellent expositions by other Chinese scholars on this issue. Of course, the Chinese government is also charged with a host of major functions in the supply of public products, construction of large-scale infrastructure projects, state assets management, employment promotion, environmental protection, family planning, income regulation and social security, which are a reflection of certain Chinese characteristics.

IV. Administrative Reform, Government Reform and Political Restructuring

What is meant by government reform? Government reform at

present is in fact a type of administrative reform. In the final analysis, it is the political restructuring that is headed for a public government and a government providing services (or simply, using the term, "customer relations management [CRM]" in e-government). Some people hold the view that the current reform in China is limited to administrative reform or even to the streamlining of government organizations, and does not extend to government reform as such. In fact, the current political restructuring touches on the expansion and reconstruction of the social order as a whole, and calls for a balancing of the demands of various interest groups, requiring increasingly higher political skills and technical support. Therefore, I am also in favor of the two relatively neutral concepts "government governance" and "institutional innovation of the government." In fact, the current structure of government and the whole political system in China were not designed and put into place for the establishment of a market economy in the first place. Some people have termed this process of change from a government in a traditional planned society to an effective government in a modern market economy society as "government switching to a new system" or "government restructuring," which smacks of an institutional transition. In my view, administrative reform, government reform and political restructuring are three concepts increasing in importance in a progressive order. In that case, the term "government reform" is a step further than "administrative reform," which is designed to improve efficiency.

V. Government Reform After the 16th CPC National Congress

The section of the report to the 16th CPC National Congress on political construction and political restructuring dealt nine issues centring on the fundamental objective of developing socialist democracy and building a socialist civilization. After the congress, Hu Jintao, the general secretary of the CPC Central Committee, urged the whole party to act upon Mao Zedong's call before the founding of the PRC for remaining modest, prudent, and free from arrogance and rashness in their style of work, and preserving the style of plain living and hard struggle. Recently he has urged the media to keep in close contact with reality, the people and life. Meeting the press during the National People's Congress session earlier this year, Premier Wen Jiabao said that the new government elected at the congress session had a plan to push forward political restructuring by starting with three areas — the democratic and scientific decision-making mechanism, performance of administrative functions in accordance with the law, and democratic supervision. He told the press that to strengthen the anti-corruption struggle he would push forward the streamlining of the government organizations and reform the system of administrative control, the reduction of the scale of administrative examination and approval, the fund management system and the personnel system. We have already seen a series of big moves made in the wake of the NPC session. The Economic Restructuring Office of the State Council was incorporated into the State Development Planning Commission to become the new State Development and Reform Commission. This was a correct move, for macro-control of the market economy is closely related to the reform. But from the medium-to-long-term perspective, the reform tasks are still very heavy. It can be said with certainty that the new government will push forward the government reform and the political restructuring in a more pragmatic and steadfast way. Of course, it is necessary to strike a balance between the effort to treat "symptoms" and those to address the "root cause" and guard against the pitfall of "treading the old path in new shoes."

Practical problems are even more complicated and difficult. But we have also seen some new bright spots and new hopes from the practice of various localities. The first and foremost point in Lu Rizhou's "Changzhi experience" (Changzhi is a city in Shanxi Province and Lu is the secretary of the CPC's Changzhi Municipal Committee) is open administration, which is the foundation for building a political civilization. However, some scholars are critical of Lu Rizhou's practice of "running the city through the media (referring to his persistent use of the *Changzhi Daily* — the journal of the CPC's Municipal Committee — to expose dereliction of duty, corruption and violations of the law by local officials)." Critics have pointed out that what the *Changzhi Daily* has done is not supervision by the public opinion in the modern sense of rule of law, for supervision by public opinion in the true sense should come from social opinion outside the jurisdiction of the government.

Shenzhen City's so-called "separation of administrative power" (referring to the system of administrative control with separation among administrative decision-making, implementation and supervision) is an even brighter spot that has attracted internal and external attention. It may very likely become a focal point of the effort of various localities to speed up the reform of the administrative system in accordance with the guidelines set forth in the 16th CPC National Congress. In addition, vigorous promotion of e-government in my view should also become an item in the government reform.

Shaoxing City in Zhejiang Province has promoted the separation of government organizations and public institutions. The latter have undergone a change in management system. For example, local radio and television stations have repositioned their surplus employees and compensated them for severance from the state payroll. In Zhejiang Province, which boasts the most developed non-public sector in the country, we have also seen a force for pushing forward the reform from the bottom to the top. The market economy calls for democratic politics — this seems to be a law. Of course, it is also particularly important to separate the functions of the government and the society. After more than two decades of reform, to develop non-governmental organizations (NGOs) is an important task in the effort to build a modern social structure. Social organizations should be non-governmental in nature, for social organizations with too heavy an official coloring can hardly play their due roles at crucial moments when they have to represent and coordinate various interest groups and major interests.

It is a heartening phenomenon in China that various theoretical views are competing and contending, which provides rich theoretical resources for our current discussions on government reform and political restructuring.

VI. Major Issues in Government Reform

Government reform touches upon many complicated problems. In my view the four "shifts" listed below are the major issues the government should concentrate its reform on:

1. A shift from the government-dominated economy to the market-dominated economy. From the government-decreed economy to the government-dominated market economy to the market-dominated market economy—this traces the major stages of the market-oriented reform in China. East Asian countries, such as Japan and the ROK, used to practice a government-dominated market economy to a great extent. The ROK has paid a heavy price for this, while the Koizumi Cabinet of Japan has put forward the concept of structural reform. To meet the requirements of the WTO and in the light of the practical experience gained in its period of government-dominated market economy, China should make an early shift from the government-dominated market economy to market-dominated economic development.

2. A shift from giving priority to economic objectives to giving priority to social objectives. Practice has shown clearly that the key to whether or not the government can play an effective role in sustained economic growth lies in whether or not it can properly address problems such as unemployment, income distribution, education, social credit and market order. With a good solution to these problems, economic development will enjoy a reliable social environment; otherwise, sustained economic growth will hardly be possible.

3. A shift from an economy based on (administrative) examinations and approvals to an economy based on services. The government should continue to narrow the scope of administrative examinations and approvals by a big margin, allowing production factors to flow, to rise and fall in market competition and form optimal combinations. It should properly handle its relationships with enterprises, the market and social intermediaries, leaving to market players and intermediaries those matters that it cannot take good care of or are outside its jurisdiction. The main functions of the government are to improve legislation, promote the effort to put government work on a legal basis, standardize the relations of property, credit and contracts in market economy conditions, maintain the market order, ensure fair competition, establish and improve the social security system, social services system and other social public products and public services, and, through e-government and other means, bring about an open government.

4. A shift from a system of administrative control to a system of carrying out administrative functions according to law. China's administrative management system features control from the top to the bottom. To meet the requirements of its WTO accession, the government should speed up the building of a legal system compatible to the socialist market economy, act strictly in accordance with the law in the performance of its functions, and ensure fair market competition by making and enforcing laws in an equitable and rigorous way, standardising the actions of various social roles and severely punishing violations of the law.

Practice over the past year since its WTO accession shows that the government has made significant progress in reforming its system of administrative examination and approval, playing a major role in creating an environment for fair competition. Continuing to take government reform as the focal point of the reform in the coming new stage in accordance with the guidelines set forth in the 16th CPC National Congress will play a major role in further promoting China's market-oriented reform process.

THE PROCESS OF THE MARKET-ORIENTED REFORM AND THE DEVELOPMENT OF NGOS IN CHINA

(April 2003)

After more than two decades of reform, China has built the basic framework of socialist market economy. The economic transition has been accompanied by certain progress in social transition in the country. Today, against the general background of economic globalization, the reform has entered the stage to tackle difficult issues, focus on the adjustment of major interests, and the social transition has likewise reached a crucial juncture. To vigorously develop NGOs is a major task confronting the process of social transition in the new period. Such is the extent of China's reform and opening-up program today that NGOs, government and enterprises have become the three major pillars supporting the modern social structure. Therefore, to develop NGOs is an objective requirement of immediate urgency.

1. In a given period in the course of China's economic transition, the development of NGOs is directly and intrinsically related to the reform and opening up. On one hand, the process of its market-oriented reform is one in which the state has fundamentally changed the past practice of taking all socio-economic affairs into its own hands in the conditions of the planned economy system as well as one of market and social development and formation. On the other hand, a full development of NGOs is one of the important indications of the improvement and formation of the socialist market economy. Viewed from this angle, while the initial formation of the socialist market economy is mainly an achievement of the basic reform to allow the market forces to play an essential role in the allocation of resources, China's market-oriented reform is far from being complete if we take into consideration the social transition, which includes the development of NGOs among its important objectives. It follows that we should speed up the structural reform which takes as its main task the adjustment of major socio-economic relations.

2. NGOs of various types have registered a certain level of growth during the reform process over the past two decades and more. But their growth has fallen considerably short of the objective requirements of the reform and opening up. This has had a negative impact on the actual process of China's market-oriented reform.

Available statistics show that social organizations of various types in China increased from more than 6,000 in 1978 to 165,000 in 1998, while non-governmental enterprises run by the non-state sector increased from zero to around 700,000 during the same period. However, the progress in NGOs so far is only the beginning. For example, Shanghai had 410 industrial and commercial chambers in the early post-liberation period, whereas it had only 123 such chambers by the end of 2001 (despite great efforts to restore them). Yet it is among the areas with the fastest growth of trade associations in the country. The fact that even Shanghai still shows a big gap compared with the early post-liberation days speaks for the current national conditions with regard to the development of trade associations.

The stunted NGO development is manifested not only numerically but also in some "congenital" deficiencies that showed up in the initial stage of their development. (1) At present, NGOs in China — whether trade associations or social organizations of other types — have a thick administrative coloring. Therefore, they cannot reflect or represent the interests of the groups they are supposed to represent. (2) Although they have reached a certain number, they are not widely representative. For example, although Shanghai leads the country in the development of trade associations, such associations only have about 50 percent coverage. (3) NGOs in China are of a relatively low standard and are not very effective. For example, a considerable number of participants in international forums on human rights are representatives of international NGOs of various types. Chinese government delegates show considerable limitations when engaged in discussions and dialogues with NGO representatives on human rights and similar topics. If Chinese NGOs had been able to adequately present the country's human rights conditions and engaged in dialogues with NGOs from other countries, they would have achieved remarkably different results and played a role which government delegates could not have. (4) Their legal status remains undetermined, despite the publication of some relevant administrative rules and regulations.

3. China has entered a new stage in the reform and opening up. Both the structural reform focusing on the adjustment of various major interests and the all-round opening to the outside world raise urgent demands on the need to speed up the development of NGOs.

In the new stage of reform, adjusting the various major interest relationships, such as the government vs. society, enterprises vs. the government, farmers vs. urban residents, and the rich vs. the poor, has become the most fundamental and most substantial content of the reform. The new stage of reform poses a major question to NGOs, that is, whether they are able to directly represent the interests of the various sections or groups of people they are supposed to represent. The situation now is different from what it was ten years ago. Today, both economic globalization and economic and social development have put NGO development as an important item on the agenda. In such circumstances, if our policy makers can take the initiative to gain a sober-minded and truthful understanding of this issue, and promote NGO development energetically, we will be able to make the best use of the situation amid the economic changes and the changes in the social structure, and bring their role as policy promoters into full play. Doing otherwise would be unfavourable to the resolution of all kinds of increasingly growing social contradictions, or even sharpen some contradictions.

To conclude, to promote development by reforming is an important feature of the course of NGO development during the period of economic transition in China.

I. Governmental Reform and NGO Development

China is at a crucial juncture in its economic transition at present. The emergence and growth of NGOs is a product of the reform, governmental reform in particular, and at the same time an important criterion for testing the effectiveness of government reform. I cite two examples here. First, how is it that till this day the separation of the functions of the government and enterprises has remained a difficult task despite the persistent call for it for more than 20 years, and that some government departments have actually been reinforcing certain powers? Who can represent the enterprises in dialogue with the government and take back those powers that are due to them from the government? A single enterprise is too weak to start a dialogue or negotiations with the government, but a trade association representing enterprises can play an indispensable role as their representative. This shows that a delayed development of trade associations and some bureaucratic tendencies are important factors leading to the mixing up of government and enterprise functions. Second, although government reform has made certain progress in a number of areas, it is far from meeting its targets whether in terms of the number of people on the state payroll or the actual process of the shift in government functions. In my view, this has something to do with deep-rooted interests. The reason why the reform of the administrative examination and approval system has been so difficult, with some government departments still clinging to their powers over matters that should not be subject to approval is that the examination and approval process may involve some exchange of interests. Therefore, I term today's government reform the four "shifts":

1. A shift from the government-dominated market economy to the market-dominated economic mode. The government role in the modern market economy is indeed very important, but for the government to be a dominant force in the market economy can cause a series of problems and contradictions, as clearly shown in the Asian financial crisis.

2. A shift in government functions from giving priority to economic objectives to giving priority to social objectives. In circumstances under which social contradictions and relations of interest are becoming increasingly complicated, only by giving priority to solving social contradictions and problems can the government provide a good social environment for sustained economic development.

3. A shift from an economy based on (administrative) examination and approval to an economy based on services.

4. A shift from a government model featuring administrative control to a government model featuring the performance of administrative functions in accordance with the law. The law controls first and foremost the government's actions and the people who wield power.

The process of shift in government functions provides much room for the development of NGOs. First, the relationship between the NGOs and the government changes: It should be a partnership instead of administrative dependence and it should be one of consultation and cooperation on an equal footing instead of subordination. Second, government reform will provide room for NGOs to play their role in the socialization of public services. The government may very well leave some of its social functions to NGOs, which have been shown by many examples to be equal to such tasks. Third, the shift in government functions will provide opportunities and possibilities for NGOs to represent various interest groups more directly and in a better way. Now, various interest groups have shown a strong desire to have their own representatives. For example, regarding the establishment of farmers' associations, an issue that has eluded a solution for a long time, farmers have begun to voice their demand. In such circumstances, the development of NGOs will have an important foundation, and the solutions to such mattes as funding and staffing will have a material basis.

II. Reform of Social Organizations and NGO Development

In the period of economic transition in China, the further growth of social organizations is directly and intrinsically related to their reform. The general objective of such a reform is to shift from the tendency of modelling on administrative organizations and wielding power to being non-governmental and socialized. Here I quote from the report to the CPC Hainan Provincial Congress held in 1998: "At present, it is necessary to do properly the work of changing the mass organizations from being 'government-run' to being non-governmental, to enable them to gradually meet the goals of self-decision in the elections of leaders, self-funding and self-determining in carrying out activities and, under the political leadership of the CPC and within the framework of the Constitution and laws, to fully exercise their democratic rights, build up their capacity for development, play their full role as a bridge between the CPC and the government on the one hand and the general public on the other, and truly represent and protect the interests of the general public." By quoting this passage, I lay the groundwork for discussing the following issues: First, is the "three selfs" principle for reforming the social organizations under the political leadership of the CPC — self-decision in the election of their leaders, self-funding and self determining in carrying out their activities — a correct definition of the direction for the development of NGOs in the period of economic transition? In my view the answer is affirmative. If social organizations are run as official or semi-official ones, where is their representativeness, their role, their vitality and their initiative? Second, how is it that the direction and principles for the reform of social organizations that were put forward 15 years ago have still not been put into practice in real earnest? It is true that it takes time to understand and accept them, but the major reason is that the serious delay in political restructuring has caused a "peaceful retrogression." What has happened in Hainan also shows that the reform of social organizations there has, instead of making progress, seen further emergence of the tendency to take administrative organizations as models. Third, can the "three selfs" principle for the reform of social organizations under the CPC leadership be finalized in the new stage of reform? In my view, in order to enable the various social organizations to really play their role at a time when social interests and social contradictions are coming to the fore daily, reform is necessary, and is taking on increasing urgency.

III. Reform of Public Institutions and NGO Growth

An important feature of China's traditional system was that the state took charge of all social undertakings. Although some reforms have been carried out in this respect over the past two decades and more, on the whole the state of affairs in which the state managed social undertakings in the same way as it did administrative organizations has not been completely changed. Therefore, the reform of public institutions in China, especially those in the field of public welfare, is most closely linked with the growth of NGOs in the period of economic transition in China. Associations, societies and scientific research institutions of various types are all closely related to this reform.

The reform of public institutions in the country is a very complex matter. I divide them into three categories: First, those clearly charged with administrative functions should be returned to the ranks of the government; second, those fully capable of operating as enterprises should be classified into the category of enterprises; third, those working for the public good, and are non-profit making and of a social nature should be turned into independent public welfare legal entities, practicing a governance structure befitting such legal entities. Take our institute for example. The China (Hainan) Institute for Reform & Development was set up jointly by the former State Economic Restructuring Commission and the Hainan provincial government as a public institution in 1991. In the following year, it began to practice a management pattern of a legal entity run as an enterprise responsible for its own profits and losses, without asking for any fund or authorized personnel quotas from the government. Our institute has, after a decade of effort, grown into a reform research institution with a special institutional advantage and sustainable development.

IV. Reform of Trade Associations and NGO Growth

At present, the reform of trade associations is facing two major issues: (1) As the market economy has developed to today's extent with the mixed-ownership sector gradually becoming its micro-foundation and micro-players, the trade associations which used to mainly represent state-owned enterprises should shift to represent enterprises of different ownerships. (2) It is imperative to change as soon as possible the tendency of these associations to model themselves after administrative organizations and win the support of enterprises by speaking on their behalf, entering into dialogues with the government on their behalf and protecting their interests. Only thus can the trade associations show a wide representation and play their full role in protecting the interests of enterprises.

V. Establishment of a Social Consultation and Dialogue System, and NGO Growth

The report to the 13th CPC National Congress, held in 1987, officially called for the establishment of a social consultation and dialogue system. It explained that people who may not always share identical interests and views needed a channel for mutual communication, and therefore it was necessary to institutionalise social consultation and dialogue to improve communication and understanding between the authorities and the general public, as well as among the general public, facilitating the flow of information in a timely, unimpeded and accurate way. Practice over the past decade or so shows that, with an effective consultation and dialogue system, representatives of different interest groups are able to articulate their opinions in a timely and direct way. Only consultation and dialogue on an equal footing and in partnership can reduce the various social contradictions and make it possible to reflect the desires of different interest groups.

A consultation and dialogue system is an important channel for NGOs to play their proper role. (1) An important condition for improving the relationship between society and the government is that NGOs of different types can communicate and engage in dialogue with government departments on a regular and timely basis, for only thus can social contradictions be resolved and risks defused. (2) Multiple beneficiaries of social interests are a general trend, and yet different interest groups have diverse demands. NGOs can thrive by representing and reflecting accurately diverse demands of different interest groups. (3) Globalization and IT application are important features of contemporary society. Therefore, a sudden event in any one country often has an international dimension, and news of a major event is instantly circulated. Against this background, establishment of a sound social consultation and dialogue system will be conducive to responding to any sudden events, strengthening social supervision and enhancing China's international image as an open society. Therefore, it is very important that the need to establish a social consultation and dialogue system should be voiced once again in the new stage of reform.

VI. New Stage of Opening to the Outside World and NGO Growth

Here I give some examples. Following its WTO accession, anti-dumping has become a focus of growing attention. How is it that only seven Chinese enterprises had responded out of a total of more than 400 anti-dumping cases (against Chinese enterprises) before China's WTO accession? An important reason was that the Chinese trade associations had not acquired their "tickets" into anti-dumping negotiations. Foreign-funded enterprises in Shanghai have asked to be able to form their own associations, which is a kind of "foreign pressure" on the existing Chinese trade associations. Another example is that as the host country of the Bo'ao Forum for Asia (BFA), China has not yet enacted stipulations on the registration of international organizations in the country. The registration of the BFA has been treated as a special case. In the future, the entry of international organizations into China will be unavoidable, and will be on a growing scale. It is already a practical problem to register them in accordance with law. I have cited these examples to show that the coming of the new reform and opening up stage has posed challenges to and offered opportunities for the development of NGOs in China. We should seize every opportunity to open to the outside world, further speed up the development of NGOs, especially industrial associations, respond to challenges with initiative, and strive to turn challenges into opportunities. Meanwhile, it is vital to make some readjustments to policies and laws according to the requirements of all-round opening to the outside world.

VII. "Running Social Affairs in Accordance with Law" and NGO Growth

At present, China manages NGOs in more or less the same way as it does administrative organizations. For example, NGOs must be affiliated to a competent authority administratively and professionally, and public institutions must have sponsoring organizations when they apply for the status of corporate entities. To make things more difficult, although non-governmental sectors may run public undertakings, public institutions that are found to possess no state assets are denied registration. When scientific and technological personnel living abroad come to China and start scientific research institutes with their own funds, they will encounter difficulties with registration. This is because under the traditional system, all public institutions were run by the state. Now for individuals and non-governmental sectors to run public institutions constitutes a new problem. It is true that it is a good thing for non-governmental sectors to run public undertakings, and a move in the right direction. However, in the absence of explicit laws and policies in this respect, people will find themselves in an impasse if they hope to do some good for the public. Therefore, we are in urgent need of relevant laws and administrative rules and regulations so that NGOs may be registered in accordance with the law and social affairs run in accordance with the law.

VIII. Political Restructuring and NGO Growth

First, we should promote a shift from a power-based society to an ability-based society in the course of renovating the political system. In this process, NGOs should be encouraged to play an effective role in the country's socio-economic life.

Second, we should bring about a gradual shift from an administrative system of one-way control to a management mechanism based on consultations and cooperation. While striving for a sound and effective administration, the government should make efforts to establish a grid-type organization. Such a mechanism will provide an important platform for the growth of NGOs.

Third, we should gradually shift from a state society to a citizen society. It is necessary to thoroughly change some outmoded concepts that are ossified in people's minds in the period of the planned economy system concerning staff employment in government departments, public institutions and enterprises, practice community self-management and self-regulation of trades, encourage people to look for jobs or start businesses on their own and foster citizens' independent moral qualities — self-respect, self-reliance and self-improvement. This will provide an important channel for the growth of NGOs.

Fourth, the most pressing task of political restructuring at present is to restrict power on the basis of democracy and the legal system, to avoid any alienation of power in the market economy. At present, the spread of corruption and its tendency to evolve into institutional corruption and corruption of a bloc type are partly the result of weak social supervision. NGOs should take it their special mission to exercise democratic supervision and restraining power. Therefore, political restructuring and the process of building a socialist political civilization will provide increasingly greater opportunities and ever-widening scope for the expansion of NGOs.

China is in a new stage of attacking difficult issues in the reform, with the adjustment of major interest relations as its basic feature. This new stage promises much room for the development of NGOs, which will not only have a great impact on China's current reform and opening up, but also become an important force for promoting the country's economic development and social progress.

WTO ACCESSION AND THE NEW STAGE OF OPENING TO THE OUTSIDE WORLD

THE NEW STAGE OF CHINA'S OPENING UP

(*May 2003*)

China's accession to the World Trade Organization (WTO) as a big developing country in the course of economic transition after 15 long years of negotiations is a strategic choice demonstrating its determination to push forward its reform and opening-up program, a strategic choice it made on its own with a view to actively participating in economic globalization, and a major strategic choice concerning its socio-economic development in the early years of the 21st century. Therefore, it is appropriate to examine some major issues concerning China's opening up in the wake of its WTO accession.

The report to the 16th CPC National Congress pointed out explicitly that, with its WTO accession, China had entered a new stage in its opening up to the outside world. There are many ways to describe this "new stage," an important one being that China's opening up will shift from one in limited spheres and areas to a multiple-range, all-round one; from a policy-type opening featuring experiments and planning to a market-dominated opening within a legal framework; and from an essentially unilateral self-opening to a mutual opening between China and other WTO members.

I. A New Situation in China's Opening Up

With its WTO accession, China will face many new situations now and in the coming few years. For example, as it pushes forward its economic internationalization as a WTO member it will face all-round international economic competition and serious challenges from some uncertainties to its economic development. Anti-dumping measures, Asian regional cooperation, the war in Iraq and the Korean Peninsula nuclear issue, if no timely and effective measures are taken, will also have certain negative impacts on China's opening to the outside world. These are all new problems confronting its opening-up policy.

1. China's opening up is advancing to an even higher level.

Determined pursuit of opening up is one of China's basic state policies. Regardless of changes in the domestic situation and the international environment over the past two decades and more, it has adhered steadfastly to the basic principle of opening up, and continuously made new advances. It has expanded its opening up in width and breadth, from establishing special economic zones (SEZs) to setting up the Pudong New Area in Shanghai, and from opening coastal cities to foreign investment to opening the areas along the Yangtze River, the land borders and inland cities to foreign funds. For example, China's total export and import volume increased from 325.2 billion US dollars-worth in 1997 to 620.8 billion US dollars in 2002, with its world ranking rising from tenth place to fifth in the same period. Its service trade has grown steadily, registering a big increase in the number of foreign tourists to the country and foreign currency earnings. It has topped all the developing countries in attracting direct foreign investment for ten successive years. Facts show that China has formed an all-directional, multi-tiered and wide-ranging opening pattern, and its export-oriented economy has developed swiftly.

Its WTO accession has marked a new turning point in China's opening up in the new century, signifying the stepping of its opening up onto an even higher stage. It will be of major immediate and profound historical significance in promoting the country's socio-economic development.

2. With its WTO accession, China has entered a new stage in its opening up.

Its WTO accession is favorable to creating a good external environment for China's reform and development. This makes it possible for China to develop an open economy on the principle of a multilateral, stable and unconditional most-favored-nation (MFN) treatment, gradually remove the discriminatory trade restrictions imposed by some countries on China and, in the course of participating in the formulation of international economic and trade rules, promote the establishment of an equitable and rational international economic new order so as to protect China's fundamental interests. Meanwhile, by fulfiling its commitments and observing the WTO rules, China will enhance its international image as a more open, responsible big country.

China's WTO accession will be favorable to pushing it to participate in economic globalization with initiative and steadiness. The WTO is a product of economic globalization and an important international economic organization that in turn pushes forward the process of economic globalization. Its WTO accession represents a decisive move on the part of China to become deeply involved in economic globalization, and a major opportunity to speed up the adjustment of its economic structure. Chinese enterprises are expected to do a better job in participating in international competition and cooperation, and absorb more funds, advanced technologies and professional skills from other countries. This will be beneficial to adjusting the country's economic structure rationally by pursuing benefits and avoiding harm at the same time as it shares the benefits of economic globalization, and to upgrading its industries so as to improve its international competitiveness.

The WTO will help make the Chinese and other countries' economies more mutually complementary. China's rich manpower and natural resources will benefit those countries that are deficient in them; and many of its adaptive technologies, management expertise and inexpensive commodities will benefit developing countries.

Therefore, China as well as other countries worldwide will benefit from the country's accession to the WTO. Opening is accompanied by negative impacts and risks, promising both opportunities and serious challenges. The current overall quality of China's economy is not high, nor is its international competitiveness. It is unavoidable that some trades and enterprises should be negatively affected by its WTO accession in the immediate wake. In particular, many aspects of our concepts, working habits, economic management pattern, and laws and rules currently in force are at odds with the rules of the WTO. Therefore, we should take its WTO accession as a motive force for promoting further ideological emancipation and boldly changing our concepts; for promoting the shift in government functions and speeding up the government reform focusing on the reform of administrative examination and approval; and promoting the reform of SOEs and the development of the non-governmental sector, and improving the overall quality of the national economy in an effort to turn negative factors into positive ones and create a new situation in China's reform and opening up against the WTO background.

3. Changes in the world political and economic situation constantly pose new problems to China's reform and opening up.

For China, the first two decades of the 21st century is a period of important strategic opportunities, which China must seize firmly and which offers bright prospects. Its development objective for this period is to build a well-off society of a higher standard in an all-round way to benefit its well over one billion people. We will further develop the economy, improve democracy, make science and education advance, enrich culture, foster social harmony and upgrade the texture of the people's life. However, without a peaceful international environment, China will not be able to meet the objective of building a well-off society in an all-round way in about 20 years. First, it should seize the historical opportunities presented by economic globalization, make full use of the coordinating mechanism of the WTO and accelerate the restructuring and readjustment of the domestic economic structure, so as to keep generating the internal motive force for sustained economic growth. Second, China is a big country, and, for that matter, a developing and responsible big power. In international affairs, it should play its due role as a large developing country. In a complex and changeable international situation it should be able to concentrate its efforts on speeding up its economic development while playing its role well as a major country. The realization of its economic and social development goals for the next 20 years is all-important to China. In this sense, the seizing of the historical opportunity to concentrate on developing the economy is the main task of China's opening to the outside world, and an issue of the first and foremost importance, an issue of historical and decisive importance bearing on the overall situation.

To realize China's economic and social development objectives for the next 20 years will depend on a long-term, stable international environment for peaceful construction. Against the general background of economic globalization, the pace of bilateral and multilateral trade liberalization will pick up greatly. Meanwhile, unilateralism and power politics have also shown a growing tendency, due to changes in certain factors. The war in Iraq has had an impact on the economy of the world as a whole, as well as those of Asia and China in particular. As a big developing country, China has the duty to play its role in and contribute to safeguarding a peaceful and stable international environment. Meanwhile, it must always concentrate on accelerating its economic development.

The process of regional cooperation in Asia will also pick up greatly alongside the pace of economic globalization. The reason why the Bo'ao Forum for Asia (BFA), which was set up only in 2001, has attracted wide attention from various countries in Asia as well as the international community, is that it serves as a high-level platform for dialogue and communication among various Asian countries in quest of cooperation and common development. At present, it has 26 members. In view of the economic, social and cultural differences between and diversity among Asian countries, the aim of the BFA is equality, mutual benefit, cooperation and a win-win situation for all. Consisting mainly of Asian countries and regions, it is also open to other regions. It mainly discusses the economy, population, resources, environment and other major issues in Asia, to create a sound regional environment for the economic and social development of the region, so as to accelerate the process of Asian regional cooperation. In keeping with the accelerating pace of its opening, China will play an ever-more important role in Asian regional cooperation. It is actively promoting such cooperation in response to the requirements of the domestic economic development and also in response to the common aspirations of many Asian countries for economic development. Asian countries are following with interest the stability of the Chinese economy, its growth prospects and investment environment, and the market opening in the wake of its WTO accession, because China's economic development and market opening will have a major impact on the process of Asian regional economic cooperation. Therefore, China should make its due contributions and play its due role in promoting Asian regional economic cooperation. The authors of the so-called theory of the "China threat" have their own hidden agenda. Facts have repeatedly shown that China's development, instead of being a threat to Asia, provides an impetus and contribution to Asian regional cooperation.

To open wider to the outside world and boost domestic demand simultaneously constitute a major issue for study in China's opening up against the WTO background. On the one hand, China has energetically developed the enormous potential of the domestic market, and changed its total supply and demand pattern, bringing about considerably favorable conditions for China to steadily open its domestic market and actively access the international market. On the other hand, it has, while energetically expanding the domestic market, made full use of favorable conditions and opportunities with regard to the external market and economic environment flowing from its WTO accession to expand the share of its products and services in the international market, utilize more foreign investment, and import advanced technologies and equipment from other countries. This has been very important for increasing effective supply. The Chinese government has advanced a basic principle calling for actively participating in international economic and technological cooperation and competition by "bringing in" and "going global." This conforms to the general trend of economic globalization and China's basic national conditions.

II. Major Features of the New Stage of China's Opening Up

On the whole, China's opening up can be divided into two major stages. The period up to its WTO accession, spanning more than two decades, constituted the first major stage. A gradual opening strategy was the hallmark of this stage. The main manifestation of gradualism was experiments to gain successful experiences for gradual and then nationwide extension. This was done in light of domestic and external conditions, and by taking into full consideration the needs of economic development and economic and social sustainability, and weighing the pros and cons. In conformity with the overall strategy for the reform and opening up, China successfully blazed a gradual approach.

Its WTO accession marked the beginning of a new stage. In other words, with its WTO accession China has entered the second major stage in its opening up. Opening its market and observing the WTO rules are among the important commitments it made in connection with its WTO accession, and also the main tasks of the new stage, which is characterized by all-round institutional opening.

The gradual opening up was based on policies to a great extent. Opening the market in accordance with the WTO requirements and observing the WTO rules constitute institutional opening up. In this sense, China's accession to the WTO marks the entry into a new stage of institutional opening up from a general, policy-based opening up.

1. China's WTO accession marks a shift from market opening in designated spheres and areas to all-round market opening.

Advancing from partial opening up to all-round opening up, and making full use of the overall advantages of the nationwide opening up. As a result of its efforts over the past two decades and more, China has gradually formed an all-directional, multi-tiered opening pattern with focal points. Its WTO accession will further accelerate the work of improving the overall opening pattern. While continuing to maintain and develop the advantages of the coastal areas in this respect, we should speed up the opening of the western regions, which have lagged far behind the eastern regions in the degree of opening due to various reasons. At present, the actual amount of foreign investment the western regions utilize each year accounts for about 5 percent of the national total only, and the total amount of foreign investment the western regions have utilized accounts for less than 3 percent of the investment in fixed assets for the whole society in these regions. This shows that in doing a better job of opening up following its WTO accession, China should adopt measures conforming to the WTO rules to greatly raise the level of opening up in the western regions, so as to make the reform and opening up an engine for accelerating the development of the western regions.

A shift from emphasizing regional opening to the emphasizing sectoral opening, and from opening general competitive areas to opening sectors with the service sector as the focal point. The shift from the regional opening strategy to the sectoral opening strategy represents an important change in the opening strategy following China's WTO accession. In particular, the service trade market with the emphasis on insurance, banking and telecommunications is the main area China is opening following its WTO accession as well as the new focus of China's participation in international competition. Compared with the developed market countries, the overall development of China's service sector is relatively backward, with its proportion in the GDP lower than that not only of the developed countries, but also of some developing countries. Therefore, when China gradually opens its service market in accordance with the timetable stipulated in its WTO commitments, this will bring enormous pressures from foreign rivals on domestic services, but will also help to introduce advanced technologies and managerial expertise from other countries and to usher in a rapid growth of China's services. The key lies in the institutional reform of the sector to suit the need to participate in international competition.

2. China's WTO accession marks a shift from the past self-opening featuring mainly unilateral actions to a two-way mutual opening between China and other WTO members.

The shift from self-opening featuring mainly unilateral actions to a two-way mutual opening is an important characteristic of the institutional opening. Now that China has become a WTO member, other member states will open their markets to Chinese enterprises to a greater extent. This will help not only Chinese enterprises to access the world market, but also foreign investment in China to have bigger scope. Against this overall background, the Chinese government has adopted a very important strategy of supporting and encouraging Chinese enterprises with the necessary conditions to operate abroad. In the new situation following its WTO accession, Chinese enterprises are facing many new problems, such as anti-dumping, as they try to come to grips with how to participate in international economic and technological competition on a higher plane and a wider scale. They will have to learn all the relevant rules about overseas operation so as to gain the initiative in international competition.

3. A shift from policy-based opening up featuring experiments at selected spots to opening up under a legal framework.

To observe the WTO rules means revising some of China's laws and rules and regulations, and formulate new ones in accordance with the relevant WTO stipulations. This is an important aspect of

China's institutional opening following its accession to the WTO. China has done a large amount of fruitful work in this respect in the past year and more following its WTO accession, winning general endorsement from the international community. China will take even bigger steps in the opening up as it further improves its legal system and management efficiency, and its legal environment for the institutional opening.

III. China's New Opening Measures Outlined at the 16th CPC National Congress

The report to the 16th CPC National Congress explicitly pointed out: "By both 'bringing in' and 'going global,' we should actively participate in international economic and technological cooperation and competition, and open wider to the outside world." This represents both an important summing-up of the successful experience in the country's opening-up program over the past two decades and more and a major strategic plan for the opening up against the background of the country's accession to the WTO.

1. To promote reform and development by opening up is the important guiding idea of China in the new stage in opening up.

Its WTO accession is, in a sense, the country's second round of opening up and reform, resulting in a situation in which opening up expedites reform. Therefore, it is necessary to promote reform by opening up, gradually removing institutional barriers to the development of the productive forces and providing the enterprises, Chinese and foreign, with conditions for open and unified competition on an equal footing. To promote development by opening up, we should make full use of our own economic and market advantages, accelerate the work of establishing an open economic system and instill new motive forces and vitality into economic development.

2. It is essential to expand trade in goods and services, implement the strategy of market diversification, and strive to increase exports.

Steps to be taken include bringing into play our comparative advantages, consolidating our existing markets and opening new ones, and expanding trade in goods and services; sharpening the competitive edge of our goods and services for export by ensuring good quality and improving their technological content and added value; optimizing our import mix and effectively regulating imports by applying WTO rules, exception clauses and arrangements for the transition period, and adopting technical regulations, standards, anti-dumping and anti-subsidy measures, and safeguards; and deepening the reform of the foreign trade system, encouraging more enterprises to engage in foreign trade, and improving the relevant taxation systems and the trade financing mechanism.

3. It is essential to absorb more foreign direct investment, and use it more effectively.

Its WTO accession greatly helps China to absorb foreign direct investment. In such circumstances, we should, while persisting in absorbing more foreign investment, concentrate our attention on using it more effectively, optimize the foreign investment mix and give full play to its important role in promoting economic growth and structural adjustment, creating more jobs and increasing tax revenues.

4. It is essential to shift the focus of our attention from "bringing in" to equal emphasis on both "bringing in" and "going global."

Due to its national conditions and actual needs, China's opening up focused on "bringing in" over the past two decades and more. But, along with changes in the overall environment both at home and abroad, it has gradually become both a necessity and possibility to develop overseas markets. "Going global" has become a necessity if China is to participate fully in economic globalization and expand its scope for economic development, as well as necessary for the country to exercise its rights in the WTO and raise the level of opening up. It is above all a need to forge Chinese-style transnationals as a way to improve the international competitiveness of Chinese enterprises.

5. It is essential to actively participate in regional economic exchanges and cooperation, and pay greater attention to safeguarding national economic security while opening wider to the outside world.

Under the impetus of the economic globalization, regional economic integration has picked up swiftly worldwide. Since the Asian financial crisis in 1997, calls for Asian regional cooperation have become louder. Economic cooperation in East Asia in particular has been speeded up, resulting in such forms of cooperation as "ten plus three" and "ten plus one." As a large Asian country, China should actively participate in and promote regional economic exchanges and cooperation, and the process of regional trade liberalization.

PROMOTE DEVELOPMENT BY OPENING UP AND MAKE CHINESE ECONOMY MORE INTERNATIONALIZED IN AN ALL-ROUND WAY

(*May 2003*)

  China's accession to the WTO will have an important and far-reaching impact on its economic development, which, in essence, needs to speed up the effort to build an open economy and make its economy more internationalized in an all-round way. It can be said that China's WTO accession marks a shift from the opening up of a general nature, that is, one focusing on developing an export-oriented economy, to the new stage of opening up with the development of an open economy as its main objective.

  Generally speaking, an exported-oriented economy refers mainly to an export-led economy. An open economy, is essentially one with intrinsic economic ties and cooperation on an international scale. From this it can be seen that the shift from developing an export-oriented economy to an open economy in opening the country further to the outside world is a profound shift from a quantitative change to a qualitative change. It shows that, with its entry into the WTO, China's economy has become more closely linked with the world economy, and the operations of the Chinese economy, while depending mainly on domestic factors, will also depend on international factors. In implementing a series of economic policies and macro-control measures, China will also have to take the trends and changes in the world economy into overall consideration, while putting the main focus of attention on its national conditions.

I. To Develop an Open Economy, We Should Absorb More Foreign Direct Investment

An active, rational and effective use of foreign investment is an important component of China's policy for opening up. China has ranked first in absorbing foreign investment for nine successive years among the developing countries. Out of the need to develop an open economic structure following its WTO accession, China finds it even more necessary to bring in more foreign direct investment, optimize its mix, use it more effectively and give fuller play to its important role in promoting the adjustment of the economic structure and economic growth, and creating more jobs. An important aspect of promoting development by opening up is to further absorb foreign direct investment. The experience of the past year or two shows that China's WTO accession has led to increased foreign investment.

1. With its WTO accession, China has absorbed more foreign investment and improved its mix.

With its WTO accession China has become obviously more attractive to foreign investors. Along with the improved investment environment in China, the country is expected to enter a period of fairly remarkable growth in terms of foreign investment in the next few years. According to some expert projections, it will absorb no less than 50 billion US dollars in foreign investment a year on average in the next five years. A report on world investment for 2002 published by the United Nations Conference on Trade and Development in September said that China continued to top the developing countries and regions in absorbing foreign direct investment, and was expected to maintain the momentum of smooth growth in the next few years.

There has been a steady growth of foreign investment. In 2001, China attracted 46.9 billion US dollars in foreign investment, 13.8 times the amount registered in 1989 and averaging an increase rate of

24 percent a year. In 2002, it actually absorbed 52.743 billion US dollars, increasing 12.6 percent over the previous year, and surpassing the United States for the first time to become the top country in the world with the greatest influx of overseas direct investment.

There has been a steady improvement of its mix. The proportion of exports from foreign-funded enterprises in the country's total export volume rose from 9.4 percent in 1989 to 50 percent in 2001; the average amount of foreign investment per project rose from 970,000 US dollars to 2.65 million US dollars during the same period; and focal areas for foreign investment spread from general manufacturing industry to basic industries, infrastructure and new- and high-tech industries. In the wake of its WTO accession, China will open its service sector to the outside world step by step, and commerce, foreign trade, telecommunications, banking, insurance and other services are becoming hot spots for a new wave of foreign investment. Transnational giants are actively investing in China, with more than 400 of the world's top 500 having a presence in the country. They have established close to 400 R & D centers of various types in China.

2. With its WTO accession, China has shifted its focus of attention from the effects of aggregate growth to those of structural upgrading in absorbing foreign investment.

Judging by the current trend, foreign direct investment in China will continue to grow in the next five to ten years at an average annual rate of 5 to 10 percent. That means that China will continue to maintain a growing trend in absorbing foreign investment for several years to come, but the historical period of rapid growth in foreign investment has basically come to an end. China will now enter a period of stable growth. Proceeding from this realistic assessment, we should, with a view to maintaining the contributions of foreign investment to economic growth, improve the output efficiency of the economy as a whole by optimizing its industrial distribution structure to offset the negative effects of a slowdown in the aggregate increase.

This means in practice a shift in the development strategy for promoting economic growth through absorbing foreign investment from paying attention to the effects of aggregate growth to paying attention to the effects of structural upgrading.

According to its commitments in connection with its WTO accession, China will open its service sector wider to the outside world. In this category are banking and insurance, wholesale and retailing, foreign trade, telecommunications, transportation and technological services. The sheer size and potential of its service market holds great appeal to foreign-funded enterprises. Therefore, investment in the service sector is expected to grow much faster than in other trades. Receiving impetus from foreign direct investment, the market-oriented reform of China's service sector will also be greatly accelerated, resulting in a marked growth of the sector.

A survey conducted in 2001 by the Development Research Center of the State Council of 136 EU-funded enterprises in China showed that EU enterprises may make new changes in their investment in China in terms of industrial structure. First, manufacturing is most likely to be the first choice. Second, investment in services related to telecommunications and transportation will grow swiftly, increasing its share in the total investment. Investment in posts and telecommunications and transportation accounts for only about 3 percent now, and 57.4 percent of the EU enterprises are expected to choose these sectors for investment in the coming years. Third, banking and insurance will be among the priority areas for investment, taking third place after manufacturing and posts and telecommunications and transportation. Fourth, fast growth of investment and a rising share of the total will also be seen in electricity and gas production and supply, and commercial wholesale and retailing.

3. Following the WTO accession, the geographical distribution of foreign investment in China will further spread from south to north and from east to west.

Now that China has become a member of the WTO, the coastal

areas of southeast China, especially Shanghai and its vicinity, will continue to be the focus of foreign direct investment thanks to their favourable location, and fairly complete infrastructure and institutional advantages. Benefiting from the large-scale development of the western region, the central and western areas will improve their environment for investment considerably as a result of the effort to speed up reform and opening up, strengthen the infrastructure, improve the ecological environment, and develop science, technology and education. Moreover, the central and western regions, the western regions in particular, offer foreign investors more generous access terms in some investment areas than do the eastern regions. Thus, it can be anticipated that foreign investment in the central and western regions will grow by a big margin in the future, and its share of the national total will also rise.

4. With China's WTO accession, foreign investment will more extensively become involved in the reorganization and transformation of large- and medium-sized state-owned enterprises and be fused with non-governmental, including private, enterprises.

The reorganization and transformation to diversify investors in large- and medium-sized state-owned enterprises, especially those in competitive fields, and introduce the joint-stock system to them will attract increasing foreign investment. Foreign investment, especially strategic investment by transnationals, will play a role in the reorganization and transformation of larger SOEs in China as one of their important strategic choices, including the use of merger and acquisition to incorporate Chinese enterprises into their global production and operation networks. At the same time, private and other non-governmental enterprises will also actively seek foreign investment in response to international competition. Especially the fast-growing, larger ones among them and non-governmental scientific and technological enterprises will receive the attention of foreign investors.

II. Seize Opportunities and Actively and Steadily Implement the "Going Global" Strategy to Develop an Open Economy

In response to the general trend of economic globalization, the Chinese government has in recent years officially defined the "going global" strategy as an important opening strategy in the new period. Since becoming a member of the WTO, China has given greater encouragement and support to those enterprises with better conditions in "going global" to expand its overseas markets. It can be said that the "going global" strategy is a necessity for Chinese enterprises to participate in economic globalization and expand their scope for economic development as well as necessary for the country to upgrade its opening-up program in an all-round way. This is even truer of the need of Chinese enterprises to improve their international competitiveness. Therefore, the Chinese government has listed the "going global" strategy as one of the three pillars of an open economy, together with foreign trade and use of foreign investment. The WTO accession has not only prepared the conditions for implementing the "going global" strategy, but also made it an urgent necessity. Therefore, we should seize opportunities, and actively implement it.

1. Chinese enterprises have achieved initial successes in "going global," but there is still a long way from the goal of developing an open economy.

By the end of 2002, China had set up 6,960 non-banking enterprises outside its territory, with a total committed investment of 13.78 billion US dollars. Contracted engineering projects in other countries were worth 114.78 billion US dollars, with the volume of business already completed amounting to 82.72 billion US dollars. Contracts for labor export were worth 29.52 billion US dollars, with the volume of business already completed amounting to 23.76 billion US dollars and the number of times workers were sent to other countries reaching 2.734 million. In addition, other forms of economic cooperation, such as resources exploitation in other countries, transnational acquisition and merger, establishment of R & D centers and agricultural cooperation have also been started and have made initial progress.

The scope of overseas operations has extended gradually from a few simple areas in the early days, such as import and export trade, shipping and catering, to production and processing, resources exploitation, contracted engineering projects, agricultural cooperation and R & D. At present, China is operating more than 200 cooperative resources exploitation projects in more than 50 countries and regions, covering oil and gas, minerals, forestry and fisheries. Personnel sent out on labor export contracts were ordinary workers and skilled workers in the early days. Now, engineers in various fields, as well as hi-tech and managerial staff are also sent to other countries.

There has been an upgrading of overseas operations. Early investment in other countries only extended to establishing representative offices. Now it has extended to establishing factories with a view to facilitating the export of Chinese-made equipment and materials, transnational acquisition and merger, transfer of property rights, listing abroad, establishing R & D centers, industrial parks and international marketing networks. Forms of operations in the contracted engineering projects in foreign countries have also spread from civil engineering sub-contracting to general contracting, project management contracting, turn-key projects and BOT.

Chinese enterprises have made only initial progress in "going global," and there is still a long way for them to go. Statistics show that at the end of the 20th century, total foreign investment worldwide was 1,000 billion US dollars. Although China tops the world in the use of foreign investment, its enterprises invested only some 60 billion US dollars in other countries, or less than 1 percent of the global total. Data show that the average ratio between the export of international direct investment and import of international direct investment is 166:100 in the case of the developed countries and 18:100 in the case of the developing countries, as against 1.5:100 in the case of China. At present, the total amount of international contracted engineering projects amounts to 1,000 billion US dollars a year worldwide, but China's share is only a little more than 1 percent.

2. The government encourages and supports enterprises under all forms of ownership with better conditions to "go global."

The key to implementing the "going global" strategy under the conditions of the modern market economy is to treat enterprises as major players, and mobilize and bring into fuller play the initiative of enterprises of various types. Enterprises, whether state-owned or non-governmental, should not only be allowed but should be encouraged to carry out transnational operations in various forms, such as forming joint-equity ventures, cooperation, holding controlling shares, buying shares, acquisition and merger and technological transfer. They are encouraged to set up factories in other countries, carry out various forms of economic and technological cooperation, and make greater use of foreign resources and markets, with a view to facilitating the export of Chinese technologies, equipment, goods and labor services. They are also encouraged to engage in design and consultancy services, contracted engineering projects, and labor cooperation with foreign countries, with emphasis on general contracting projects, large engineering projects and turn-key projects involving the export of complete plants and technological and service exports, expanding the scale and improving the standards of contracted engineering projects and labor cooperation in foreign countries.

3. The government should create various favorable conditions for enterprises to "go global."

To improve its international competitiveness after entering the WTO, China must lose no time in developing a group of internationally competitive transnational corporations. On the whole, Chinese enterprises are still some way from attaining the objective of "going global." Therefore, large enterprises which are in a position to "go global" should put in place as soon as possible a management mechanism and a competition mechanism in response to international competition. Using capital as the linkage, we should energetically encourage trans-sectoral, trans-regional and trans-ownership enterprise reorganization, gradually forming a batch of large enterprise groups with independent intellectual property rights and key competitiveness, and improving their ability to participate in international competition.

To gradually form a group of strong transnational corporations is an important task for China in establishing an open economy following its WTO accession. To this end, government departments have the duty to provide various favorable conditions for enterprises to "go global." For example, they should intensify their efforts to formulate and improve the relevant laws and regulations with which to effectively guide and manage efforts of enterprises to "go global"; they should formulate relevant laws and regulations designed to provide a good environment for the enterprises in this respect; and they should establish and improve the incentive, guarantee and regulatory systems at an early date, and urge the enterprises to quicken their steps of reform, and bring about a change in mechanism and management so as to meet the needs of "going global."

III. Seizing Opportunities and Striving to Build a "World Workshop" by Speeding Up the Development of the Manufacturing Industry

The overall capacity and standards of the manufacturing industry, especially equipment manufacturing, decide the economic strength, national defense capabilities and overall strength of a country, as well as its ability to participate in global economic competition and cooperation. They also determine the process of a nation, especially a developing nation, to realize modernization and national rejuvenation. As a developing country just entering the middle stage of modernization, China must be soberly aware of the importance of raising the overall capacity and competitiveness of the manufacturing industry, especially those of equipment manufacturing, to its development. China's WTO accession has provided the most important condition for a quicker development of its manufacturing industry and a direct impetus for improving its level of internationalization. In light of the current trends and against the background of economic globalization, it can be anticipated that in 10 to 15 years' time China's manufacturing industry will attract world manufacturing industry with its special international competitive edge, and a "world workshop" will sink roots in Chinese soil, and grow for a long time to come. It should be noted that the quickening steps of economic globalization and China's accession to the WTO have provided the country with a very rare historical opportunity to develop its manufacturing industry.

1. China is not yet a "world workshop," but has the condition to become one with hard efforts.

To be frank, China is not yet a "world workshop," and still has a considerably long way to go before it can become one. The main gap lies in the fact that first, its economic aggregate is still very small and so is its proportion in the world total. According to government statistics, the output value of its secondary industry (the construction industry included) in 1999 was close to 500 billion US dollars, only about 5 percent of its manufacturing industry in output value. Second, the enterprises are not big enough. There are far too few Chinese enterprises that are capable of leading the world manufacturing industry. There were 11 Chinese enterprises among the world's top 500 in 2001, but none of them was in the manufacturing industry. Third, the technological standards of Chinese enterprises are not high enough. Less than 5 percent of the machinery products are up to international standards, the added value of the new- and high-technology industries accounts for only 4 percent of the GDP, and the labor productivity of China's traditional industry is only one-third of the world average, and several dozen times less efficient than that of the developed countries.

However, China has the conditions and a foundation from which it can build a "world workshop" through hard work. Now that it is in the WTO, it will make further use of its comparative advantages to speed up its pace of building such a "world workshop."

(1) The country has an overall advantage and tremendous room for development in its efforts to build itself into a "world workshop" and the trend of becoming a "world workshop" has become ever more conspicuous against the background of economic globalization. It is a realistic and objective assessment that it will basically become a "world workshop" after 10 to 15 years of effort.

(2) The country has an internal need for building itself into a "world workshop," which is becoming increasingly more pressing. Not only is industrialization based on the international standards of the manufacturing industry, but also socio-economic development, especially employment, will depend on the vigorous development of manufacturing industry. It is a strategic choice for China's socio-economic development to build itself into a "world workshop" after years of effort.

(3) In gradually building itself into a "world workshop" in the course of opening its market in an all-round way, China will provide not only good and inexpensive manufactured goods to Asia and the rest of the world, but also satisfy the enormous domestic market demand. When China becomes a "world workshop" it will be the result of its efforts to display its comparative competitiveness in international competition, and beneficial to forging stronger economic and trade cooperation with other countries.

2. It is essential to seize opportunities, blaze a new trail in a pioneering spirit, and strive to turn China into a country with a strong manufacturing industry.

At present, Chinese manufacturing industry is facing a new

opportunity for development, and is at a critical juncture. Against this special background, and in face of immediate needs, we should carefully study how to make good use of our overall advantages, and implement the strategy for industrialization focusing on manufacturing industry, in response to the general trend of economic globalization. A top-priority task now is to improve the policies, institutions and social environment for the development of the Chinese manufacturing industry compatible with the need to build a "world workshop" and, using its WTO accession as a motive force and working in a pioneering spirit, blaze a new trail with Chinese characteristics to make the country strong through upgrading its manufacturing industry.

(1) Manufacturing industry will remain the dominant force behind China's industrialization for the next 20 to 30 years. The state needs to formulate a strategy for industrialization focusing on the development of the manufacturing industry and in response to the challenge of economic globalisation, and map out a medium- and long-term plan for the development of the manufacturing industry. Unlike the past ones, the new industrialisation plan should have two basic prerequisites: the goal of building a "world workshop" and projections with regard to the international and domestic markets.

First, we must formulate and implement the relevant industrial policies, such as speeding up the development of heavy machinery manufacturing, especially the equipment manufacturing industry, renewal of industrial equipment and technological transformation, and development of technology-intensive and high- and new-technology industries, so as to promote the structural upgrading of China's manufacturing industry.

Second, we must establish and improve the IT system for China's manufacturing industry, so as to promote the development of the manufacturing industry by applying IT.

Third, we must formulate a strategic plan for the use of resources in the development of the manufacturing industry, bearing in mind the target requirements of building a "world workshop."

Fourth, we must study and put forward a plan for optimising the structural organization of China's manufacturing industry, promote its reorganization, and improve the key competitiveness of enterprises.

(2) The key to building a "world workshop" lies in absorbing a large amount of foreign investment on the basis of China's own comparative advantages. The relevant government departments should come up with policies and measures to encourage foreign investors to develop China's manufacturing industry, so as to promote the flow of global manufacturing industry to China.

First, we must seize the historical opportunities, and further improve the policy environment for absorbing foreign investment, with the emphasis on the manufacturing industry. For example, we must get rid of administrative monopoly, lift restrictions on market access, encourage outside investment in the infrastructure which serves the manufacturing industry, lift restrictions on the training market and encourage outside investment in high- and low-end training markets, so as to improve intellectual support for the manufacturing industry.

Second, we must set up free trade zones or free export processing zones for the manufacturing industry in areas with better conditions and adopting various forms compatible with international practices. In addition, we must apply low tariffs, zero restrictions and other free trade zone policies within the WTO framework selectively to areas with a heavy concentration of manufacturing industry, such as Shanghai and the Pearl River Delta, making these areas the country's "beachheads" and bases in its endeavor to build itself into a "world workshop."

In addition, the establishment of similar free trade zones or free export processing zones focusing on the manufacturing industry in some western cities, such as Chengdu, Chongqing and Xi'an, can be considered in the course of implementing the strategy of large-scale opening up of the western regions. Establishing manufacturing centers in the western regions with foreign investment is aimed at turning them into relay stations for industrial gradient transfers from overseas and China's coastal areas, and growth poles and "dynamos" for faster western economic development.

Third, we must carry out extensive cooperation among the four areas across the Taiwan Straits — the Mainland, Hong Kong, Macao and Taiwan — taking advantage of the strengths of each. It is necessary to take a wide range of measures to propel the industrial complementarities and transfers among the four areas. The relevant quarters should try to reach an early consensus with Taiwan, Hong Kong and Macao on rules of origin, intra-regional trade protection, lower trade barriers and intra-regional free circulation of manufactured goods. The four areas should energetically develop intermediaries, so as to lower trade costs, especially the information trade cost, and improve the competitiveness of China's manufacturing industry in the international market.

(3) A basic condition to turn China into a "world workshop" is to develop the overall innovation capacity of its manufacturing industry. The state should pay special attention to education and R & D in this respect.

First, the state should increase expenditures on vocational junior colleges, to expand the supply of trained workers. It should lift restrictions in this field, and diversify investment in such education by bringing in foreign investment and non governmental investment. In addition, it should encourage enterprises to invest in engineering education through tax reduction and exemption, and establish a continued education system.

Second, the state should pay more attention to R & D in the manufacturing industry. The government departments concerned should establish global manufacturing industry research centers as soon as possible, set up R & D funds for manufactured goods in areas where the conditions are ripe, and encourage enterprises to set up their own R & D funds through tax reductions and exemptions, so as to develop the technological innovation capacity of enterprises. In addition, it is necessary to introduce relevant preferential measures to encourage transnational corporations to set up R & D centers in China. Certain preferential tax policies should be adopted to support the integration of colleges, research institutions and enterprises in the course of transforming traditional manufacturing industry by adopting high- and new-technologies and advanced technologies.

Third, it is essential to pay special attention to bringing into play the role of Chinese technological personnel, adopt various forms to encourage them, and give appropriate rewards for their inventions and innovations. At the same time, greater efforts should be made to protect intellectual property rights and enforce the relevant laws, and bring about an institutional environment favorable to sales of advanced manufacturing technologies, in order to speed up the diffusion of technologies.

(4) Outside investment and non-governmental investment are important forces for developing the country's manufacturing industry. It is essential to introduce more liberal policies that will allow non-governmental investment to play a greater role in the manufacturing industry.

First, in response to the new situation following China's WTO accession, the government, while providing foreign investment with easier access to the manufacturing industry in China, should lift all restrictions on non-governmental enterprises that wish to access some branches of the manufacturing industry and related areas, and lower the thresholds for enterprises, especially non-governmental manufacturing enterprises.

Second, it is necessary to support the development of non-governmental manufacturing enterprises through banking, taxation, capital market and other means, resolutely cancel all discriminatory policies against such enterprises and create a favorable policy and institutional environment for their development, so as to end the monopoly of some branches by the state-owned sector.

(5) On the whole, SOEs are still the leader of China's manufacturing industry, playing a very big role. It is essential to speed up their reform with the improvement of their key competitiveness as the objective.

First, we must speed up the reform of the property rights system of state-owned manufacturing enterprises, gradually lower the portion of state shares in manufacturing enterprises through allowing other investors to participate, and establish and improve the effective corporate governance structure on the basis of diversifying property rights.

Second, we must remove as soon as possible the barriers existing in the manufacturing industry between different departments and between different regions, so as to promote trans-regional mergers and the reorganization of enterprises. This calls for reforming and improving the state assets management system, and making enterprises truly independent players in market competition; and encouraging and supporting mergers and the reorganization of enterprises in an effort to make manufacturing enterprises bigger and stronger, and improve the scale efficiency of Chinese manufacturing enterprises and their key competitiveness.

(6) The building of a "world workshop" requires a free and efficient environment for foreign trade. In this regard, it is necessary to speed up the reform of the foreign trade system, and gradually bring about an environment favorable for manufacturing enterprises to engage in import and export.

First, we must expedite the transition from the examination and approval system to a registry system with regard to the obtaining of foreign trade licenses, taking China's WTO accession as the turning point. This will allow manufacturing enterprises under various forms of ownership to ultimately have the independent right to export their manufactured goods for direct participation in international competition. In accordance with China's WTO commitments, the country undertakes to practice a registry system with regard to the obtaining of foreign trade licenses in an all-round way within the three-year transition period following its WTO entry. For the moment, the government should expeditiously abolish some irrational rules, and establish a registry system for the obtaining of foreign trade licenses compatible with international practices.

Second, we must reorganise state-owned foreign trade enterprises according to classifications and in keeping with the overall plan for the strategic readjustment of the national economy. Except for a tiny number of commodities which the state has designated for state monopoly, sole-state-funded operations should withdraw from the domain of foreign trade as quickly as possible.

Third, at a time when international trade competition is sharpening daily, and commodity prices are fluctuating rapidly, so that trade opportunities may slip away very easily, the government should establish a quick, balanced feedback mechanism and a dynamic adjustment mechanism, as well as a trade barrier pre-warning, monitoring and contingency system at a higher level for coordination among various ministries and commissions.

Fourth, we must give timely protection and support to some newly-emerging industries with major strategic significance for the development of the national economy in accordance with the WTO agreement on safeguards, and in light of the changing international market. Of course, the applicability of the WTO safeguards clauses is tied to compensation terms, so they should be applied with the utmost prudence.

As long as we seize the historical opportunities, formulate a correct strategic plan in good time, and practice flexible and effective policies and measures, we will certainly be sure that the Chinese manufacturing industry makes full use of its overall advantages, and achieves rapid development. This is something of vital importance to China's industrialization program, having a bearing on China's economic and social development.

PROMOTING REFORM BY OPENING UP, SO AS TO SPUR THE PROCESS OF CHINA'S ECONOMIC TRANSITION

(May 2003)

Why has China's accession to the WTO aroused wide domestic and international repercussions? International comments on the occasion of the first anniversary of China's WTO accession were positive. I believe the reason for this is twofold: First, China is a large developing country with a vast domestic market and a sustained economic growth; and second, it is also a large country in the process of transition from the traditional planned economy to the market economy. The fact that, as a large country in the process of economic transition, China has been able to bring itself into the mainstream of the world market economy within a reasonably short period of time is itself noteworthy. Therefore, the most profound, the most substantive and the most far-reaching aspect of China's WTO accession is, in my opinion, that the event represents China's second round of reform and opening up. With it, the country has entered a new stage in the course of opening up and reform.

The decision to accede to the WTO was a strategic choice the Chinese government made on its own with the aim of spurring its process of reform and opening up. Specifically, it is aimed at addressing deep-rooted contradictions and structural problems by opening up on a deeper level and obtaining a further motive force for sustained economic growth through institutional transition and structural upgrading, so as to improve the country's competitive edge as it promotes reform by opening up. Happening at the critical juncture for the country's transformation of its economic structure, the WTO accession will provide a fresh impetus for the market-oriented reform. First, opening up has promoted reform. The remarkable progress in many fields, including government reform, over the past year or two has amply demonstrated that its WTO accession has provided a fresh motive force for propelling China's reform and a very important motive force for the transition process. Second, the post-WTO economic reform has reached a higher level as it has been carried out in accordance with internationally accepted economic rules, and the market-oriented reform has been carried out on a higher level in an all-round way, with the aim of establishing a market economy system compatible with the international multilateral trade system and international management. Thus, the biggest post-WTO challenge is the market-oriented reform, and the most important move is to accelerate this process.

With its WTO accession, China's opening up has advanced from the general competitive areas to all-sector opening up with the emphasis being laid on the service sector. Therefore, the state monopolies are facing a tremendous challenge. Judging by this, the reform of the state monopolistic industries and service sector will be greatly accelerated in the coming years. It can be said that reform in the telecommunications, civil aviation, railways, banking, insurance and other services and areas of the infrastructure which used to be monopolized by the state sector was moving with great difficulty a few years ago. However, a big breakthrough has been achieved in the past two years. Leaving aside whether or not the split of the telecommunications industry into two corporations, south and north, along geographical lines is consistent with the principles of the market economy, it represented a big stride forward in breaking the previous monopoly. Much headway in the reform is expected in the coming three years in infrastructure and the service sector, thanks to the thrust provided by China's WTO accession.

1. Speeding up the reform of state-owned commercial banks

With China's WTO accession, the state-owned commercial banks will face tremendous pressures and challenges because of the heavy burdens left over from history and a slow shift in their operating mechanism. Whether or not the state-owned banking enterprises, especially the state-owned commercial banks, can withstand the test of the WTO accession will depend on: (1) whether or not they can successfully address the question of numerous undesirable assets so as to diffuse the banking risks; and (2) whether or not they can proceed to bring into being a new banking system, and speed up the process of market-oriented reform in the banking industry, so as to improve its international competitiveness.

2. Speeding up the reform of infrastructure

In the wake of its WTO accession, China will gradually open up its telecommunications, railways, electrical power, civil aviation and other infrastructure areas within a limited period of transition. Adapting the infrastructure areas to the new situation is a process involving very heavy tasks: breaking the administrative monopoly featuring the mixing up of the government and enterprise functions and at the same time preventing the formation of new monopolies of a market type in the transition process; paying attention to shifting and adjusting the functions of the government while developing market competition players in such areas; and breaking the traditional economic management system while expeditiously establishing a new government regulatory system and framework suited to market competition. In the light of the actual contradictions confronting infrastructure reform following the WTO accession and drawing on international experience, it is essential to address such major issues as market opening, anti-dumping, reshaping of competition players, speeding up the government regulatory system, and establishing an effective corporate governance structure.

3. Removing market segmentation and establishing a unified and open market order, taking the WTO accession as the turning point

The process of economic globalization is also one in which a worldwide unified market takes shape at an accelerated pace. To establish a "unified, open, competitive and orderly big market" is an important institutional guarantee for participating in economic globalisation. The extent of market segmentation and disorder resulting from administrative monopoly has prevented the market forces from playing a due role in optimizing the allocation of resources and stood in the way of adjusting the economic structure and improving competitiveness. This situation is not beneficial to China's participation in international competition. There is a pressing need to remove the administrative monopoly and market segmentation, and rectify and standardize the market order. The work to be done includes: (1) removing market segmentation and bringing about a nationwide unified and open market; (2) rectifying and standardizing the market order to meet the requirements for a unified and open market for fair competition; and (3) strengthening legislation and law enforcement with a view to standardizing the market order.

4. Government reform: a focal point in the wake of China's WTO accession

Under the conditions of the modern market economy, government reform and the shift in government functions are carried out to suit the process of constant participation in economic globalization. Judging by the practice over the past year since the WTO accession and forecasts for the years to come, government reform will be one of the focal points of the reform. This is the requirement of China's market-oriented reform process, its WTO accession, and, even more so, the deepening of the reform. Given the extent of the market economy in China today, what is most important is to bring about a fundamental change in the government role, especially following the

WTO accession, which means that China must follow the internationally accepted economic rules, and change or thoroughly change the "rules of play" under/of the planned economy through institutional arrangements. For example, first, the government must change the role it has played as a kind of market player. The government is still playing a partial role as a market player with regard to the state monopolies and the state sector as a whole. Second, there must be a change in the government functions. We have been urging the government to perform its public functions. What is meant by public functions? The formulation and implementation of rules are an important content of the public functions. Third, the stage that China's economic transition has reached today demands that the government change its role, perform its proper function of maintaining social stability. This puts government reform in a more prominent position than enterprise reform.

5. The building of a legal system against the WTO background

The aim of the WTO multilateral trade agreements is to remove as soon as possible the trade barriers erected by its member governments in the forms of tariffs, quotas, regulatory legislation, and other domestic legislation and administrative measures, as well as other inappropriate factors adversely affecting international free trade and equitable competition, and gradually push forward the process of trade liberalization. The legal significance of these agreements is that they require the member governments to correctly use the safeguards in their respective countries as allowed by the WTO rules, and restrain them in doing so. To ensure that China, now a WTO member, correctly applies the WTO agreements within its territory and brings its domestic laws and rules as well as its administrative procedures in line with the WTO agreements will bring major changes to the country's efforts to build a legal system.

First, China must speed up the revision of relevant domestic laws and regulations and bring them into accord with the WTO requirements. China's WTO accession mainly concerns the legislation and standardization of the economic reform to ensure that the relevant laws, decrees, regulations and policy measures conform to the WTO rules and its own commitments, and that these are implemented in a unified way throughout the country. Therefore, it is essential to review the laws currently in force to identify those stipulations that are obviously at odds with the WTO rules and China's commitments, and complete the work of revising or abrogating them within the set time. In the past year and more, the Chinese government has done much work in this respect, winning approval from the international community.

Second, it is necessary to speed up protective legislation in connection with China's WTO accession. It is necessary to enact a batch of laws and regulations standardizing economic activities in the fields newly opened in implementation of its market access commitments, so as to improve the legal system without leaving any legal gaps for unlawful enterprises to exploit through taking advantage of "grey areas." In order to protect domestic enterprises, it must take full advantage of the relevant WTO clauses and the "grey areas" when enacting legislation, and help speed up the development of domestic industries by lessening the negative impact from foreign industries. For example, it is advisable to make a safeguards law (or regulations) as well as anti-dumping and anti-subsidy regulations in accordance with the WTO agreements on safeguards, and establish an industry complaint mechanism and a standard investigations procedure to make them more effective.

In addition, it is essential to strengthen law enforcement in connection with the WTO accession, which invariably requires the eradication of artificial factors from economic activities and improvement of the legal system. Its WTO accession has placed even higher demands on the government, requiring it to reform its administrative management system, improve its administrative efficiency, increase its transparency, perform its administrative functions according to law and strengthen law enforcement.

6. The WTO accession and speedy formation of an institutional environment for attracting and using talented people

Competition in the modern economic and technological fields boils down to competition for talented people. Strategies for developing and using human resources are sources of economic growth, both national and enterprise-wise. China's WTO accession has touched off a competition for talented people, a challenge which China has to face squarely. For example, the competition for talented people will extend from Chinese students trained abroad to the best brains within the country. It is a pressing task to keep them by bringing about an institutional environment favorable for attracting and using them. Therefore, to speed up the development of human resources is a major strategy for responding to the WTO challenges.

The WTO accession has pushed China's reform and opening up to a new stage. I believe that in the next few years China's market-oriented reform will advance more rapidly than originally anticipated, playing an important expediting role in the country's economic and social development.

CHINA'S WTO ACCESSION AND ASIAN REGIONAL ECONOMIC COOPERATION

(*May 2003*)

Along with economic globalization, the process of regional economic integration will also advance at a much faster pace, and become an important force for propelling economic globalization. In fact, 55 to 60 percent of world trade is carried out within various types of regional organizations. As far as the WTO rules are concerned, not only is regional economic cooperation compatible with the rules the WTO has formulated and advocated for multilateral trade but the two are also mutually reinforcing. As things stand now, to participate in economic globalization, a country must first of all start economic exchanges and cooperation within its own region, with which it has the closest ties. Since the outbreak of the Asian financial crisis in the 1990s, more and more Asian countries have come to realize the importance of regional cooperation in dealing with crises and promoting growth. Thus, Asian regional economic cooperation has shown a quickening trend in recent years. While acceding to the WTO, China has taken some measures and shown a more positive posture in speeding up Asian regional economic cooperation.

I. China's WTO Accession: Its Major Impact on Asian Regional Economic Cooperation

China has a pivotal influence on Asian regional economic cooperation, because of its population size, resources and economic aggregate as well as its position in international politics and economics. After the outbreak of the Asian financial crisis, China stuck to its policy of not devaluing its currency, demonstrating a positive posture and its important role in Asia's economic cooperation. In the wake of its WTO accession, China will further open its markets and investment fields to the outside world, allowing other countries and regions to have more opportunities to conduct economic and trade cooperation with the country, and in wider areas. This will enable Asian countries, especially Southeast Asian ones, to gradually reduce their dependence on the European and US markets, accentuating China's role in Asian regional economic cooperation. It can be said that China's WTO accession will have a many-faceted important impact on Asian regional economic cooperation:

1. It will offer more opportunities to Asian countries and regions to access the Chinese market.

First of all, China's WTO accession will give a vigorous impetus to sustained economic growth. China will be able to maintain a 7-percent annual economic growth rate in the next 20 years or so, quadruple its GDP for the year 2000 by the year 2020, and industrialize its overall economic structure. Therefore, China will increase its domestic demand for capital, energy and raw materials to meet the needs of its industrialization program. Secondly, it will lower tariffs by a big margin, and lift quotas in the next few years. Asian countries and regions will benefit by increasing their exports to China. Expanded production and export of China's labor-intensive goods will generate greater demand for capital- and technology-intensive goods and raw materials that China imports from Asian countries and regions. This shows that Asian countries and regions will be among the first to benefit from China's WTO accession.

2. It will benefit the opening up of trade and investment in Asia.

In order to ensure the long-term and stable development of the

Asian economy, expanded trade and markets within the region will be vital to promoting regional economic cooperation. The fact that Asian countries and regions are at different economic development stages provides broad scope for the growth of trade and investment. As economic reorganization and transfers of industries progress, industry-wide and corporation-wide trade will enjoy broad prospects. Prompted by the regional demand, Asian enterprises in general desire to strengthen cooperation and open up trade and investment. Although there are controversies over the relationship between regionalism and multilateralism, regional trade agreements usually stipulate higher requirements on the obligations to open up than multilateral ones. As a WTO member, China may enter into bilateral or multilateral negotiations on the basis of regional trade agreements. Following China's accession to the WTO, deeper entry into the Chinese market may become an important motivation for other countries to start negotiations with China or its neighbouring countries (on the basis of regional trade agreements), which will also have a major impact on the facilitation of trade among Asian countries and regions.

3. It will benefit the coordination of views and positions among Asian countries and regions in the multilateral trade system.

Developing countries in Asia have always played a very important role in the world multilateral trade system, which is dominated by the US, EU, Japan, Canada and other developed Western countries. With China now a WTO member, developing countries will be able to exert a bigger influence in world trade through consultations and cooperation, and become more active in the multilateral trade system, contributing further to the development of world trade.

II. Participating in Asian Regional Economic Cooperation and Exchanges More Actively

With its WTO accession, China will play a more important

role in Asian regional cooperation. In such circumstances, it will strengthen economic cooperation and exchanges more actively with Asian countries and regions. For example, various types of regional economic cooperation organizations may be set up within the WTO framework, so that China can interact with the regional economy effectively and push forward the growth of the Asian economy.

1. Actively promoting trade liberalization with Asean

A free trade area is an important form of economic globalization, with two major features: First, the members of the group remove tariffs and other trade barriers among themselves; second, each member independently retains its external trade policies, especially tariff policies. The establishment of a free trade area accords with the WTO rules, and is very conducive to promoting regional trade liberalization as well as economic globalization.

The members of the Association of Southeast Asian Nations (Asean) are China's close neighbours, and both they and China are developing countries. China's trade with Asean has grown fairly rapidly in recent years. By 2000, the bilateral trade had reached 39.5 billion US dollars-worth, with Asean being China's fifth-largest trading partner, having an 8.3 percent share of China's goods trade market, while China was Asean's sixth-largest trading partner, having a 3.9 percent share of Asean's foreign trade. China and Asean combined have a total population of 1.7 billion people, and a GDP of 2,000 billion US dollars. A study shows that once a free trade area is established between China and Asean, Asean would be able to increase its investment in China by 48 percent, and its own GDP by 0.9 percent, while China would be able to increase its exports to Asean by 55 percent and its GDP by 0.2 percent. In fact, a China-Asean free trade area would not only increase regional trade, but also promote an influx of investment from without as well as intra-regional investment. At the same time, China would greatly increase its investment in the Asean countries.

On November 4, 2002, the China's premier and the leaders of

the ten Asean countries jointly signed the China-Asean Framework Agreement on All-round Economic Cooperation, signifying a new historical stage for economic and trade cooperation between China and Asean. The key to establishing a China-Asean free trade area is to strictly observe the WTO rules, minimize the exclusiveness of a regional economic union, and energetically create conditions to speed up the process of the free trade area. Within the framework of the free trade area, efforts should be made to strive for substantial breakthroughs in liberalizing agricultural, tourism and banking services transactions over the next two years.

2. Active participation in sub-regional cooperation in Northeast Asia

The northeast Asia economic rim focusing on China, Japan and the Republic of Korea, and the European and North American economic rims are world's three major economic rims. The total output value of China, Japan and the ROK in 2000 reached 6,000 billion US dollars, while the total output value of the ten Southeast Asian countries was only 675 billion US dollars. The northeastern economic rim is enormous in market scale and growth potential and northeastern regional economic cooperation is very important to the three countries alike.

There exists a solid foundation for regional cooperation among the three countries. Sino-Japanese economic and trade relations occupy an important position in China's overall economic and trade relations with foreign countries. The two countries are mutually important partners in economic and trade cooperation, with Japan being China's largest trading partner for seven consecutive years and China being Japan's second-largest trading partner. Japan is one of the main sources of China's foreign investment and technology imports. Since China and the ROK established diplomatic relations in 1992, bilateral trade had grown sharply — from 5.06 billion US dollars in 1992 to 24.04 billion US dollars in 1997. The trade volume suffered a fall in 1998 due to the Asian financial crisis. But since 1999 bilateral trade has once again shown a good growth momentum and the

ROK becomes China' fourth-largest trading partner. China, Japan and the ROK have all the conditions to further their cooperation in regional economic relations, strategy and security.

China's WTO accession will help the process of northeastern Asia regional economic cooperation. Some scholars have thus proposed that China may build closer regional economic cooperation with other countries in Northeast Asia in three stages: As the first step, the three countries could establish a trade ministers' meeting mechanism to promote economic, trade and banking cooperation among them, and study ways to prevent trade friction. Meanwhile, it is necessary to promote exchanges and cooperation among industrial and commercial circles of the three countries, and set up a commercial forum with the participation of prominent figures from the economic circles of the three countries with the purpose of drawing up some large-scale development plans that would use capital, technologies and human resources from the three countries. In addition, fact-finding missions on economic and trade affairs, investment and the environment may be exchanged to help forge closer regional economic ties. As the second step, the three countries could establish and refine the regional division of labor among their industries, in an effort to make their industrial structures mutually complementary, and share resources. They may experiment with setting up free trade zones in some cities in the three countries, to prepare the ground for establishing a regional union. As the third step, a formal free trade area zone could be set up, with the ultimate aim of setting up the Northeast Asia Economic Community or Common Market.

3. Strengthening regional economic ties with Russia, South Asia and Central Asia

It is necessary to adopt a long-term perspective on China's economic cooperation with Russia. Before Russia accedes to the WTO, China and Russia should, on the basis of fast-growing economic and trade cooperation, further expand the fields and total volume of trade, strengthen economic and technological cooperation and technological trade, start large economic and trade cooperative projects in energy, aviation and other areas, and begin and expand direct investment in each other's country. Vigorous efforts should be made to create conditions for Russia to join some multilateral regional economic cooperation organizations in Asia, which will be beneficial to Asian regional economic cooperation and to economic and trade cooperation between China and Russia.

There exists a fairly good foundation for regional economic cooperation between China and South Asia. China should take its WTO accession as a turning point for further strengthening and expanding its economic and trade relations with South Asia. In recent years, South Asia and Southeast Asia have been discussing the idea of setting up a free trade area adjacent to China's border regions. China should actively get involved in this, provide necessary infrastructure for the South Asia free trade area through the construction of the Pan-Asia Railway, and continue to provide economic assistance within its capabilities.

China's accession to the WTO has also provided important opportunities and conditions for its regional economic cooperation with the six Central Asian countries. The Shanghai Cooperation Organization, embracing China, the Central Asian countries and Russia, stands astride the continents of Europe and Asia with a vast market scope and rich resources. It is possible for China and the six Central Asian countries to strengthen their economic and trade cooperation within the WTO framework, and explore the possibility of setting up a regional economic cooperation organization of a substantial nature.

III. Economic and Trade Relations Between China's Mainland, Hong Kong, Macao and Taiwan Within the WTO Framework

There are four Chinese members in the WTO now with the accession to it of China's mainland and Taiwan, plus Hong Kong and

Macao as separate Chinese tariff territories. Due to China's special circumstances, the WTO accession of both sides of the Taiwan Straits will gradually bring about major changes in the economic and trade relations among China's mainland, Taiwan, Hong Kong and Macao. This requires us to face reality, take a long-term point of view, and explore in an objective way the trends of the economic and trade relations among the four.

1. Expediting economic and trade cooperation among the four cross-Straits entities, in keeping with the general trend of Asian regional economic cooperation

First, free trade arrangements among the four cross-Straits WTO members should and can go faster than the actual pace of Asian regional economic cooperation. The four parties should reach consensus on this point, and take specific measures as soon as possible.

Second, free trade in the industrial category among the four can start first. It is possible to make substantial breakthroughs in tourism, agriculture or banking.

Third, it is essential to take a principled stand on the practice of the "one country, two systems" concept, and at the same time show a certain degree of flexibility. For example, it may be possible for the Macao Special Administrative Region and the Zhuhai Special Economic Zone, under the prerequisite of adhering to the basic principle of "one country, two systems," develop Hengqin Island by cooperating in such a way that we may term it "one country, three systems" under the principle of "one country, two systems."

Fourth, the free trade arrangements between China's mainland and Taiwan should be oriented to the general trend of Asian regional economic cooperation and, proceeding from the overall interests in sustainable development on both sides of the Taiwan Straits, and seek early breakthroughs in some areas under the prerequisite of adhering to the "one China" principle. This will benefit development of both.

2. Strengthening economic and trade cooperation among the four Chinese WTO members across the Taiwan Straits and making important contributions to promoting the Asian regional economic cooperation

China's sustained rapid economic growth is a contribution to Asian economic development and, to an even greater extent, helps the country to play an important role in Asian regional cooperation. Forging even stronger and closer economic and trade cooperation among the four Chinese WTO members across the Taiwan Straits will greatly enhance China's position and role in Asian regional economic cooperation. If the GDPs of China's mainland, Hong Kong and Taiwan are added up, then the total will reach 1,531.9 billion US dollars, exceeding the total GDP of the major Asian countries (excluding Japan), which stands at 1,425 billion US dollars. If and when the four places are integrated economically, their economic strength is expected to rise to fourth place in the world. The total volume of imports and exports will reach 1,059.9 billion US dollars, equalling the total for the major Asian countries (excluding Japan), or slightly higher than Germany's figure for 1999. This is one indication of the economic strength the four places can reach if they are integrated. At the same time, it also shows that by strengthening economic and trade cooperation, the four places will be able to make major contributions to Asian regional economic cooperation.

Resolutely opening up to the outside world is China's long-term basic state policy and an inevitable path for speeding up its economic and social modernization, and improving the country's competitiveness. China's WTO accession is at once a major culmination of its reform and opening up over the past two decades and more, and an important motive force for speeding up the reform and opening up in the future. As long as we act according to the correct guidelines set forth by the 16th CPC National Congress, promote reform and development by opening up, speed up the building of an open economy, and improve the standards of opening up in an all-round way, we will be able to take advantage of the impetus from the opening up and reform, and participate in international competition and cooperation on an even larger scale and at an even deeper level, thus greatly improving the country's competitiveness.

THE CONCEPT OF A "CHINA FREE TRADE AREA"

(November 2001)

— The prospects for economic and trade relations among China's Mainland, Hong Kong, Macao and Taiwan within the WTO framework

There are four Chinese members in the WTO now, with the accession of China's mainland and Taiwan, plus Hong Kong and Macao as separate Chinese customs territories. Due to the special circumstances of China, the WTO accession of both sides of the Taiwan Strait will gradually bring about major changes in the economic and trade relations among the four — China's mainland, Taiwan, Hong Kong and Macao. We should face reality, take a long-term point of view, explore the trends in economic and trade relations among the four within the WTO framework in an objective way, and make basic assessments.

Establishment of the "China Free Trade Area." The gradual establishment of a free trade relationship featuring unimpeded flow of the factors of production among the four Chinese WTO members can give concrete expression to the special relationships and realities among them as one country with several customs territories and adapt to the general trend of economic and trade relations among them following the WTO accession of both sides of the Straits.

I. Establishment of "China Free Trade Area": An Important Choice for Integrating the Economic and Trade Relations Among the Four Chinese WTO Members Against the General Background of Economic Globalization

1. The quickening process of regional economic cooperation and intensified trend of regional integration against the background of economic globalization

Economic globalization is the mainstream of current world economic development. The chief measure most developing countries have taken in response to the challenge of globalization is to promote trade liberalization and structural reform of their domestic economy in compliance with the requirements of an open economy. In this process, regional economic integration has become more and more an outstanding trend and phenomenon. On the one hand, the European Union (EU) and the North American Free Trade Area (NAFTA), which are already in existence, are the areas in the world with the strongest economies and will expand their scope along with their economic growth. On the other hand, many new regional integration organizations are in the making, with many more countries showing an interest in regional integration. For example, the Free Trade Area of the ten Asean countries that are headed for the goal of trade liberalization, the concept of an Asean 10 plus 3 Free Trade Area, the concept of an Asean, Australia and New Zealand Free Trade Area and the concept of a Latin American Free Trade Area. All this shows that the trend toward regional economic integration has been intensified against the background of economic globalization. As various countries participate in economic globalization, the first and foremost problem they face is how to participate in the economic integration and opening up of the regions with which they are most closely linked.

2. Objectively assessing the economic and trade relations among the four following the WTO accession of China's mainland and Taiwan

The WTO accession of China's mainland and Taiwan will bring new opportunities for economic cooperation and development in this region, pushing to a new stage their cooperation in trade, investment, economy and banking. On the one hand, a big reduction of the mainland's tariffs will help Hong Kong, Macao and Taiwan to increase export of their goods to and investment in the mainland; on the other, bound by the WTO rules, the three places, especially Taiwan, will inevitably relax restrictions on investment and imports from the mainland. In fact, the rise of the mainland's economy and daily-closer economic ties among the four places are something meriting great attention in the overall economic development pattern in Northeast Asia.

The WTO accession of China's mainland and Taiwan poses a challenge to the current economic and trade relations among the four Chinese WTO members across the Taiwan Straits, which is manifested mainly in the fact that investment from Hong Kong, Macao and Taiwan in the mainland does not show a strong competitive edge in terms of industry, and will be subject to challenges from transnational corporations in the mainland market in the wake of the WTO accession. The Law of the People's Republic of China on Protecting Investments by Compatriots from Taiwan, which the National People's Congress adopted in 1994, and the Detailed Rules on Implementing the Law on Protecting Investments by Compatriots from Taiwan, published by the State Council in 1999, while protecting investments made by Taiwan businessmen, have also extended various types of preferential treatment. With the WTO accession, the central government will have to either abolish or revise these preferential policies, or grant the same treatment to investors from other countries, which will weaken the competitive edges of enterprises funded by investment from Hong Kong, Macao and Taiwan in the mainland market.

According to the WTO rules, any sovereign country or any region having independent authority over its trading policies may apply for membership. Taipei, Hong Kong and Macao are all separate customs territories of China. We should try to find a new pattern of relations among the four places within the WTO framework and jointly promote the goal of free trade.

To construct a free trade area embracing the four tariff territories within the WTO framework is an important way to solve the question of economic and trade relations among the four places. Section 8 (b) of Article XXIV of the General Agreement on Tariffs and Trade (GATT) says: "A free-trade area shall be understood to mean a group of two or more customs territories in which duties and other restrictive regulations of commerce...are eliminated on substantially all the trade between the constituent territories in products originating in such territories." Such a group has two salient features: (1) It eliminates tariffs and other restrictive regulations of commerce among its members; (2) each of its members independently retains its external trade policies, especially tariff policies. The "China Free Trade Area" refers to an economic and trade mechanism embracing China's mainland as a sovereign state and three separate customs territories (Taiwan, Hong Kong and Macao), a mechanism by which each member eliminates tariffs and other trade restrictions in relation to the other members, and independently retains its external trade policies. Such a framework would make it possible to continue with the current preferential economic and trade treatment as an embodiment of the special relations featuring "one country with four territories," and at the same time conform to the WTO's basic rules.

3. It is a general trend to promote the economic integration of the four.

Regional economic integration is a general trend. Among the main forms of regional economic cooperation are free trade area, common market, customs union and economic integration, which vary in the extent of cooperation.

Economic contacts among the four places in the Taiwan Straits area have multiplied in recent years. Investment from Hong Kong and Taiwan in the mainland has kept growing. Hong Kong and the mainland have become Taiwan's two-biggest markets after the US. Its exports to the mainland comprise about one fourth of its total exports, and its investment in the mainland is about half of its total external investment. Its economic and trade ties with Hong Kong have a long history and have a major significance. The four places share the same cultural background. Thus, a regional economic entity has naturally evolved among them. A report published by the International Monetary Fund and the World Bank a few years ago referred to the four places as the "Chinese economic area."

In fact, the idea of taking economic integration across the Straits as the focal point for the promotion of economic integration among the four places — and even an economic integration of Chinese communities — has been kept alive ever since it was proposed in the 1980s. In the 1990s, Chinese scholars in the four places and overseas came forward with dozens of concepts and names concerning the establishment of a Chinese economic area.

4. The construction of a "China free trade area" will greatly enhance China's position and role in the regional integration process.

Statistics show that China's mainland is home to the world's seventh-largest economy after the United States, Japan, Germany, Britain, France and Italy. But if the GDP of China's mainland, Hong Kong and Taiwan (not including Macao) is added up, then it totals 1,531.9 billion US dollars, exceeding the total GDP of major Asian countries (excluding Japan), which stands at 1,425 billion US dollars, and surpassing the figures of Britain, France and Italy. If the four places across the Taiwan Straits are integrated economically, their economic strength as a whole is expected to rise to fourth place in the world. The total import and export volume will reach 1,059.9 billion US dollars, equal to the total import and export of major

Asian countries (excluding Japan) and slightly higher than that of Germany in 1999. These figures are an indication of the economic strength that the four places would show following integration.

Among the world's top ten countries and regions in 1999 in terms of foreign exchange reserves, China's mainland ranked second, with 145.7 billion US dollars; Taiwan third, with 95.7 billion US dollars; and Hong Kong fifth, with 88.9 billion US dollars. If the three figures are added up, the total comes to 330.3 billion US dollars, far surpassing Japan, Germany and the United States, and giving the area the largest foreign exchange reserves in the world.

After the 9/11 event in the United States, economic growth in most Asian countries slowed down, with some countries and regions even sinking into economic recession. In contrast, China has kept a steady and rapid economic growth momentum during this period. The main reason for this is the fact that the country has stuck to its policy of boosting the domestic market, and persisted in deepening structural reforms. In the face of the world economic depression, to promote economic and trade cooperation and speed up the process of regional economic integration is of special significance and urgency for keeping sustained and steady economic growth in the four places.

II. Establishing a China Free Trade Area: A Strategic Move to Speed Up Investment and Trade Liberalization in the Four Places

1. Gradually realizing the general objective of investment and trade liberalization

As an exception to the most-favored-nation treatment principle, Article XXIV of the GATT allows its constituent territories to establish customs unions and free trade zones among themselves, with the aim of enabling them to forge closer economic and trade cooperation, have a rational division of labor and be mutually complementary in terms of resources and industries, so as to advance trade liberalization and globalization.

The objective of a China Free Trade Area is trade and investment liberalization, in order to maintain long-term, sustained growth momentum of the economy in the four constituent territories. The essence of economic and trade cooperation among the four places is division of labor and cooperation, so as to take advantage of each other's strengths. Cooperation should not be limited to low tariffs and zero restrictions in the trade in goods, but should also include consensus on the rules of origin within the area, industrial cooperation, and service and investment liberalization.

2. Common general preferential tariffs on trade in goods

Decisions should be made on categories of common goods in the free trade area, and a scheme of lowered common tariff rates should be enacted. A timetable for trade liberalization specifying a gradual reduction or phase-out of tariff rates — say to gradually cut tariffs across the board to zero to 5 percent in five to ten years – should be adopted. All parties concerned should undertake not to introduce or erect new trade barriers, and proceed to reach agreement on the objective of establishing a free trade area, that is, China's mainland, Hong Kong, Macao and Taiwan. Common general preferential tariffs should be applied to each other within the area, while each independently decides on the tariffs it levies on other WTO members outside the area. In fact, the conditions for applying common general preferential tariffs on trade in goods are basically ripe: Hong Kong and Macao are basically free trade zones; and Taiwan is already very open, with its average nominal tariff rates dropping from 31 percent in 1982 to 6 percent in 1998 and actual tariff rates from 8 percent to 4 percent. It has acceded to the WTO in the capacity of an advanced region, and is expected to lower its general tariff level after its full WTO accession to 3.5 percent, on a par with the OECD countries; China's mainland has committed itself to speeding up the pace of its trade and tariff system reform, and reducing nominal tariff rates by a big margin to somewhere between 3 and 4 percent, and eliminating all tax reductions and exemptions. It can be said that the construction of a scheme of common general preferential tariffs in a China Free Trade Area is a very realistic idea.

3. Consensus on rules of origin

For the members of the area to enjoy greater preferential treatment or lower tariffs than non-members, it is also necessary to bring about a four-party consensus on the "Rules of Origin of the China Free Trade Area" beyond the above-mentioned trade arrangements under general preferential tariffs. The Asean Free Trade Area has set a successful example for us in this respect. On December 11, 1992, the Asean nations signed in Jakarta the Rules of Origin for Common Effective Preferential Tariff (CEPT). Under the CEPT scheme, goods made in Asean nations that satisfy the local content requirement of 40 percent are eligible for preferential tariff rates upon presentation of certificates issued by the competent authorities of the exporting nations when they are directly exported from one intra-regional country to another. Some people hold the view that the CEPT is a kind of trade protectionism, because it applies only to Asean nations and is tantamount to a trade barrier in a disguised form vis-a-vis non-Asean nations. But there is no denying that it accords with WTO rules. If the four Chinese WTO members can reach a consensus on the rules of origin they will be able to ensure the economic interests of all parties in the area and at the same time attract more foreign investment to the area.

4. Taking advantage of each other's industrial strengths, and stepping up industrial cooperation

With the WTO accession of China's mainland and Taiwan, industries in the four places that can complement each other should strengthen cooperation among themselves, in order to lessen the adverse impact of the WTO as far as possible. In terms of comparative and relative advantages, China's mainland, Hong Kong, Macao and Taiwan all have their respective strengths and weaknesses. For example, relatively speaking, the mainland's manufacturing industry enjoys rather low labor costs, and has obvious comparative advantages in the production of labor-intensive products. Hong Kong's service sector, including tourism, information and banking, is in the front ranks of the world in terms of professional standards. Hong Kong has a complete legal system, and its lawyers are well versed in the Chinese and English languages, giving Hong Kong an advantage as a center for legal arbitration for Chinese and foreign business people. Taiwan is fairly well developed economically, and needs to extend its industrial chain beyond the island. It is experienced in developing a market economy, has fairly abundant capital, and needs to make investment outside the island. In addition, it suffers from a relative shortage of labor power, and needs to bring in high-quality workers from outside. Macao's main economic pillars are tourism, lottery (accounting for more than 45 percent of the local GDP), and export-processing industries in such fields as garments, textiles and toys. It opened its service sector a long time ago, but its processing industries are small in size and limited in range. Moreover, it depends for direct investment on the mainland (45 percent) and Hong Kong (25 percent). The four places are at different development levels, showing a great potential for vertical economic division of labor or cooperation, as their economies are mutually complementary. The establishment of a China Free Trade Area would offer great prospects for the four places to take advantage of their industrial strengths and step up their industrial cooperation.

5. Advancing the liberalization process of the service sector focusing on banking and insurance

On the basis of the General Agreement on Trade in Services (GATS), the four constituent territories could actively seek ways to strengthen cooperation in the service sector among themselves, eliminate restrictions on the trade in services, and expand the scope and depth of trade liberalization in services. At present, one fifth of the world's trade is in services. In view of future development trends, trade in services will grow faster than that in manufactured goods, and it will also generate demand for manufactured goods. The central government has already committed itself to opening banking, insurance, telecommunications and other services in an all-round way within five years following China's WTO accession, and gradually phasing out the existing trade barriers of a geographical nature. The mainland's trade in services takes up a very small share of the world's total. Therefore, to open its service market is an important way to promote growth and create more jobs. Taiwan and Hong Kong enjoy advantages in such services as banking, law, finance, accounting, trade and telecommunications. The "learning effects" will help the relevant sectors on the mainland to quickly improve their standards.

6. Strategies and steps for constructing a China Free Trade Area

We may build a China Free Trade Area in several stages: Stage One: constructing a free trade area embracing the mainland, Hong Kong and Macao; Stage Two: constructing a free trade area embracing the mainland, Hong Kong, Macao and Taiwan; and Stage Three: constructing a multilateral trade strategy for actively participating in and advancing trade liberalization in our region and beyond while working for a China Free Trade Area. For example, the Chinese government has decided to establish the Asean-China Free Trade Area by the year 2010.

We may show appropriate flexibility with regard to relevant content. We may identify some priority areas for the near-term cooperation, such as opening tourism to promote cooperation in that area; promoting the development of human resources and expanding information services and cooperation in that area; and promoting opening and cooperation in the agricultural sector. The mid- and-long-term objective is to lower import tariffs, eliminate various non-tariff barriers, and advance trade liberalization in goods and services, as well as investment in terms of capital and technologies.

With regard to the specific time for implementation, the year 2003 may be considered for the establishment of a free trade area embracing the mainland, Hong Kong and Macao, when the Asean Free Trade Area comes into being. Around year 2005, a China Free Trade Area embracing the four places could be established. If such arrangements can be made, China's economy will play a greater role in advancing economic integration in East Asia, Southeast Asia, and Asia as a whole.

III. Establishment of a China Free Trade Area Conforms to the General Trend of Development in the Economic and Trade Relations Among the Four.

1. The impact of constructing a China Free Trade Area on the economy of Hong Kong, Macao and Taiwan

(1) Impact on Taiwan's economy. After both sides of the Taiwan Straits acceded to the WTO, restrictions of the international market on their goods, especially those made on the mainland have been reduced, greatly expanding China's export trade. According to the WTO Secretariat, there will be an annual growth rate of 6 to 26 percent, contributing 2.9 percentage points to China's GDP and increasing it by more than 200 billion yuan RMB in output value, not to mention the creation of millions of jobs. Such growth prospects will prompt Taiwanese businessmen to invest more in the mainland. At the same time, the growth of Taiwan's economy will also bring more business opportunities in the form of cross-Straits economic and trade cooperation. According to a study conducted by Taiwan's Economic Construction Commission, in the circumstances in which neither side across the Straits invokes the exception clauses after both sides have acceded to the WTO, Taiwan's GDP will grow by 1.72 percent, and its trade surplus will be cut by 2.7 billion US dollars between 2000 and 2004.

Some mainland and Taiwan industries will face challenges in the wake of the two sides' WTO accession. For the sake of their common interests, some mutually complementary industries on both sides of the Straits will be forced to strengthen their cooperation. Take agriculture for example. After Taiwan acceded to the WTO, increased imports of some agricultural produce due to lower tariffs and removal of non-tariff barriers led to the reduced production of such items and smaller output value, forcing a large amount of agricultural produce and capital to look for outlets elsewhere. The two sides of the Straits can address the adverse impact of their WTO accession only by strengthening their agricultural cooperation and turning to good account the differences in the stages of their agricultural development and natural endowments.

In the information and telecommunications sector, at present the mainland is the computer consumer market promising the greatest potential in the world. Its telecommunications sector has registered a very rapid annual growth rate since the 1990s, far exceeding the GDP growth rate. Since 1996, the mainland has become the largest import market for Taiwan's transmission equipment, absorbing about 46.9 percent of its exports; Southeast Asia is the second-biggest importer, with 28.7 percent of the total. As a result of the adverse effect of the Asian financial crisis, some enterprises on the island have sought to open markets in other areas, and its exports to Southeast Asia dropped. The mainland's market opening will help Taiwanese business people to expand their operations.

(2) The Impact on Hong Kong's economy. With its WTO accession, China's economic aggregate and foreign trade will grow quickly. As the mainland's largest trading partner and supplier of overseas investment, Hong Kong will undoubtedly benefit from this.

In the manufacturing sector, Hong Kong can make use of the mainland's favourable conditions in R & D, human resources and land, and combine them with its own advantages in trading networks and market promotion, to develop hi-tech and high value-added industries and upgrade its manufacturing industry.

The mainland's adjustment of its economic structure will add a new dimension to the modes of economic cooperation between the two places. IT application, as represented by the cyber-economy, will inject new vitality into the economic and trade relations between the two places.

In the investment field, the mainland's pace of opening its service sector is quickening. Medium-sized and small firms in Hong Kong have international experience and professional standards in providing specialized services in fields such as accounting, law, banking, insurance, transportation, logistics, information and consultancy. On account of their advantages in capital, technologies, managerial expertise and marketing outlets, they may establish closer and more varied cooperation with enterprises on the mainland, in a joint effort to open the domestic and international markets, which are daily merging more closely.

(3) The Impact on Macao's economy. Macao's economy will face new development opportunities. There will be a big increase in the number of tourists from the mainland, boosting its tourism-lottery industry and giving Macao an opportunity to adjust its economy and upgrade its industries. For example, a shift from labor-intensive to technology- and capital-intensive industries; a gradual shift away from the mode of production featuring sole dependence on European and American markets and the textile industry in an effort to diversify products and markets; and a transition toward culture-based industries and tourism while reducing the importance of the lottery in the economy. The mainland's economy will back up Macao's economic development by providing not only a vast market and rich labor power but also raw materials, energy supplies and food.

2. Prospects for short-term cooperation in the China Free Trade Area

(1) Speeding up tariff reduction and exemption in the China Free Trade Area within the WTO framework. China's mainland has undertaken to gradually reduce its tariffs, for example, cutting tariffs on agricultural produce to 17 percent on average within three years, to 9.4 percent on average in the case of industrial goods as a whole and zero tariffs for many hi-tech products. If Taiwan, as the producer of many agricultural and hi-tech products can benefit from the tariff reductions and exemptions ahead of schedule, it will greatly help its development of relevant products.

(2) The mainland's move to open its markets makes it possible to speed up cooperation in the allocation of resources within the area, make industries mutually complementary and upgrade them. Following its WTO accession, China's mainland will open wider to the outside world, opening markets in more areas, especially the service sector. The service sector in the mainland is not well developed, and thus promises an enormous potential for growth. Banking, insurance, telecommunications, wholesale business, investment and management consultancy, software development, law, accounting and other areas will all open both to Sino-foreign joint ventures and sole foreign investment. Because the mainland, Taiwan, Hong Kong and Macao have the same cultural background and enjoy geographical advantages, the mainland on the one hand can open these areas to Taiwan, Hong Kong and Macao ahead of other WTO members, while Taiwan, Hong Kong and Macao, on the other hand, are in a better position to enter these areas than other members. The mainland boasts rich resources, labor power and a vast market, while Hong Kong, Macao and Taiwan have ample capital, advanced managerial expertise and applied technologies. A mutually complementary use of these intra-regional advantages will result in a rational allocation of resources and constant industrial upgrading in the interests of economic development, to yield maximum returns at minimum cost and bring about a more rational industrial distribution for the common prosperity of the regional economy.

(3) The intra-regional economy will further thrive. Trade exchanges, capital flow, manpower flow, scientific, technological, economic and trade exchanges and cooperation among the four places will be speeded up, leading to the formation of an area with swift development in the Asia-Pacific Region. This, in turn, will promote the long-term development of the economies of the two sides of the Taiwan Straits and of Hong Kong and Macao, and speed up the process of Chinese regional economic integration.

THOROUGH NATIONAL TREATMENT FOR FARMERS

PROPOSALS ON GIVING FARMERS NATIONAL TREATMENT

PROPOSITION OF THE ISSUE

(*January 2002*)

When China was under the traditional system of planned economy, the main feature of the farmer-related policies was the separation of town from country. Despite the remarkable progress in narrowing the difference between town and country thanks to the reform over the past two decades and more, there has not been a total, fundamental change in this dual system.

1. With regard to the economic relations between town and country, there still exists a "price scissors" to some extent, putting the farmers at a disadvantage.

For example, statistics show that during the 16 years between 1979 and 1994, the government took away approximately 1,500 billion yuan RMB from the farmers through the "price scissors." In addition, during the same period the farmers paid 175.5 billion yuan RMB in agricultural taxes while receiving 376.9 billion yuan RMB in various government aid-agriculture funds. Thus, the government netted approximately 1,298.6 billion yuan RMB from the farmers through the "price scissors," averaging 81.1 billion yuan RMB annually, 5.2 times the pre-reform figure, which stood at 15.5 billion yuan RMB.

2. With regard to the institutional arrangements between town and country, the household registration system, the agricultural taxation system and other systems that have been in practice for 40 years

are still serious institutional obstacles to bringing together the town and country for coordinated development.

3. With regard to income distribution, the farmers have actually borne heavier financial burdens than urban residents.

For example, according to the statistics made available by the Office of the Working Group in Charge of Taxes and Fees Reform under the State Council, the total amount of taxes and fees paid by the farmers in 1998 amounted to 122.4 billion yuan RMB, which included agricultural taxes, surcharges, agricultural special product taxes, taxes for slaughtering animals, all kinds of fees and levies to support education and other local undertakings, as well as local administrative fees.

4. Due to the current rural economic development level, rural inhabitants have failed to enjoy the same rights to the social security benefits as urban dwellers.

5. Due to delayed reforms, rural inhabitants cannot enjoy a full range of basic rights or exercise them fully.

I. Reforming the Agricultural Taxation System in Accordance With the Principle of Equal Treatment to Town and Country to Unify Urban and Rural Taxation Systems as Soon as Possible

1. China's agricultural tax system, based on the Regulations of the PRC on Agricultural Taxes adopted on June 3, 1958 at the 96th meeting of the Standing Committee of the First National People's Congress, has been in force for more than 40 years. It is already irrelevant to the new situation in the country's reform and development as a result of the establishment of the market economy and deepening rural reform.

2. The collection of agricultural tax in the early period following the founding of the PRC in 1949 was determined by the basic national

conditions at the time. During the 1950s and 1960s agricultural taxes made up a considerable proportion of the national tax revenues. At present, agricultural tax makes up only a very tiny proportion, at about 5 percent. So, the preconditions for abolishing it are basically ripe.

3. The objective of the agricultural tax system reform is to unify the urban and rural tax systems, as most countries in the world do. To do so, it is essential to abolish the various taxes and fees designed specially for the farmers, treating the farmers as individual industrial and commercial businesses by applying to them value-added tax and personal income tax.

International practices are:

(1) Agricultural policies of the overwhelming majority of countries feature preferential tax treatment for farmers and farm workers engaged in agricultural production;

(2) Agriculture is entitled to more preferential tax treatment and support;

(3) The same types of tax apply to all enterprises and individuals, without separate tax types for agriculture.

II. Granting Equal Citizens' Rights to Farmers by Abolishing the Household Registration System Separating Town from Country

China began to practice the household registration system in 1958. Before then, there was a period of free migration; the period between 1958 and 1978 was one of strict control; and the period since 1978 has seen limited relaxations.

1. Since the 1980s, and especially in recent years, some localities have taken measures with regard to the reform of the household registration system and achieved successes in many aspects. But the reform has great limitations: First, the reform of the registration system has left intact the systems that are related to the status of the

farmers, such as the employment system, education system, financial system and social security system; and second, those rural inhabitants who have moved to cities cannot afford the high living standards there.

2. Proceeding from the actual conditions in rural development, the household registration system must be reformed thoroughly, ending the "separate administration of cities and the countryside through dual policies in the same country."

3. In order to modernize China's countryside through changing the social structure, it is essential to incorporate the flow of rural population in the whole society into the national social migration so that changes in occupation, residence and social status will take place at the same time.

III. Ensuring Same Labor Rights and Employment Opportunities to Migrant Workers

The Ministry of Agriculture estimated that 88 million rural laborers were on the move as migrant workers in 2001, applying the definition that a migrant rural worker is one who is employed for more than three months away from his/her home town. According to the new definition, at least 120 million rural inhabitants are estimated to be moving between town and country.

1. It is essential to eliminate discriminatory policies against the migrant rural workers in cities. For example, restrictions with regard to household registration, status, jobs, their children's education and social security must be eliminated and an open labor market unifying town and country should be gradually established, so that urban and rural inhabitants are equal before development opportunities.

2. Urbanization should be accelerated. As the country's urbanization is seriously retarded, there is a great potential for absorbing more surplus rural laborers through urbanization. To develop small

towns is among the effective ways that China has adopted to advance urbanization. The movement of surplus rural laborers from farms to small towns will propel the comprehensive development of rural economy and offer more opportunities for farmers to increase their income. County towns should be assigned a full role in the process of urbanization. Therefore, comprehensive reforms at the county level are very important.

3. All kinds of restrictions on the mobility of migrant rural workers must be eliminated, and conditions should be created for providing social security services to farmers who have moved to cities and found jobs there and education for their children. In addition, steps should be taken in the course of urbanization to provide reasonably full employment opportunities to farmers who have moved to cities and make sure that they have equal rights to jobs.

IV. Granting Same Land Rights to Farmers as Those of State Land Owners and Other Urban Land Owners

1. It is essential to fully protect the farmers' basic rights to land. First, it is necessary to prevent the state from encroaching on their rights in requisitioning their land. An outstanding example is that their rights and interests are far from being protected in the primary land market, that is, when the state requisitions land from them. Second, it is necessary to prevent encroachments on their rights in the course of rural land transfer. Strict restrictions should be imposed on some corporations entering the domain of agricultural production and purchasing a large amount of land from farmers at low prices. Third, it is necessary to prevent rural grassroots cadres from taking advantage of reallocation of land resources for "rent-seeking" or from encroaching seriously on farmers' land rights through other means.

2. It is essential to further define farmers' land rights so that they

truly enjoy the contractual right of land integrating the right to ownership, use, usufruct and disposal. The disposal right, in particular, should be granted to the farmers on condition. To allow the farmers to enjoy the contractual right of land integrating the four rights is in fact to recognize their right to land use that is in the nature of real right.

V. Ensuring Rural Inhabitants Same Right to Compulsory Education as Urban Inhabitants by Improving the Financial Transfer Payment System

Compared with urban areas, rural compulsory education at the grassroots is in a bad situation. At present, money spent on education generally makes up 50 percent of the fiscal expenditures at the county level, 70 percent at the township/town level and even more in economically undeveloped areas. In recent years the outlays of the central treasury for rural areas have in fact dropped, and so has the proportion of aid-agriculture funds in the total fiscal expenditures, from 13.4 percent in 1978 to 8.3 percent in 1997. Under the new situation, China should improve the transfer payment system to keep rural compulsory education going.

VI. Creating Conditions to Enable Urban and Rural Inhabitants Gradually to Enjoy Same Social Security

1. With the development of the market economy in the countryside, land has gradually diminished its function and role as the basic social security for the farmers. Therefore, farmers are likewise faced with market risks and the same degree of risks in their livelihood. De-agriculturalization, urbanization and other factors have placed

higher demands on social security for the rural population. The current rural social security based on land is becoming more and more irrelevant to the needs of economic and social development.

2. At present, in order to advance the urban social security program, the shortfalls in the old-age pension fund and the expenditures of local governments for paying subsistence allowances for urban residents are partially made up for by the central treasury and sales of state assets. State assets are assets of the whole people; the farmers should not be excluded from them for ever but should gradually be allowed to enjoy equal right to them.

3. It is necessary to launch pilot projects on rural old-age pension and rural medical insurance systems funded jointly by the state, the collectives and the farmers according to a rational sharing of burdens and on subsistence allowances for farmers in combination with rural poverty reduction projects and other subsidy programs sponsored by civil administration organs.

VII. Enabling Farmers to Establish Organizations Representing Their Interests — Farmers' Organizations

1. It is necessary to guide farmers in forming various types of special-purpose cooperative economic organizations on a voluntary basis so as to enable them to enter markets as members of organizations and lower risks and business costs of their products on the markets. This will help rural economic development and social stability.

2. It is necessary to establish farmers' associations at various levels to represent the farmers' interests on the basis of self-management at the village level. Farmers' associations should have the same political status and social functions as the women's federations, trade union federations and other mass organizations.

Conclusion

1. To grant comprehensive national treatment to farmers is the main objective of the second round of reform in China's countryside.

2. We must run the work of granting national treatment to farmers throughout the entire process of building a well-off society in an all-round way.

3. We must resolve the question of national treatment for farmers step by step, starting now, and in issues for which the conditions are ripe.

INCREASING FARMERS' INCOME NEEDS NEW IDEAS

(*June 2002*)

In China's new stage of development and against the background of the country's accession to the WTO, the issue of the countryside, farmers' income in particular, is directly related to the system and structure of the national economy. Although the rural reform has been going on for more than 20 years, no substantial breakthroughs have been made in some major aspects, so that the long-term and institutional contradictions adversely affecting farmers' efforts to increase their income have not been fundamentally solved. Priority given to industrialization has failed to lead to a simultaneous progress of urbanization and rural modernization. Structural contradictions have come to the fore in the course of urban and rural economic development. Therefore, a real solution to the problem of farmers' income should neither rely on the traditional mechanism of increasing output and raising prices nor limit the efforts to agriculture or the rural economy itself. We propose that we should, bearing in mind the objective of increasing farmers' income, speed up the efforts to address the outstanding contradictions in the urban-rural economic structure, and advance the rural reform in an all-round, coordinated way.

I. Granting and Ensuring Farmers' Property Rights in Legal Terms, so as to Provide Them with a New Motive Force for Increasing Their Income

1. Mobilizing and protecting farmers' initiative by granting

and protecting their property rights. Resources and property rights are the preconditions for generating incomes, with the size of a person's income to be determined by how many resources he or she can dispose of and how well the property rights are protected. An important factor that has affected farmers' income is the limited resources and property rights of farm households and poor protection of their property rights. In the rural surveys and comparative studies conducted in recent years, we have found that the disparity in income between the farmers in the eastern and western regions lies not so much in income from household operations as in the wide gap in income from wages and property. For example, Zhejiang Province in east China is listed at the bottom in the country in terms of per-capita amount of land but is in the front rank in terms of per-capita income for farmers (4,253.67 yuan), only after the income of farmers on the outskirts of Shanghai (5,596.37 yuan) and Beijing (4,604.55 yuan). In terms of income from property, farmers in Zhejiang top the country; per-capita income of farm households in the western region in the form of wages is only 60.7 percent of the national average, and 33.7 percent of the eastern region, and the average income of a farm household in the western region from property is only 27.97 yuan, only 62.1percent of the national average and 37.8 percent of that of the eastern region. The disparity in income in the form of wages and from property reflects the disparity between farmers in the eastern and western regions in terms of human and capital resources, and property rights.

Protection of resources and property rights are also decisive factors for economic and political democracy at the grassroots. Chinese history has repeatedly proved that whenever the state practices correct policies with regard to land and property, the farmers display high enthusiasm and register a high income level. In the near- and long-term point of view, the key to mobilizing and protecting their enthusiasm is to grant and protect their property rights, and at the same time develop economic and political democracy in an effort to create a good institutional environment for increasing their income.

2. Establishing rural relations of property rights in legal terms as a fundamental way to address the problem of increasing farmers' income. (1) It is necessary to establish farmers' property rights relations over land in legal terms, truly granting the right to use land resources to farmers. The formulation or amendment of the "Rural Land Contract Law," the "Law on Agriculture" and the "General Rules of Civil Law" should aim to address some major issues bearing on the overall situation and long-term interests: First, it is essential to take the granting and protecting of a long-term and secure land-use right to farmers as the fundamental aim of the legislation, so as to truly "grant long-term, secure right to land use to farmers." Second, farmers' right to land use must be confirmed in a form of real right rather than creditor's right. To do this, the state should make up its mind to grant to them the right to inherit and mortgage land-use right. (2) It is necessary to confirm and register the house and land property owned by farm households and township enterprises, issue property rights certificates and protect real right. Compared with the urban land policy and laws, the house property of farmers, the result of accumulation over generations, does not have house property certificates, nor does the house and land property of township enterprises. This is absolutely unfair. Relevant laws should have explicit stipulations that the house and land property of farmers and township enterprises is real right, which should be confirmed and registered for legal protection. (3) As the human resources of farmers are becoming an increasingly important source of income, it is necessary to change the dual economic structure separating town from country, and grant equitable property rights of human resources to farmers so that the value of their human resources can be realized. (4) It is necessary to protect farmers' usufruct.

II. Innovating Institutional System for Increasing Farmers' Income by Reconstructing the Two-tier Management System Integrating Unified and Separate Management

At present, the two-tier management system in many places only applies to farm household management, while the collective economy remains in name only. In some other places, what remains of the collective economy — some plots of land (for example, the so-call "land reserved for unforeseen use") and assets (for example, township enterprises run in the name of collectives) — is contracted out to individuals as the main source of income for the collectives, instead of concentrating on providing pre-production, in-production and post-production services to farm household operations. The total separation of the collective economy and farm household management has seriously hampered the growth of farmers' income. It is an inevitable choice to reconstruct the two-tier rural management system integrating unified management with separate management.

1. We must persist in the household management system for a long time to come and build up farmers' capabilities to accumulate funds, invest and conduct negotiations. The household contract management system and the collective land are a cornerstone that has been laid by the rural reform and should be kept stable under the current policies without any wavering. It is necessary to grant to farmers the real right over the use of land and earnestly protect it, grant to farm households status as legal entities, and gradually build up their capabilities to accumulate funds, invest and conduct market negotiations so that they can participate in market activities as a legal entity.

2. We must reconstruct the form of combination of farm households with the collective economic organizations, taking household management as the core. Household management is the core of the collective economic organization of a community and its main form of realization. It is necessary to find a proper form to combine the collective economic organization with farm households through an effective organizational framework. Diverse forms of combination may be employed to suit different levels of development and conditions in various areas. For example, in an economically developed area, the collective economic organization of a community can focus on developing unified management that includes the scattered farm household operations as its organic component elements, thus bringing into full play both the advantages of unified management and the initiative of farm household operations. In economically less-developed areas, the scattered farm household operations are the main form while the unified management of the collective mainly provides services at the pre-production, in-production and post-production links, and, by so doing, links the scattered household operations into an organic whole for the benefit of bringing the potential of the household management system into the fullest play.

3. We must transform the structure of property rights of the collective economic organization of a community and its organizational structure to turn it into an incorporated cooperative that accords with the requirements of the market economy and is internationally accepted. Its transformation or reorganization should be done along two main lines:

First, moving in the direction of becoming an independent economic legal entity after going through a restructuring of property rights, a market player at the micro level full of institutional vitality. First, the collective economic organization of a community has its independent property rights over land and other collective property and should be given legal right to freely dispose of its property within the limits set by the state with regard to its use. Second, contractual relations between the collective economic organization and the farm households should be recognized in legal terms. The law should ban administrative organizations from encroaching on farm households' right to the use of land by adjusting land; at the same time it should support the collective economic organization in enjoying the ultimate legal ownership, disposal right and management and control right and collecting contraction fees from farm households while paying land taxes to the state in the capacity as the owner. Third, with regard to other common property of the community, it may, in accordance with the existing practices, be converted into shares to be apportioned to farm households, which enjoy usufruct. The collective economic organization should be allowed to absorb non-governmental capital, applying the rules of the joint-stock system.

Second, moving closer to the internationally acknowledged cooperative organizations after going through the transformation of the organizational structure to become an "incorporated cooperative" with special characteristics. Macro policies and relevant laws should provide, at least, for: first, the category and legal status of the collective economic organizations of communities, which should be confirmed through registration and certification; second, defining such organizations as "incorporated cooperatives," to follow the examples of Germany and Japan; third, their right to enjoy tax reductions and exemptions and state investment as a way to compensate the losses they incur in performing their functions of community construction and management; and fourth, the permission to allow such organizations to enter economic fields suitable for them to display their advantages of management of scale.

4. Rationalizing the intra-community relations between the collective economic organization and various special-purpose cooperative economic organizations. As the collective economic organization of the community has a foundation in terms of property rights that have existed for a long time, the various special-purpose cooperative economic organizations within the community are not yet in a position to replace it in performing its functions. Therefore, state policies should permit, encourage and support a free development of various special-purpose cooperative economic organizations within a rural community and, at the same time, support the collective economic organization of the community to develop in an orderly way its own cooperative economic organizations of various types. When the conditions are ripe, the various types of special-purpose economic organizations within the community may be incorporated into the ranks of the collective economic organization of the community through restructuring property rights in an effort to reorganize all cooperative economic organizations within the community.

III. Preparing a Good Organizational Carrier for Farmers to Participate in Market Competition and Increase Their income by Vigorously Developing Rural Cooperative Economic Organizations

1. The cooperative system is the best form for Chinese farmers to get reorganized. In face of the need that Chinese agriculture participates in economic globalization, Chinese farmers are in urgent need of getting reorganized in accordance with the internationally acknowledged principles of cooperatives. These principles include: voluntary and open membership, with freedom to join and withdraw from the cooperatives; democratic management with one vote for each member; only limited returns on the capital contributed as membership dues, with a large share of the profits going to expand the cooperatives and augment their public accumulation funds; self-management and independence; education and training; and cooperation among cooperatives. A cooperative in a true sense is first and foremost an enterprise but, apart from seeking the maximum profits as enterprises generally do, it should also try to meet its members' needs of social and cultural development and promote a sustained development of the community. More importantly, the organizational form of the cooperatives respects the wishes of the farmers without doing harm to the household management system.

2. It is necessary to study and enact law on rural cooperatives as soon as possible on the basis of actual conditions in China and in light of international experience. The proposed law should provide for the legal status of the cooperatives as a legal entity, their principles and aim, scope of business, membership, membership training, capital structure, distribution of dividends, financial control and supervision, registration and change, conglomeration, dissolution and financial liquidation. This will put the operations of millions of cooperative economic organizations in the countryside on a legal basis. As the legislation on rural cooperative economic organizations involves the revision or enactment of the General Rules of the Civil Law, Law on Real Right and Law on Agriculture, overall planning and early preparations should be made and people summoned together to start studies.

3. It is necessary to adopt different development policies to suit the development levels of different areas and encourage farmers to form various types of special-purpose cooperative economic organizations in accordance with their needs and desires. In developed areas, it is necessary to transform the organizations for the industrialised operation of agriculture into cooperatives. The so-called "corporations plus households" model in the industrialised operation of agriculture has two main problems: first, there has not yet been a rational industrial division of labor as most such corporations are concentrated on farming and breeding without extending the industrial chain; and second, such corporations have failed to form a mechanism by which they share risks and interests with farm households and some of them have instead derived their main profits by exploiting farmers. The fundamental way out for the industrialized operation of agriculture lies with the adjustment of industrial structure and transformation of agricultural operation organizations into cooperatives.

In economically less-developed areas, vigorous efforts should be made to develop various types of special-purpose cooperative economic organizations providing pre-production, in-production and post-production services to farm households. For example, first, to set up special-purpose cooperative economic organizations to provide such services to farm households as storing, shipping and selling their agricultural and sideline products, supplying agricultural means of production, and providing mechanised plowing and harvesting services; second, to transform the traditional organizations into cooperative economic organizations, for example, supply and marketing cooperatives may turn into special-purpose cooperatives by absorbing farm households as shareholders and some associations and societies may develop into cooperatives by taking in farmers as members; third, to vigorously develop agricultural and sideline product processing enterprises within communities along the lines of cooperatives, for example, by turning the most influential ones among them into joint-stock cooperative enterprises that take in farm households as shareholders; fourth, to allow and support farmers in forming cooperatives by pooling their land as shares. Such cooperatives aim to develop cooperation between land contractors and between land contractors and other economic organizations under the prerequisite that their right to use the land they have contracted will remain unchanged for a long time to come and on the basis of their contractual right of land or land management right; and fifth, efforts should be allowed and encouraged to develop rural cooperative funds aimed at providing financial services to farm households within the community.

IV. Speeding Up the Reform of Rural Political and Social Structure to Provide a Strong Guarantee for Farmers' Efforts to Increase Their Income

1. Standardizing the relationship among the government,

enterprises and farmers. The government should respect farmers' rights and create conditions for them to increase their income. First, we must restrict the ultimate disposal right of the government over collective rural land, and guarantee the completeness and exclusive ownership of the collective property rights of the villages and cooperatives; guarantee against the loss of farmers' rights and interests in the course of land transfer; and respect the farmers' right to make management decisions on their own. Second, the government should create conditions for farmers to rest and build up their strength. For example, it may reduce and exempt agricultural taxes in poor areas, and abolish the agricultural special-product tax, which was designed to restrict non-grain production during the days when the policy of "taking grain production as the key link" in agriculture prevailed; and it should make great efforts to relieve the farmers of the burden of financing social undertakings in the countryside by increasing its expenditures on agriculture and the construction of rural infrastructure, so as to increase the supplies of public products for rural communities.

2. It is necessary to speed up social reform in response to the increasingly heavy task of reorganizing rural culture amid the stratification in the countryside and uneven transition of the rural structure. The rise of township enterprises and community service organizations, the formation and growth of farmers' economic organizations or complexes based on kinship ties, geography or trade, and farmers' freedom to seek jobs — all this has brought changes to their status and led to differentiation of groups. It has broken up the original social order, values and code of conduct of the villages and cooperatives, resulting in a "mixed system" in which diverse interest groups, a multi-tier social structure and diverse values exist side by side. The existence of a mixed system provides diverse choices for different social interest groups in determining their roles and positions in society while it is in transition, and therefore diverse channels for realizing different social interests, thus reducing institutional conflicts. Meanwhile, however, the abrupt social transition has led to mutual conflicts of diverse interests and values. This can be taken as one of the main reasons for the sharply rising social contradictions in rural areas.

The key to speeding up the reform of the rural social structure is to balance the relations among various interest groups, the most important objective being enabling farmers to achieve common prosperity. Property right is the foundation of all rights, and the property right and economic capability of farmers are the prerequisite for realizing their democratic rights. The key to ensuring an equal sharing of economic and political rights at the grassroots by the farmers is to enable them to have equal property rights and gradually achieve common prosperity on this basis. Therefore, the main task of rural social reform is to create equitable economic opportunities for the farmers and vigorously advance democracy at the grassroots level on the basis of balancing the relations among different interest groups through such means as reforming the income distribution system of communities and establishing effective social insurance systems.

V. Establishing and Improving the Government System of Supporting and Protecting Agriculture Compatible with WTO Rules, so as to Create Conditions for Farmers to Increase Their Income

1. A top priority is to establish and improve a commercialized agricultural services system. First, the government should make great efforts to transform circulation at the county and township levels, turning the supply and marketing cooperatives, grain purchasing stations, tobacco purchasing stations, timber companies, seed companies and rural credit cooperatives into independent market players making management decisions on their own and creating out of them a pre-production, in-production and post-production service system. Second, it is necessary to establish a responsive market information feedback and service system covering the production, consumption and circulation of agricultural produce, to provide market information to farmers at a price. Third, it is necessary to increase agricultural science development and innovation input, improve agricultural science innovation and promotion network, and gradually convert agricultural technical promotion stations, animal breeding and veterinary stations, forestry stations, farm machinery stations, economic management stations, water conservancy and electrical pumping stations and all other facilities with better conditions into profit-seeking enterprises.

2. It is necessary to make the best use of the "green box" policies, taking the provision of agricultural infrastructure and other public products and rural education and training as the focus of support. China's focus for making use of the "green box" policies is to increase the total input, and adjust and improve the structure of the domestic support system for agriculture, focusing the support for agriculture on projects of "general government services" that are compatible with the WTO rules. Focal areas are construction of agricultural infrastructure, provision of public products, and rural education and training.

3. It is necessary to make full use of the protective role of customs duties. As a developing country, China can establish a rational customs duties level in accordance with the relevant WTO provisions and by adjusting customs duties within the transition period, and make full use of the utilizable protection space provided by customs duties to give priority protection to a few agricultural products identified for their importance to the national economy and the people's livelihood, such as grain (rice, corn and wheat).

4. It is necessary to change the beneficiaries of China's subsidies to agricultural produce, shifting gradually from consumers to producers. China's price subsidies are provided by the state in the realm of commodity circulation or in the realm of consumption in order to stabilize the basic livelihood of urban residents. The principal type is subsidies for agricultural produce, which are in fact subsidies to urban residents, or the realm of circulation, while the farmers in general have almost nothing to gain; the practice of giving subsidies to the grain purchasing and marketing enterprises is not only disadvantageous to their cost accounting, but also prone to the transfer or loss of subsidies. The enormous amount of price subsidies has added to the state financial burden. The country should change the beneficiaries of subsidies to agricultural produce in the future, shifting gradually from consumers to producers. At the same time, it is necessary to standardize the realm of circulation and ensure an unimpeded flow of goods, rationalize the prices of agricultural produce, and eliminate price distortion in purchasing and selling agricultural produce.

5. It is necessary to establish an agricultural insurance system to boost the farmers' ability to manage risks. Agricultural insurance is among the important means available to China to protect agricultural production and increase farmers' income following the country's WTO accession. As a coordinated policy for supporting and protecting agriculture, it has an especially important role to play. I suggest that, first, setting up a state agricultural insurance corporation at the national level to render support to agriculture by reinsuring rural mutual-aid federations or other insurance organizations in various provinces and autonomous regions throughout the country. The central treasury can set up a state agricultural insurance fund by allocating funds in proportion to the actual agricultural insurance business each year in order to subsidize agricultural insurance; second, the state should set up rural insurance mutual-aid societies at the county level as grassroots agricultural insurance organizations. This will enhance farmers' awareness of insurance, and bring the initiative of localities and farmers into play. As international experience shows, the agricultural insurance program must integrate services in science and technology, supply and marketing, credit, relief, meteorology, disaster and other damage reduction, and insurance.

VI. Intensifying Rural Banking Reform to Meet the Growing Needs of Agriculture and the Countryside for Funds, and Providing Stable Banking Support for Farmers to Help Them Increase Their Income

The change in the growth pattern of agriculture and the rural economy, and farm household management in China has placed ever-greater demands on banking support. The current rural banking system and the capacity to invest and lend cannot keep up with such demands. The rural banking sector has become a bottleneck in agricultural and rural economic development.

1. It is imperative to find an expeditious solution to the contradiction between the shortage of rural funds and the diversion of rural capital to non-agricultural use by introducing a policy restricting the outflow of rural bank savings through banking institutions. There is an acute shortage of funds in rural areas. At the same time, a considerable portion of this limited supply flows to cities or non-agricultural undertakings. According to statistics, farmers' deposits in rural credit cooperatives and regular banking institutions are on the increase year by year, but the proportion of loans that farmers obtain from them in the farmers' deposits is decreasing year by year — from 41 percent in 1994 to 19 percent in 1998, which means that the credit cooperatives lent to farmers less than one fifth of what the latter had deposited. For a time, this scissors differential showed a widening tendency. It should be stipulated that rural deposits in rural banking and non-banking institutions, including those of farm households, should be mainly used for the development of agriculture, the countryside and the farmers.

2. The key to providing farm households and township enterprises with easier access to funds is to develop rural non-governmental banking services, and establish and improve a credit guarantee fund system. Because the rural banking market suffers from limited development and a shortage of capital, a situation compounded by institutional obstacles, most farmers and township enterprises do not have access to loans from regular banking institutions, so there has been an abnormally swift development of private borrowing and lending of money. Surveys show that between 1996 and 1998, loans obtained by farm households from the private financial sector exceeded 70 percent of the total money they borrowed. Farmers and township enterprises find it difficult to borrow money because the rural banking institutions ask for a 100 percent security for a loan, while farmland, large farm machinery, draught animals and housing cannot be mortgaged. This has led to an abnormal growth of private borrowing and lending in rural areas, and resultant serious problems like usury. In the circumstances in which the state can only provide limited financial support to the countryside, the state should, first, permit and standardize the presence of primary credit, vigorously develop rural non-governmental credit cooperatives, and allow farmers to raise funds through special-purpose cooperative economic organizations, so as to diversify rural banking institutions; second, establish farmers' credit guarantee funds and improve rural credit guarantee mechanism for small rural enterprises; and third, reform and innovate the organizational system of rural credit cooperatives, renovate the forms of loans of rural banking institutions, micro-credit in particular.

VII. Fundamental Way to Help Farmers Increase Their Income: Cities to Absorb More Rural Surplus Labor by Expanding the Urban Economic Scale

1. Farmers' employment is the most outstanding problem in the 21st century, and the key task of developing non-agricultural sectors and urbanization is to transfer surplus rural labor power. Farmers' income growth is directly related to their employment. The main reason why agriculture and the rural areas cannot provide a fundamental solution to the problem of slow growth of farmers' income is that their ability to create jobs has been greatly weakened. Employment pressures from rural surplus labor necessitate faster urbanization. It is imperative to lift all those urban policies that exclude farmers from finding residence and employment in cities. It is imperative to completely get rid of the institutional arrangements that separate town from country, giving farmers the same treatment as urban residents. Measures to be contemplated may include: acknowledging the tremendous contributions of farmers to the urban economic system through the "price scissors," and, when state-owned assets are reduced, setting aside a share as settlement and pre-job training funds for the farmers who have moved to cities; eliminating the discriminatory regulations related to employment of farmers in cities and arranging for welfare and social security of migrant rural workers in accordance with the modern employment system; and reducing or abolishing various discriminatory charges so as to create a good social environment for farmers who have moved to cities to work or do business.

2. Accelerating urbanization is the key to breaking the dual economic structure of town and country. At present, the gap between urban and rural areas is further widening, and the dual structure has seriously impeded the sustained and sound development of the national economy: slow development of the urban economy resulting in a slower pace of absorbing rural labor power; and a shrinking rural market with a weak purchasing power, which has made the consequences of the surplus urban productive forces more pronounced. If China's rural population always stays above 800 million (50 percent of the total population of 1.6 billion), the per-capita shortage of rural resources will not be changed fundamentally. If half of the national population stay in the countryside just to produce enough food, their income cannot be expected to rise significantly, and the national objective of basically modernizing the country will fail. Therefore, China will have to transfer 100 million rural laborers (about 300 million rural inhabitants) to cities by year 2030. This will be a very arduous task, for which plans must be made now and vigorous steps taken to speed up urbanization.

3. It is necessary to mobilize the entire urban economic system to support agriculture and open the rural market in order to expand the urban economic scale. China's urban development strategy must include the opening of the rural market. To support the development of agriculture, the countryside and farmers is not an extra burden on the urban economy and the national economy as a whole, but rather their intrinsic need for a sustained, rapid and stable development. China's overall national strength can be enhanced only when the farmers are shifted from the traditional economic system to the modern urban economic system, allowing them to create more wealth with the support of the urban economic system, and enabling the urban economic system to release its full potential for creating wealth so that the urban and rural economic systems can develop harmoniously by supporting and complementing each other.

4. It is necessary to pay attention to the important role of the county economy in the development of both the urban and rural economies. The county economy and the rural economy are so closely linked that, to a considerable extent, to develop the county economy is to develop the rural economy. At the same time, as the county economy is where the urban and rural economy meets, to develop the county economy will be of very important significance in addressing the current employment pressures on farmers and lightening their burdens. The development of the county economy calls for a swift shift in the focus of the country's strategy from development of small towns to construction focusing on county seats. It also calls for putting in proper perspective the efforts to increase county revenues and farmers' income. In economic work of a county, top priority should be given to building up farmers' ability of self-accumulation and self-development. Their low ability of self-development is the fundamental restraint on the development of agriculture and rural economy. Therefore, the first and foremost task for county economic development is to increase the income of the farmers, while the increase of county revenues comes second.

GIVING LAND-USE RIGHT TO FARMERS

(January 2002)

After more than 20 years of reform in China, the framework of market economy has taken shape initially in the countryside, with farm households gradually becoming active market players and the overwhelming majority of farmers having obtained the contractual right of land and the right to land use with an assurance that this will remain unchanged for 30 years. The long duration of the right to rural land use and its properties as capital and real right have been basically established as a kind of direction for development. The current outstanding problem is that, without sufficient legal protection, farmers' long-term right to land use is prone to various charges in certain circumstances. For example, the practice of household management has incurred constant censure again in recent years. This shows that the adoption of legal means to build a complete range of systems in China covering rural land property rights, land market and land management has become an important part of the work to deepen rural reform, gear the rural economy toward the market, and improve the legal system as regards the countryside.

Here I will focus my discussion on nine questions concerning the legal protection of farmers' right to land use.

1. Stabilization and protection of farmers' right to land use have become an outstanding contradiction bearing on rural economic development and social stability, and speedy legislation on the protection of farmers' rights and interests in land is a pressing task. The actual institutional arrangements with regard to rural land have shown a considerable deviation from the written laws, policies and decisions of the central government, for example, shortening duration, encroachment on the farmers' rights to land ownership, use, usufruct and disposal, and periodic readjustments to the land that farm households have contracted. In recent years especially, in the course of the structural adjustment of agriculture, industrialization of agriculture, management of scale and urbanization, some localities have terminated contracts arbitrarily, taken land back without compensation, and illegally transferred, rented out or taken over for use land which farmers have contracted, or forced farmers to pool their land as shares, interfered in their decision making or encroached on their lawful rights with regard to land. All this has artificially aggravated the land scarcity, led to spiralling land disputes, and soured farmers' attachment to land, constituting an outstanding contradiction and problem affecting the development of the rural economy and social stability. Therefore, it is all the more necessary at present to reaffirm the rural land policy of the CPC, and strengthen supervision over the enforcement of the state laws and regulations on land and, in particular, accelerate the making of a new law on farmland, so as to ascertain and protect legally the long-term, secure right of farmers to land use.

2. The most important objective of the legislation on farmers' right to land use is to establish their relations of property rights to land. I am of the opinion that the collective ownership of rural land means common ownership by the farmers. A "rural collective" can be understood to mean that all farm households or members are joined together into a whole to enjoy the ultimate legal ownership of the land they possess, and right to management and control, and usufruct. It can also be understood to mean that each member of the collective has a fair right to own and use land. Collective land ownership can likewise be divided into stock shares, with everybody having an equal share, so that land is capitalized. Land shares may become capital in forming share-holding cooperative enterprises with or without other capital, or become land resources which farmers may directly own and use. In other words, farmers' right to land use is in essence their property right to land. The projected law should recognize and further clarify farmers' land property relations. As Engels pointed out in his *Origin of the Family, Private Property, and the State*, "A contract requires people who can dispose freely of their persons, actions, and possessions, and meet each other on the footing of equal rights." After more than 20 years of reform, it is time now for China to institutionalize and define in legal terms the farmers' actual land property relations. Only when this issue is really solved will there be a solid foundation for giving real land-use right to the farmers.

3. The name of the new law should be the "Law on the Right to Use Rural Land." The new law on rural land should use real right instead of creditor's right to affirm farm households' contractual right of land. Its name should be the "Law on the Right to Use Rural Land." The farm households' contractual right of land in reality is virtually in the nature of real right, embracing the right to ownership, use and usufruct and a partial disposal right, except for the right to mortgage. The growing tendency to turn the rural land-use right into real right should be affirmed in the new law. The "Law on the Right to Use Rural Land" can better address the actual contradictions facing the current rural land system, and better accord with the actual conditions with regard to the land-use right that the farmers have obtained.

4. Farm households' right to land use is a string of rights which should be clearly defined in the new law on land. Their right to land use is one, in the sense, of property right, and consists of: (1) the exclusive ownership of the land which farm households have contracted, that is, the right of actual control, while the collective needs only to collect land rent from the users, and has the ultimate legal ownership and land management right; (2) the right of farm households to independently use and manage the land free from interference from any organization or individual; (3) the right of farm households to the distribution of residual products; and (4) partial land disposal right of farm households covering the compensatory transfer of land-use right, sub-contracting, renting out, pooling of land as shares, mortgage and inheritance. Legislation on rural land should move along the lines of "fairness of the use right, respect for independent decision making, protection of usufruct and standardization of disposal right."

5. Strict restrictions should be imposed on land readjustments throughout the duration of use which should last at least 30 years. Facts show that as long as land readjustments proceed unimpeded, farmers' land-use right cannot possibly be guaranteed. Jiang Zemin, CPC General Secretary, made a statement when he inspected Anhui Province in 1998 that "The contract period should be extended and remain unchanged for another 30 years, and beyond that there will be no need to change either." A legal provision should be made embodying the gist of his statement and using such phrasing as "The farmers' land contract period should remain unchanged for at least 30 years" to affirm and emphasize the point. The new law should also provide for strict readjustment of land during the 30-year contract period, upon the expiration of which users may renew the contract in accordance with the law.

6. It is necessary to make clear stipulations on the transfer of land-use right and the land market. The transfer of farmers' right to land use is already a reality, and there are numerous cases of this. It is an objective need of agricultural development that farmers' right to land use should change hands on the basis of stabilizing the household management system. A circular issued by the CPC Central Committee last year (2001) on the transfer of farm households' right to land use set forth clear-cut principles and policies on the topic. It is a good document and its main policies should be affirmed in the form of a law. The transfer of rural land should be carried out under the prerequisite of persisting in and stabilizing the household contract management system for a long time to come. It should follow the principle of acting in accordance with the law and on a voluntary and compensatory basis. Restrictions should be placed on industrial and commercial enterprises in directly managing land in the countryside and land transfer should take place among farm households. The law should make specific stipulations on these points so that there will be a good market mechanism for the transfer of rural land-use right.

7. In the new situation, legislation on rural land and the legal protection of farmers' right to land use should focus on addressing the current outstanding contradictions. (1) We must correctly understand and handle the relationship between the management of scale and household management. At present, agricultural population still makes up 64 percent of the national total. Only when agricultural population is reduced to a certain extent will it be possible for the management of scale to develop gradually. Therefore, only small-scale household management can be practiced in China in the present stage, while optimum-scale management is a long-term process of development that can only be based on the household management system. (2) We must correctly understand and handle the relationship between land transfer and protection of farmers' right to land use. The point of departure in establishing the land market is to gradually replace administrative adjustments of land with market regulation, with a view to addressing the land shortage question. A clearly-defined real right and an undisputed land boundary are the necessary conditions for land to enter the market, just as a long term and stable right to land use protected by law is the basis for land transfer. It should be seen that the role of the land market is limited, for without making more non-agricultural jobs available to farmers there will not be a large amount of land up for market exchange nor will the household management system be transformed, through land transfer, into management of scale in keeping with large-scale, socialized production. Therefore, the use of administrative means to promote land transfer must be strictly forbidden. (3) We must correctly understand and handle the relationship between the adjustment of agricultural structure and protection of farmers' right to land use. The starting point and the end-result of the effort to adjust the agricultural structure are to improve quality and efficiency. The adjustment of the agricultural structure and industrialization of agriculture definitely does not mean the concentration of landholdings or a new collectivization movement in a disguised form. The fact that farmers have a long-term and stable right to land use is more conducive to raising the productive forces, structural adjustment, and the effort of agriculture to meet the WTO challenge. (4) We must correctly understand and handle the nurturing of "dragon-head" enterprises (as the leaders in the industrialization of agriculture) and protect farmers' right to land use. In the light of the actual conditions in China, it is essential to address the problem of such "dragon-head" enterprises contending for land with farmers. In the course of the industrialization of agriculture featuring "corporation plus farm households," special attention should be paid to preventing farmers being reduced to the status of helpless hired hands or tenant farmers of such corporations. The "dragon-head" enterprises should play a role in the storage, processing, shipping and marketing of agricultural produce, and the operation of specialized agricultural produce markets and commercialized services for agricultural production. The core of their development is the formation of a rational upstream-downstream products exchange mechanism and interest distribution mechanism among the people engaged in the production, processing and marketing, so that farmers enjoy their lawful rights and interests as equal market players, and share profits from the processing and circulation of agricultural produce.

8. Speeding up legislation concerning rural land, and improving law enforcement. The collective ownership of rural land and household management are a basic economic system suited to China's conditions, showing a very strong adaptability and vitality. Therefore, we have always insisted on and stood for the "granting to farmers a long-term and secure right to land use," promoting the conversion of this right into capital and real right, and enabling it to attain a legal status as a basic state policy. At present, two laws concerning the rural land system are being drafted. One is the Law on Rural Land Contract and the other is the Law on Real Right. Both tend to base rural land ownership on farm households, and put it on a long-term basis. We look forward to the early promulgation of these two laws. We also hope that efforts will be made now to improve the environment for implementing them. For example, strengthening publicity and education concerning rural land policies and laws; restricting the power of the basic-level governments, and township and village cadres to make decisions concerning land; resolving the current rural land disputes, and easing the tension between cadres and farmers; cracking down on rural evil forces and stopping them from illegally encroaching on farmers' lawful land rights; and punishing in accordance with the law violations of farmers' land rights.

9. The legal protection of farmers' right to land use must be combined with the strengthening of democracy and democratic participation at the grassroots level. The legal protection of farmers' right to land use requires the strengthening of democracy and democratic participation at the grassroots. It should be noted that democracy at rural areas is based on the farmers' secure land rights, because when the farmers are not in a position to protect even their land-use right that the state laws and policies have granted them they have no way to exercise their democratic political rights. On the other hand, if and when they can correctly exercise their democratic political rights, they are sure to be able to protect their legal land rights.

NEW TOPICS IN THE REFORM OF CHINA'S INFRASTRUCTURE AND PUBLIC UTILITIES SECTOR

NEW TOPICS IN THE NEXT-STEP REFORM OF CHINA'S INFRASTRUCTURE AND PUBLIC UTILITIES SECTOR

(*November 2002*)

China faces new contradictions and challenges in its next-step reform of the infrastructure and public utilities sector.

I. It is urgent to establish a standard corporate governance structure in the infrastructure and public utilities sector after industrial reorganization in the sector.

The reality is that the enterprises after industrial reorganization in the infrastructure and public utilities sector have remained exclusively state-owned or the state controls the shares. It is still an arduous task to establish a modern enterprise system in which the post-reorganization enterprises or enterprise groups will operate in compliance with the Company Law.

1. Reform of the property rights system in the course of reorganizing the infrastructure and public utilities sector. How to proceed from the practical situation and deepen the property rights system reform in the sector with clearly defined equity relations and beneficiaries.

2. For exclusively state-owned or absolutely state-controlled enterprises, how to establish and ensure corporate property

rights in the true sense, and bring about the separation of ownership from corporate property rights.

3. To improve the corporate governance structure and to build a rational structure of board of directors, so as to form a rational mechanism for power division, and checks and balances.

4. In accordance with the requirements of entrusted or authorized management, no interference should come from any related government department or state assets management department in the forming of company's board of directors, staffing or operations.

In view of the conspicuous contradictions in the present situation, the priority of the reform in the next stage in the infrastructure and public utilities sector shall be given to the establishment of a corporate governance structure, which will serve as a basis not only for building an improved mechanism for fair competition in the sector, but also for propelling the government reform to separate its functions from enterprise management.

II. To facilitate non-governmental capital's access to the infrastructure and public utilities sector, the country is in urgent need of policies which will support and encourage non-governmental investment in the sector.

In terms of major principles, there are no more policy barriers to non-governmental capital entering into the infrastructure and public utilities sector. But the actual picture still shows a disproportionately small share of non-governmental investment in the sector. A nationwide review of non-governmental investment in 2000 in such infrastructure and public utilities fields as transportation, urban construction and social development revealed that none of the 14 regions surveyed, including Beijing, Shandong and Shanghai, reached a proportion of 10 percent for non-governmental investment in such fields. Construction in China's infrastructure and public utilities sector suffers an enormous shortage of funds. For the Tenth Five-Year Plan (2001-2005), the urban infrastructure construction alone will need an investment of about one trillion yuan, of which 200-300 billion yuan will be invested by the central and local governments, while about 70 to 80 percent of the resources will depend on loans, foreign investment and non-governmental investment.

It is necessary to adopt a variety of policies and measures to support non-governmental capital's influx to the infrastructure and public utilities sector, in view of the present developments of the non-public sectors in China, as well as the need to develop the infrastructure and public utilities sector. Based on the practical experience in Wenzhou and some other places, I would suggest the following relevant policies:

1. The application of different market access policies to competitive and non-competitive trades in the sector, relaxing control on market access to non-competitive trades.

2. The establishment of a system of fiscal subsidies on interest payments, under which a portion of financial allocations or financial credits is converted into funds for subsidizing interest payments on loans for infrastructure projects.

3. The raising of long-term funds for construction of infrastructure projects, making use of the long-term bond market and stock market.

4. Effecting a shift in the financing pattern of infrastructure projects from relying solely on increasing funds to the practice of not only keeping up a steady increase in funds but also making efficient use of available facilities to raise new funds. To this end, we may at any time sell part of the already built facilities or equities or management rights to recover capital to be put back into infrastructure projects, thus carrying on the construction of the projects on a rolling basis.

5. Construction projects promising economic returns should be managed as enterprises. To do this, the owners of such pro-

jects should establish joint-stock corporations on the basis of multi-partner collaboration, diversified sources of investment, construction with borrowed capital, and issuing stocks and shares.

III. The reform of government rules and regulations has become an important component of government reforms, and is also one of the priority tasks of the subsequent reform in the infrastructure and public utilities sector.

Against the overall background of economic globalization, an important trend in the reform of economic rules and regulations in developed countries is to relax restrictions. China is currently at a critical junction for economic transition, and its reform of government rules and regulations has a dual task of opening markets and breaking monopolies on the one hand, and of building scientific and effective government rules and regulations on the other. An important objective of advancing the reform of government rules and regulations is to get rid of monopolies, introduce competition, and effectively manage markets through rules and regulations. At a time when monopolies are still prominent, government rules and regulations should aim to get rid of administrative monopolies instead of protecting new monopolies.

Government rules and regulations should serve the public interests of society and the interests of consumers. At a time when monopoly can not yet be totally removed, government reform of rules and regulations must in no way represent groups of specific interests, but should guarantee that all consumers benefit from the reform.

Several key relationships must be well addressed in carrying out the reform of government rules and regulations:

1. The relationship between economic globalization and the reform of government rules and regulations. Against the background of economic globalization, the reform of rules and regulations should be fundamentally oriented to relaxing government control, opening market access to the infrastructure and public utilities sector, and strengthening the market competition mechanism. With China's accession to the WTO, the reform must adhere to this basic direction.

2. The relationship between relaxing and tightening rules and regulations. Proceeding from China's realities, we should attend to both the relaxing and tightening sides of the issue, do away with outdated rules and regulations and at the same time consolidate and reconstruct the existing ones.

3. The relationship between the subject and the object in the reform of rules and regulations. The government is the subject who formulates rules and regulations, while enterprises are the objects to observe them. It is essential to separate government functions from enterprise management and management of public institutions, and to separate the government from supervisory organizations. The aim is to bring about a kind of new relationship in which "enterprises can operate independently; trade associations are self-regulated in providing services; and supervisory organizations carry out supervision according to law." This will ensure the independence and transparency of agencies charged with the work of carrying out rules and regulations.

IV. Anti-monopoly in China's infrastructure and public utilities sector and its legislation should be accelerated.

China is currently working on the enactment of an Anti-Monopoly Law. The infrastructure and public utilities sector is the focal field for anti-monopoly. Judging by the developments of reform in the infrastructure and public utilities sector, I would propose the following issues for discussion regarding anti-monopoly in this sector, and legislation in this field:

1. Whether administrative monopoly should be listed as an "exception to application"

According to anti-monopoly laws in various countries, anti-monopoly mainly targets three kinds of monopolies: One refers to a single company's monopoly of the market; another concerns several companies' monopoly by agreeing on apportioning the market; and the last is collaboration among different companies to monopolize the market. Administrative monopoly does not fall into any of these categories. In view of the fact that most cases of monopoly in China's infrastructure and public utilities sector are directly related to administrative monopoly, the country's anti-monopoly legislation should therefore provide for prohibiting administrative monopoly.

2. The relationship between the administrative supervisory organization and the anti-monopoly agency in the exercise of power

While there is no special anti-monopoly agency in China, the law enforcement power for anti-monopoly in the infrastructure and public utilities sector has all along resided with government departments and industrial supervisory organizations. With progress in breaking up monopolies and introducing competition in the sector, anti-monopoly and anti-monopoly agencies hold a prominent position in the sector's industrial governance structure, the industrial supervisory organizations cannot exercise anti-monopoly power on their own, and the industries in the sector still need strong supervisory organizations. It is necessary to rationally define, through legislation, the terms of reference for anti-monopoly agencies and supervisory organizations.

3. The relationship between anti-monopoly legislation and legislation on industries in the infrastructure and public utilities sector

Since the anti-monopoly law shall apply to a scope beyond the infrastructure and public utilities sector, it is impossible to make specific anti-monopoly provisions for each and every industry of the sector when they differ widely from each other. It is, therefore, necessary to formulate or revise, on the basis of the Anti-Monopoly Law, specific laws such as the civil aviation law, the electric power law, the railways law, and the regulations on telecommunications, so as to make specific legal provisions for anti-monopoly in different industries of the infrastructure and public utilities sector.

Accelerated advancement of the reform in the infrastructure and public utilities sector is of vital importance to the sustained growth of China's economy. The practice over the past few years has proved that propelling the sector's reform side by side with proactive financial policies contributed significantly to the rapid economic growth during that period. Facts also tell us that the next-step reform of the sector will directly help increase the economic growth in the coming five to ten years. For example, first, efforts to encourage and support non-governmental capital and foreign capital to invest in the infrastructure and public utilities sector and to markedly increase their proportion in the sector's total investment will play a key role in increasing investment growth; secondly, breaking monopoly in the sector and curtailing irrational price increases for public products will directly contribute to consumption growth; thirdly, accelerated development of the sector's industries in the process of reform will significantly increase the proportion of transportation, posts and telecommunications in the GDP, and correct the structural deviation which has restrained China's sustained economic growth, thus increasing the international competitiveness of the country's economy. The advancement of reform in the infrastructure and public utilities sector is, from any perspective, playing an increasingly important role in China's economic growth. We can say that to propel the reform in the infrastructure and public utilities sector is an objective requirement for China's continued economic growth. In-depth discussion at this symposium on the new topics concerning the reform in the infrastructure and public utilities sector will play a positive role in promoting the reform in the sector.

CHINA'S WTO ACCESSION AND NEW BREAKTHROUGHS IN THE REFORM OF THE INFRASTRUCTURE AND PUBLIC UTILITIES SECTOR

(*October 2001*)

Following its accession to the WTO, China will progressively open up, within a limited transition period, its industries in the infrastructure and public utilities sector, including telecommunications, railways, electric power and civil aviation. It will be a tough task to accelerate the reform of the infrastructure and public utilities sector in order to keep up with the situation. Efforts should be made not only to speed up breaking the administrative monopoly featuring the mixing of government and enterprise functions, but also to prevent the emergence of new monopolies of a market type in the process of transition. Attention should be paid not only to transforming and adjusting government functions, but also to cultivating and shaping market competition players in the sector. And it is necessary not only to break in good time the traditional economic control system, but also to build as soon as possible a new governmental control system and framework suited to market competition. In view of the actual contradictions that China faces in its reform of the infrastructure and public utilities sector following its WTO accession and in light of international experience, it will be of considerable practical significance and urgency to further engage in in-depth discussions regarding such major topics as market opening, anti-monopoly, re-shaping competition players and accelerating the reform of the governmental control system.

I. We must fully recognize and assess the urgency of reform in the infrastructure and public utilities sector after China's WTO accession.

China has achieved important progress in its reform of the infrastructure and public utilities sector over the past 20 years. But it still has a considerably long way to go before it meets the requirements of economic reform and the demand of competition and opening of the sector following its accession to the WTO. We must have a full understanding of the importance and urgency of the reform in the infrastructure and public utilities sector, against the overall background of the world economy after China's WTO accession, and in particular after 9/11.

1. Accelerating the sector's reform is an urgent requirement for improving the competitiveness of industries in the sector.

China's accession to the WTO indicates that market-oriented reform, or in other words, reform and opening up, has become an international obligation that China must duly fulfil. The process of China's reform and opening up is irreversible. It is in this sense that I have termed China's WTO accession its second round of opening up. The opening-up pattern prevailing after China's WTO accession will push forward the reform of the infrastructure and public utilities sector.

China clearly lags behind the developed countries in infrastructure and public utilities sector at present, not just in terms of technology, equipment and management, but more importantly in its poor international competitiveness due to a high degree of state capital monopoly in this sector. Since the infrastructure and public utilities sector accounts for a fairly large proportion in China's economic aggregate, the competitiveness of the sector's industries will have a significant impact on the overall competitiveness of the economy. It will become a general trend for China's market-oriented reform following its WTO accession that as the country increasingly participates in international market competition its reform will move from general competitive fields deeper into such infrastructure areas as telecommunications, electric power, civil aviation and railways, where monopoly is more prevalent.

2. As opening up promotes reform, China's WTO accession calls for accelerated reform of the infrastructure and public utilities sector.

Since 1990, China has sped up its opening of the infrastructure and public utilities sector. For example, foreign businesses are permitted to become involved in the construction and operation of civil airports; they are also encouraged to construct and manage railway transport technology and equipment, local railways and their bridges, tunnels and ferry facilities, as well as to provide machinery and equipment for highways and ports, and their designing and manufacturing technologies; foreign and domestic companies are encouraged to establish joint ventures to operate international shipping business, and joint ventures are allowed to operate expressways; pilot projects have started to actively use foreign investment in, among other areas, water transport; foreign businesses are permitted to participate in urban subway projects.

There are only two to three years from now to China's accession to the WTO and to the deadlines for lifting protection of certain trades, leaving very limited time and space for the infrastructure and public utilities sector to readjust itself and develop. Therefore, the infrastructure and public utilities sector should build its competition mechanism in the quickest possible way, and advance its development and improve its competitiveness through reform.

3. Accelerating the reform of the infrastructure and public utilities sector will have an important effect on the sustained growth of China's economy.

In response to a tendency toward deflation, the Chinese government has, since 1998, implemented an expansive fiscal policy to increase its investment in the infrastructure and public utilities sector. This policy has produced a positive effect on preventing economic decline and improving the macroeconomic environment. Between 1998 and 2000, the government issued 360 billion yuan of state bonds for this purpose, and planned to issue an additional 150 billion yuan of bonds in 2001, of which 50 billion yuan was earmarked for infrastructure investment in the western region. The problem is, first, facing a huge demand in the infrastructure and public utilities sector, the government's resources are limited; second, the government cannot be the main source of investment, which should be enterprises and society. Economic growth can only be temporary and limited if the stimulation of economic growth relies mainly on the government issuance of state bonds and expansion of government direct investment without mobilizing non-governmental sources. A fundamental reason for the failure to mobilize non-governmental sources is that the threshold of the sector's industries is too high for non-governmental capital to access the market. Therefore, the government should open the infrastructure and public utilities sector for investment, relax restrictions on market access, adopt diverse measures, and fully mobilize the initiative of non-governmental and other social sources for investment, so that such investment will gradually enter the infrastructure and public utilities sector on a large scale. Only thus can the backward state of infrastructure be improved more speedily and a solid foundation laid for a long-term and stable development of the economy.

At present, economic growth in the United States, the European Union and Japan has slowed down in different degrees, which will have an adverse impact on the economies of countries around the world, including that of China. The 9/11 terrorist attack, as another adverse factor, will undoubtedly delay the recovery of the US economy and the world economy as a whole, although some economists estimate that it will not affect China's GDP growth rate too much. These factors will have a great negative impact on the speed of the growth of China's economy.

Compared with the generally competitive industries and the manufacturing industry, industries in China's infrastructure and public utilities sector have a much greater potential for investment and development. With China's accession to the WTO, this sector will become extremely attractive to foreign investment and non-governmental capital. The endeavor to speed up the sector's reform, open the market and remove the barriers to foreign and non-governmental capital, particularly at a time when the international economic environment is not so favorable, will have an important impact on China's continued economic growth and macroeconomic stability for a number of years to come.

II. We must fully recognize and assess the important effect of market opening on promoting effective competition in the infrastructure and public utilities sector.

1. Breaking monopoly and introducing competition are a top priority in China's reform of the infrastructure and public utilities sector at the present stage.

Recent years have seen a beginning of the breaking of monopoly in the infrastructure and public utilities sector, an initial pattern of market competition, and certain progress in the industrial reorganization and transformation of enterprises into corporations. For example, in China's telecommunications sector a vertical division of business has been carried out, and a pattern of competition among China Telecom, China Unicom and other corporations has initially taken shape in the basic telecommunications and Internet areas. In value-added telecommunications, operation licenses have been issued to 3,028 enterprises. In civil aviation, aviation enterprises have been separated from airports, and merging and reorganization among air transport enterprises as well as their transformation towards the shareholding system are making positive progress. In the electric power industry, a pattern of multi-investors for power plants has already taken shape, and pilot projects have started to separate plants from power grids, and to allow enterprises to make decisions independently on power generation and to sell electricity to grids at competitive prices. The railways sector has initially separated its main operations from its ancillary occupations, and established six major railway non-transportation enterprises and five independent passenger and cargo transportation companies. As a result of industrial reorganization and enterprises' corporation-oriented transformation, a group of competitive enterprises in the infrastructure and public utilities sector have been successfully listed in capital markets both at home and abroad.

At present, many problems exist in the infrastructure and public utilities sector. For example, the functions of the government and enterprises are mingled, property rights are not clearly defined, and trade monopoly still exists. Among these problems, low economic efficiency due to monopoly has, particularly, retarded development of the infrastructure and public utilities sector. In those infrastructure industries that are naturally monopolistic, such as cable telecommunications, electric power, railway transportation, tap water and gas supply, a control system featuring the mixture of government and enterprise functions and government monopolized operations still prevails in varying degrees. Such administrative monopoly is a kind of institutional monopoly that strangles competition mechanisms. It obviously differs from economic monopoly, which results from production concentration through free competition. The dominant players of administrative monopoly are the government and its administrative agencies, which can take all kinds of measures to put up access barriers in order to safeguard the monopolistic position of their own enterprises. Some local governments even go so far as to legitimize their monopolistic position by making local regulations. After China's accession to the WTO, the top priority of the reform in the infrastructure and public utilities sector is to get rid of administrative monopoly, open the market and let the market forces play a full role.

2. Opening markets and promoting competition have greater substance than ever against the WTO background.

Opening markets is the most substantial measure to promote effective competition in the infrastructure and public utilities sector. China's present efforts in splitting or reorganising industries in the infrastructure and public utilities sector have, in most cases, not changed the property rights pattern, with the state still being the sole source of investment. Industries in this sector are in the nature of public welfare ones to a certain extent, and hence need government inputs. But international experience has indicated that the government is by no means the only effective investor. Besides government inputs, investment from non-governmental sources should be allowed to enter this sector, and ways and means such as bidding and subsidies should be employed to attract a great amount of such investment. For example, non-governmental capital has accounted for 70 percent of the total investment in building infrastructure in the Wenzhou and Taizhou areas of Zhejiang Province, playing a major role in advancing economic development in the region. As a non-public enterprise, the Sichuan Haite Group has, only a few years after obtaining a license for aircraft maintenance, not only acquired a considerable market share in China, taking the lead in a good number of fields, but also started to enter the international market. These cases are evidence that it is not just imperative but also possible and economically feasible to open the market of the infrastructure and public utilities sector. With China's accession to the WTO, these sectors will inevitably open to foreign investment. In this process, the government should take the initiative in creating conditions for opening the sector to Chinese non-governmental investment earlier than or simultaneously to foreign investment, broadening the channels of domestic non-governmental capital for accessing the sector.

A rational price mechanism is the prerequisite for building up an effective competition pattern. Adequate market opening is an important condition for establishing a rational price competition mechanism. Opening the market is the fundamental way to spur enterprises to improve their services and reduce costs, and proceed to promote rational competition among them.

III. We must fully recognize and assess the important role of the reform in introducing a shareholding system in advancing the reorganization of enterprises in the infrastructure and public utilities sector.

1. Reorganizing enterprises in the infrastructure and utilities sector should be combined with reforming property rights.

At present, enterprise reform in monopolistic industries is still being carried out basically within the original operating system of state monopolies, and likewise the ways to introduce competition are basically the splitting or reorganizing of SOEs. However, such reforms, due to their limitations, cannot fundamentally change the state of low efficiency and poor competitiveness in this sector.

Practice has proved that the effort to advance the industrial reorganization of the infrastructure and public utilities sector must be combined with the reorganization of proprietary rights, so that sources of investment can be diversified and the situation of a single state property right and governance for enterprises can be fundamentally changed. Against the background of its accession to the WTO, China needs, in the face of international competition, to further deepen the reform of its SOEs and transform their management mechanism. On the other hand, it should change policies that discriminate against non-public sector's access to the market and introduce non-state operators, thus giving rise to a situation in the infrastructure and public utilities sector in which both state-owned and non-public enterprises, as well as enterprises operating with foreign investment compete with and stimulate one another.

2. It is necessary to accelerate the reform to establish shareholding system in the infrastructure and public utilities sector.

It is essential to adequately understand the important role of the reform in introducing the shareholding system when promoting the entry of non-state sectors into the infrastructure and public utilities sector. The introduction of the shareholding system should be carried out to quicken the pace in doing away with administrative monopoly and improving the status of low efficiency in the sector. Under the conditions of market economy, there should be flexible arrangements regarding the proportion of state-owned equities. In fact, a smaller proportion of state-owned equities, if rationally planned, will be beneficial to competition in and development of the infrastructure and public utilities sector.

Experience both at home and abroad has shown that pushing forward the shareholding system in this sector has a lot of advantages. For example, it is possible to pool a great amount of funds within a relatively short period of time; it can enable managers with technical know-how and managerial expertise to enjoy independent management rights. Binding investors' obligations closely with their rights, the shareholding system makes it possible to improve the efficiency and economic returns of infrastructure projects under construction; it is conducive to building up a government control system which separates government functions from enterprise management; it is conducive to building strict corporate governance; it will help strong enterprises and core enterprises to form modern enterprise groups through capital markets using capital as the linkage, thus optimizing market players' competition stance. Therefore, the shareholding system should become the dominant form of ownership in the infrastructure and public utilities sector. With respect to infrastructure industries and facilities in the transportation, telecommunications and energy sectors that are expected to become profitable in the future, the shareholding system should be vigorously promoted for the construction of new projects, thus accelerating the process of reform towards the shareholding system in the infrastructure and public utilities sector.

At present, it is necessary to adopt a variety of effective forms to press ahead with the introduction of the shareholding system in this sector. First, infrastructure industries and facilities in transportation, telecommunications and energy that have prospects of making profits in the future should be gradually converted to the shareholding system, depending on the maturity of conditions. Second, enterprises that can be transformed into standard stock sharing corporations should strive to become listed on the stock market at an early date. Third, if an entire enterprise cannot switch to the shareholding system for the moment, some parts may go ahead now and other parts may follow later. Fourth, for enterprises where conditions are not ripe for the time being, the shareholding system can be introduced in stages, by first issuing convertible bonds. Fifth, when conditions are ripe, bonds should be issued to a wider scope of investors, employing diverse forms to socialize investment in the infrastructure and public utilities sector, and creating conditions for introducing the shareholding system to the sector.

3. Speeding up the shift in sources of investment is an essential task in the reform of the infrastructure and public utilities sector.

The government cannot become the main subject for investment or dominant operator in the infrastructure and public utilities sector, either in terms of investment or in terms of market-oriented reform in the sector. Compared with non-governmental capital that amounts to the tune of trillions of yuan, the government investment's contribution to new economic growth is limited. Hence, to effect a gradual transition from government to non-governmental sectors as the main subjects of investment is a vital approach to speeding up development in the infrastructure and public utilities sector and also a key to maintaining the vitality of the sector.

Based on practical experience, non-state capital can enter the infrastructure and public utilities sector through the following channels and approaches: First, encouraging non-governmental capital to enter the infrastructure and public utilities sector by way of conglomeration, joint operation, raising funds and buying shares. At the same time, the threshold for non-governmental capital to enter this sector should be lowered by dividing a project into components. Second, great attention should be paid to bringing into play the important role of stock markets. Third, we should fully utilize and draw on international practices, such as BOT (build, operate and transfer). Fourth, we should denationalize operation rights and put the operation of state-owned assets on a non-state basis.

IV. We must fully recognize and assess the importance of building a government control system which tallies with market opening.

1. Under the conditions of an open market, it is necessary to define as early as possible the basic functions of the government regarding its control over the infrastructure and public utilities sector.

Effective government control provides a premise and a foundation for safeguarding effective competition in naturally monopolistic industries. At present, the Chinese regulation departments do not have enough binding force over the monopolies, nor are their ways of control soundly based on laws or regulations. On the one hand, China has to relax the administrative control which used to prevail in the planned economy; on the other hand, in order to cater to market competition, it is necessary to improve methods and instruments for control and, with regard to the content of control, improve its functions and rebuild the control system. China's reform of government control should lay equal stress on relaxing control, introducing competition and rebuilding control. To tally with market opening, further improvement of the government economic control functions is the first and foremost task in propelling the reform of the government control system.

In light of international experience, in a government control system where government functions are separated from enterprise management, the functions of government control should include the following elements:

(1) Relevant regulations for government control should be formulated. That is to say, according to the technological and economic characteristics of specific industries in the infrastructure and public utilities sector, the government should make provisions in the form of regulations for such matters as the setting up of control agencies, their responsibilities and powers, and major readjustments of market structure, so as to fix the basic framework for a new system of government control.

(2) It is necessary to issue and change the licenses granted to enterprises.

(3) It is necessary to decide control prices, and supervise their implementation.

(4) It is necessary to exercise control over market access.

2. We must establish independent and specialized supervision organizations as soon as possible.

Supervision organizations differ greatly from general governmental ministries and departments. While definitions of independent supervision organizations vary with different countries, independent supervision organizations share at least the following features: (a) They have considerable flexibility in financial affairs; (b) There is no conflict of interests between supervising organizations and the corporations to be supervised; (c) Supervision organizations are fully independent when making decisions, free from political or administrative pressure; (d) Supervision organizations must have a strong professional capacity. As supervision is a kind of highly complex work, supervision organizations should have their own capacity to carry out technological appraisals.

Regarding the setting up of supervision organizations, some experts have called for the establishment of a centralized organization, trying as far as possible to pool under the new control organization all those control functions shared by different governmental departments. However, since industries in the infrastructure and public utilities sector are highly technical and specialized, it will be more appropriate to establish in given industries of the sector separate, specialized control organizations, leanly staffed but highly efficient. In addition, as control will certainly involve economic, political, technological and legal aspects, it will be necessary to recruit widely the service of experts in the work of government control, thus forming a specialized control organization that enjoys broad social participation and comprises trade administration experts, technological specialists, economists and jurists.

3. We must build up and improve a legal system for competition and control, and raise the standard and efficiency of government control on the basis of a legal system.

At present, China's control of the infrastructure and public utilities sector mainly relies on government administrative coordination, instead of standardization and regulation by law. This is not compatible with the objective requirements of China's accession to the WTO and China's dovetailing with international practices. In order to keep up with the need to open the markets, legislation work should be speeded up with regard to the infrastructure and public utilities sector.

It should be pointed out that with China's accession to the WTO, the formulation and implementation of an anti-monopoly law will be of particular importance. At present, the major contents of the anti-monopoly reform in the infrastructure and public utilities sector is to break administrative monopoly and introduce market competition. It is possible that market-based monopolistic forces may come into being in the process of reforming and reorganizing monopolistic industries. With the coming of transnational corporations after China's accession to the WTO, it is also likely that new market monopolies will arise through competition on the market. It is only through relevant legislation that market monopoly can be overcome and settled. China's accession to the WTO makes the legislation to standardize the competition order a most pressing task. The drawing up of the anti-monopoly law and other relevant laws should take such a background into full consideration, and move ahead more rapidly.

REFORM IN THE INFRASTRUCTURE AND PUBLIC UTILITIES SECTOR AND CHINA'S OPENING-UP DRIVE

(*January 2002*)

With China's accession to the WTO, the country's infrastructure and public utilities sector, including telecommunications, railways, civil aviation and electric power industries, will all open up to the outside world step by step within a limited transition period, and participate in international market competition. These areas boast larger-scale industries with a high concentration of state capital. The long-standing monopolistic operations in these industries have led to low efficiency and poor international competitiveness. On the other hand, infrastructure and public utilities are the areas that have seen a comparatively faster development and enjoy broad markets and good growth prospects. It is certain that in these areas domestic enterprises will face powerful competition from big international companies. To face up to the competition and challenges from the international market, keep up with the situation following China's accession to the WTO and meet the WTO requirements, it is necessary to make, in light of international practices, rapid and appropriate adjustments regarding market players at the micro level, market structure, government control system and mode of control, and improve the competitiveness of all trades in the infrastructure and public utilities sector.

I. Speeding up the reform of infrastructure and public utilities sector is an objective requirement for China's observance of the basic WTO rules and fulfillment of its commitments.

First of all, the essence of the WTO rules is to standardize the operation of a market economy, and see to it that these rules are implemented. With regard to the WTO rules, we can simply summarize them with 12 Chinese characters, meaning "to formulate rules, open markets and settle disputes," and the core is to formulate the rules of the market economy. In this sense, the essence of WTO functions or rules is to practice a market economy and standardize its modes of operation and institutional environment for operations worldwide. The purpose of the WTO in opening markets and handling disputes is to supervise over its members, and make sure that these members are effectively practicing market economies in line with its rules. In this sense, the function of the WTO is, in the simplest terms, to standardize the market economy.

Second, the essence of China's accession to the WTO is to practice a market economy in an all-round way, and to dovetail its economic system with the mainstream of the world economy. Before its reform and opening up, China practiced a planned economy and carried out construction behind closed doors. It was out of the question then to talk about dovetailing with the mainstream of the world economy, or to talk about participating in international economic competition. After China started to implement its reform and opening-up program, the first thing it did was to open its doors in carrying out national construction, and then declared its intention to practice a socialist market economy and open wider to the outside world, with the aim of increasing its economic strength more rapidly and linking itself with the world economy. As a big country, China should create the conditions to tie itself closer to the world economy. It is particularly so today when economic globalization, no matter how many advantages or disadvantages it may bring, has become an unavoidable trend, whether or not China is able to use its accession to the WTO as a turning point to accelerate its dovetailing with the mainstream of the world economy. This will be an issue of great importance for China's sustained economic development.

Third, China's accession to the WTO shows to the whole world that China's market-oriented reform, or, in other words, its reform and opening up, has become an international obligation that China must duly fulfill. Therefore, the process of reform and opening up has an irreversible nature. China is committed to "observing the rules and opening markets" in connection with its accession to the WTO. China will observe the rules of the market economy, open its domestic market and gradually dovetail its economy with the mainstream of the world economy in accordance with the WTO rules.

It is exactly in sense that we say that China's accession to the WTO is the country's second round of reform and second round of opening up. What is most fundamental about the impact and significance of China's WTO accession is that it will greatly push forward China's reform process.

Since 1990, the Chinese government has speeded up its opening to the outside world in the infrastructure and public utilities sector. This was prompted by the need to overcome the shortage of domestic investment in infrastructure since this sector had become a bottleneck for China's economic development. Hence, introducing foreign investment has become an important policy tool for promoting infrastructure building. In the "Guidelines for Foreign Investment in Industry," the Chinese government expressly indicates that foreign businesses are permitted to participate in the building and operation of civil airports, with the proportion of foreign investment in airport construction being allowed to reach up to 48 percent, and in civil aviation enterprises up to 35 percent, along with voting rights not exceeding 25 percent. During his visit to the United States in April 1999, Zhu Rongji, Premier of the State

Council, signed the "PRC-USA Aviation Agreement." This agreement complied with the trend in international civil aviation for the liberalization of the skies and commercialization of airports, marking a new stage in the opening of China's civil aviation services. With China's accession to the WTO, the infrastructure and public utilities sector will surely open wider to the outside world in both width and depth.

In its negotiation process for its accession to the WTO, China signed with various WTO members bilateral or multilateral agreements on the scope and timetable for opening its markets. These agreements have a strong binding force. Among them, the agreement on trade in infrastructure and public services contains the most important items of all the relevant agreements. For example, the USA-PRC bilateral agreement on China's accession to the WTO in the area of telecommunications provides that China has, for the first time, agreed to open its telecommunications to direct investment. China will therefore become a member of the basic telecommunications agreement. With regard to the principles of administration, China agrees to abide by competition-supportive principles as included in the basic telecommunications agreement, and agrees to the plan of technological neutrality arrangement, which means that foreign service-suppliers may use any of their selected technology to provide telecommunications services. With respect to the scope of services, China will gradually eliminate all geographical restrictions on paging and value-added services within two years, eliminate restrictions on mobile phones within five years, and eliminate those on domestic phone lines within six years. The main telecommunications service channels in Beijing, Shanghai and Guangzhou, which account for about 75 percent of China's total domestic telecommunications business, will immediately be opened to all telecommunications service suppliers. Upon its accession to the WTO, China will immediately lift restrictions on value-added and paging businesses in Beijing, Shanghai and Guangzhou, and one year later it will gradually open 14 other cities — Chengdu,

Chongqing, Dalian, Fuzhou, Hangzhou, Nanjing, Ningbo, Qingdao, Shenyang, Shenzhen, Xiamen, Xi'an, Taiyuan and Wuhan. After another two years, the whole country will be open. In this area China permits up to 30 percent of foreign investment share. After one year, the permitted share will be raised to 49 percent. As for value-added and paging services foreign businesses can have a share of 50 percent after two years. As for mobile phone and data services, one year after China's WTO accession, foreign investors are allowed to hold a share of 25 percent, and three years after, a share of 35 percent, five years after, a share of 49 percent. In this area, one year after China's WTO accession, Beijing, Shanghai and Guangzhou will be opened first; three years later, the 14 cities of Chengdu, Chongqing, Dalian, Fuzhou, Nanjing, Ningbo, Qingdao, Shenyang, Shenzhen, Xiamen, Xi'an, Taiyuan and Wuhan will be opened; five years later, the opening will be expanded to the whole country. In the fields of domestic and international services, three years after the accession, foreign service suppliers may possess a 25-percent share; five years later, they may possess a 35-percent share; and six years later, a 49-percent share. In this area, three years after China's accession to the WTO, Beijing, Shanghai and Guangzhou will be opened first; five years later, the 14 cities of Chengdu, Chongqing, Dalian, Fuzhou, Hangzhou, Nanjing, Ningbo, Qingdao, Shenyang, Shenzhen, Xiamen, Xi'an, Taiyuan and Wuhan will be opened; and six years later, the whole country will be open to overseas investment. The WTO accession arrangements allow for a very short transition and buffer period for the reform of the infrastructure and public utilities sector. Therefore, speeding up the reform and opening of the infrastructure and public utilities sector is not just needed for the sector's self development, but is more a kind of objective requirement due to changes in the external environment after the country's accession to the WTO. If our infrastructure and public utilities sector wants to join the mainstream of the world economy, it must fulfill its commitments, abide by the WTO rules and open its market.

II. It is an inevitable choice for China to speed up reform in the infrastructure and public utilities sector and increase its competitiveness to participate in economic globalization.

Looking back on the reform process over the past 20 years and more, we can see that China has made outstanding achievements in the reform of general competitive industries and relevant areas. But in the area of infrastructure and public utilities, where a high degree of monopoly by state capital exists, the reform has lagged behind, and yet this area and its relevant government supervision system are the most important aspects of the work for making the economic transition and linking up with international rules. Furthermore, the all-round opening up after China's accession to the WTO has set a deadline for the reform of the infrastructure and public utilities sector, leaving very limited time and space for the sector to accomplish the reform. Of this, we must have a clear understanding.

After China's accession to the WTO, the country's reform and opening up will also enter a new stage, in which its economy will link up with the world economy, and cooperate and compete with transnational corporations. In the short term, the infrastructure and public utilities sector will face both shock waves and opportunities. Compared with the developed countries today, our infrastructure industries are obviously in disadvantageous position in terms of technology, equipment, human and financial resources, managerial expertise and market development. More importantly, China's infrastructure and public utilities sector has not yet have a sound competitive mechanism, the enterprises have not yet been tempered in a really competitive environment, the management system of our infrastructure industries is way behind that in a fully market-oriented economy, and there are inadequate legal instruments to standardize trade behavior. Therefore, it is certain that our infrastructure and public utilities will encounter shock waves after China's accession to the WTO. But shock waves can also be beneficial for development, because enterprise development is motivated by profits and pushed by competition pressure, and competition is an effective way to raise our own level. There are only two to three years left to the deadline set for removing protection for certain trades, leaving very limited space to the infrastructure and public utilities sector for self-adjustment and development. In this limited period of time, industries and enterprises in the infrastructure and public utilities sector should enhance their awareness of crisis and urgency, and make full use of the pressure coming along with the country's accession to the WTO to push forward reform boldly and resolutely, and try to speedily accomplish the basic task of introducing non-governmental capital and building a competition mechanism in the sector. Reform should be used to propel the priority development of the infrastructure and public utilities sector and improve the sector's own competitiveness, so as to mitigate as far as possible the negative impact of foreign capital inflow on the sector.

As the infrastructure and public utilities sector accounts for a considerable proportion of China's economic aggregate, the competitiveness of the sector has great weight in the overall competitiveness of the country's economy. Therefore, it will be an inevitable trend in China's market-oriented reform that, while participating in international market competition, the reform must be expanded from the general production and circulation areas to such particularly difficult areas as infrastructure and public utilities, and from general competitive areas to highly monopolistic infrastructure and public utilities such as telecommunications, electric power, civil aviation and railways, with the aim of raising the overall competitiveness of the country's economy. In this sense, it can be said that the reform in the infrastructure and public utilities sector, which features breaking monopoly and introducing competition, is an extension of the reform and reorganization of the state sector from competitive industries to monopolistic industries, signifying that China's reform of the government control system and the state sector has entered a new stage.

III. Speeding up reform in the infrastructure and public utilities sector and propelling the market-oriented process of investment and financing in this sector are the essence of China's macroeconomic policies under the pressure of insufficient effective demand.

The fact that China has intensified its investment in the infrastructure and public utilities sector to facilitate sustained economic growth has now become a focus of attention both at home and abroad. Expanded investment in this sector at a time of economic transition bears not only upon efforts to change the backward state of the sector, but also upon efforts to upgrade China's industrial structure and improve the overall quality of our national economy. It will also have an important impact on the reform of the basic industries, and the entire related infrastructure and public utilities sector (including areas and industries where the state sector holds a dominant position: state security, public works, monopolistic trades, resource-based industries, as well as essential processing industries, pillar industries and infant industries). In the market economy, it is imperative to continue with the reform in the infrastructure and public utilities sector. The rationale for such a viewpoint is that the in-depth development of the reform in this sector will have a positive effect on the sound growth of the national economy: When its rich potential develops to a certain stage and has generated and will continue to generate important qualitative change, the infrastructure and public utilities sector will become the leader of the nation's economic growth; the infrastructure and public utilities sector has already become an important component of the force for increasing market demands and initiating market consumption; and a profound change has taken place in industrial structure and organizational forms of enterprises in the sector, which is taking an ever more important position in the strategic reorganization of state assets. Hence, expanding investment in the infrastructure and public utilities sector must go side by side with accelerating the reform of the sector, so that infrastructure can be more cost-effective, more competitive and more sustainable. This will truly make expanded investment play its full role in contributing to China's economic growth.

In view of the deflation tendency occurring in China, the government has, since 1998, implemented a proactive fiscal policy to expand investment in the infrastructure and public utilities sector. This policy choice has not only averted an economic decline and greatly helped improve the macroeconomic environment, it has also reflected the inherent demands of China's economic development on the infrastructure. As far as the inner relationship between infrastructure and economic growth is concerned, we can say that, when a country's economic development reaches a certain level, it will be necessary to increase infrastructure availability accordingly and this is the time when increased investment in infrastructure will yield much higher marginal returns than any equivalent amount of investment in other fields can do. The problem is, in face of huge demands for investment in the infrastructure and public utilities sector, the government's capacity is limited, and the government cannot possibly be the main subject of investment, which should be enterprises and society at large. If non-governmental investment is not initiated, government efforts alone to stimulate economic growth by expanding its direct investment with money from issuing state bonds can only produce a temporary and limited effect.

The long delay in bringing in non-governmental investment is due fundamentally to China's administration and operation systems in the infrastructure and public utilities sector, which are seriously unfit for meeting the development needs of the sector, and to the high industrial thresholds, which have restricted the market access of non-governmental capital. Therefore, it is imperative to open up investment areas in infrastructure, relax restrictions on market access and take diverse measures to fully mobilize the initiative of the non-governmental sector and other sectors of society for investment, so as to facilitate the entry of non-governmental capital on a large scale and thus quickly changing the backward state of China's infrastructure. Only thus can a foundation be laid for long-term and stable economic growth.

IV. The imbalance in the industrial structure is a deep-rooted reason for unsustainability of China's economic growth, and the reform of the infrastructure and public utilities sector constitutes an important link in correcting the industrial structural deviation retarding China's economic growth.

Tertiary industry, including transportation, posts and telecommunications, banking and insurance, education, science and technology, is not only an intermediate link connecting the primary and secondary industries with markets, but also an essential condition for developing the primary and secondary industries. The fact that our secondary industry's output accounts for an excessively large proportion of the economy is the result of lopsided efforts at industrialization under the traditional planned economy. While China has achieved a certain level of market economy development, its industrial growth has not been able to regain its relatively high speed due to market constraints, and it is unavoidable that the economic growth which used to rely mainly on industrial growth has been affected adversely. A fundamental change has taken place in the world economic structure, in which the proportions of both primary and secondary industries, with manufacturing industry as their main component, are on a gradual decline, while the proportion of the service industry, including banking, tourism and telecommunications, has already risen to 50 percent, or even to about two-thirds in a few countries. International experience shows that the basic service industries play a special and pivotal role in raising labor productivity, reducing production costs and improving the quality of life. Especially along with the development of the modern economy, infrastructure facilities as an important component part of the overall national strength likewise play such a role in the national economy. World Bank experts' studies have proved that infrastructure capacity increases simultaneously with economic outputs; that is, every one percent increase in the stock of infrastructure will bring up the gross domestic product by one percent. However, since the 1990s the proportions of China's transportation, posts and telecommunications, banking and insurance, as well as science and technology in the country's GDP have all remained very low or even dropped in some cases.

An analysis of China's current situation shows that the delayed development of transportation, posts and telecommunications and other areas of the infrastructure and public utilities sector is directly related to the delay in the reform of this sector. Since China's reform and opening up were started, some trades and places have introduced non-governmental funds and foreign capital on a limited scale into the construction of infrastructure projects for development purposes. On the whole, however, the market-oriented reform in the infrastructure and public utilities sector has not seen any substantial breakthrough, and a market competition mechanism has not yet been established. It is precisely the administrative monopoly in the infrastructure and public utilities sector that has led not only to short supply of infrastructure facilities, shortage of products and poor quality of services at expensive prices, but also to excessive investment, oversupply and vicious competition in some more competitive trades, such as the manufacturing and processing industries, and retail businesses, thus increasing the investment risks of enterprises, gravely divorcing the supply structure from the demand structure, and leading to low efficiency in the distribution of resources. This is the direct reason why our economy as a whole has failed to switch to the track of sustained growth supported by improved economic efficiency. The current phenomenon of deflation in our national economic operations indicates that China's economic development must be underpinned by a considerable readjustment of the economic structure, and the reform of the infrastructure and public utilities sector provides favorable conditions for the readjustment of the industrial structure. The flow of nongovernmental funds into the infrastructure and public utilities sector through the market-oriented reform will not only end the situation in which supply falls short of demand in the sector but also bring about the readjustment of the industrial structure by changing the investment structure.

V. The development of the market economy and social stability place new demands on public products, and accelerating the reform in the infrastructure and public utilities sector is an effective way for the government to guarantee the supply of public products.

Since the 1950s, along with the progress in science and technology and growth in social wealth, people's living standard has improved constantly and their demand for public products is also on a constant increase. People need a safe and stable social environment, efficient and developed infrastructure of good services, a harmonious ecological environment and good welfare benefits. In the face of an ever increasing demand of the public, developed countries in the West have, one after another, carried out market-oriented reform and privatization in public utilities such as water and power supply, telecommunications, aviation, etc., which used to be vertically operated by state monopoly, by turning over the supply of these public products and services to private capital, while the government has focused more on such public products as medical care, education, social security and other welfare expenditures, in order to increase the efficiency in supplying public products and services, improve the quality of services, meet the requirements of the public and reduce the burden on financial expenses. Such reform has not just immensely promoted development of infrastructure and public utilities, but also resulted in an improved social welfare as a whole and a stable social development.

Funds are the crux of the matter in China's infrastructure construction. In accordance with the World Bank estimate, China's investment in infrastructure in the mid-1980s accounted for 4.4 percent of the GDP, and in mid-1990s the percentage increased to 7.5. The World Bank has forecasted: in order to keep a continued high growth of the GDP, the country's investment in the infrastructure and public utilities sector in the next ten years shall have to make up 8 to 9 percent of the GDP and its total amount shall reach 740 billion US dollars, of which 200 billion US dollars will be used for building energy infrastructure. In the meantime, the proportion of China's fiscal expenditures in the GDP was on the decrease steadily. Between mid-1980s and mid-1990s, the proportion of fiscal expenditures in the GDP dramatically decreased from 25 percent in 1987 to 8.9 percent at the end of the period under review. During the same period, investment demand kept on increasing in both absolute amount and proportion in the GDP, which increased from 15.8 percent in 1989 to 25.3 percent in 1993. It is due to a declining capacity of government financial investment that non-state sector has, since the start of the reform, been able to make up a considerably high proportion of investment in general trades. The infrastructure and public utilities sector, however, has still mainly relied on the state inputs because the reform in this area has lagged behind, resulting in a low proportion of non-state investment. Hence, the fundamental way to address the shortage of funds in building infrastructure and public utilities and to increase the supply of products can be none other than to accelerate the market-oriented reform in the sector.

In the area of public products supply, the Chinese government had for a long time focused more on the productive and profitable infrastructure facilities in the economic sector, while its inputs in social security, culture and education, environmental protection and other public undertakings had remained chronically insufficient. Furthermore, in allocating inputs for the area of public utilities, the government did not make a distinction between business-based projects and non-business projects. As a result, the range of public products kept expanding, creating a heavy burden on the treasury, which found it more and more difficult to cover the expenditures. This had not only retarded the development of infrastructure and prevented it from playing its due role as a new growth point in contributing to economic growth, but also handicapped the development of public utilities to an extent that the growing demands of the general public for public products cannot be satisfactorily met. Only when the government stops doing something can it do something else better. In the infrastructure and public utilities sector, only when the government lightens the burden on the treasury through reform by handing over part of traditional public products that are more competitive and profit-oriented to the non-governmental investment, can it shift those fiscal inputs originally earmarked for productive and profit-oriented areas to basic education, health, culture and other public services as well as to the improvement of the social security system. At the same time, efforts should be made to strengthen macroeconomic control with a view to ensuring a more coordinated and balanced economic structure and constantly upgrading it, and to effect a fundamental change in the mode of financial inputs to guarantee that the government will focus on the supply of most effective public products to the entire society, thus creating most important conditions for ensuring economic development and social stability.

BREAK MONOPOLY AND INTRODUCE COMPETITION TO ESTABLISH AN ADEQUATE MARKET COMPETITION MECHANISM

(January 2002)

Over recent years, China has achieved positive results in its reform of the infrastructure and public utilities sector, as the reform extends its feelers more deeply into the sector. But monopoly is still the major contradiction that our reform in the sector has to confront. Whether or not we can accelerate the process of breaking it and introducing competition under the context of China's accession to the WTO has important implications on increasing competitiveness of the industries in the sector.

I. Speeding up the process of breaking monopoly and introducing competition mechanism is still the first priority in China's current reform of the infrastructure and public utilities sector.

One of the main achievements that China has gained in its reform of the infrastructure and public utilities sector over recent years is reflected in the fact that the vertical integrated monopolized operations have begun to be broken up, a market competition pattern has initially taken shape, and remarkable progress has been made in industrial reorganization and in transformation of enterprises into corporations.

At present, there exist many problems in the infrastructure and public utilities sector, for example, government functions are mixed up with enterprise management; property rights are not clearly defined; trade monopoly; poor quality of services; high operation costs; obvious tendency to seek group interests; serious waste of resources and so on. The various phenomena of low economic efficiency are glaring examples of how monopoly has bottlenecked the reform and development of China's infrastructure and public utilities sector. In those naturally monopolistic infrastructure industries, such as cable telecommunication, electric power, railway transport, tap water and gas supply, up to now a control system featuring a mixture of government and enterprise functions, and government monopolistic operation is still basically practiced. Under such a system, the government is the maker as well as supervisor and implementer of the control policies and at the same time the monopolistic operators of specific businesses. That is typical of administrative monopoly. Administrative monopoly is a kind of institutional monopoly that strangles competition mechanism. It obviously differs from economic monopoly as a result of a concentration of production through free competition. The dominant players of administrative monopoly are the government and its administrative agencies. They use all means to put up barriers to market entry in order to protect the monopolistic position of the enterprises in their own systems. Some local governments have gone as far as to legitimize it by making local regulations. The following examples show how it mainly works: use of administrative regulations to control market entry of new enterprises. That is, a relevant government department may block the entry of new enterprises under the pretext of maintaining economy of scale and preventing disorderly competition, so as to entrench the existing enterprises in the monopolistic operational position. Not only main business is under monopolistic operation, but also the relevant products are monopolized. Taking advantage of their monopolistic position, these enterprises also practice so-called "tied-up" operations. To give just a few examples, installing gas piping is "tied-up" to selling cooking utensils, installing telephones is "tied-up" to selling phone sets, some even "tie up" railway goods delivery to charging insurance premium on highway transport.

The main drawbacks of administrative monopoly are: conditioned to an environment of monopoly operations for a long time, such enterprises lack vigor for competing and a flexible operation mechanism, are not service-sensitive and their operation costs are high. What is more, with their monopolistic position, enterprises can set monopoly prices far higher than the costs and in so doing, they can turn part of the consumers' surplus into that of the producers, so as to make monopoly profits. Such practices will certainly result in a distortion of social distribution efficiency and an infringement on consumers' interests. In order to overcome these drawbacks and resolve the various contradictions in the infrastructure and utilities sector, the key again lies in introducing competition to build up sufficient market competition mechanisms.

In addition, with China's accession to the WTO, flaws in the vertical integrated monopoly as a deep-rooted contradiction and control system in the infrastructure and public utilities sector are revealing themselves ever more conspicuously. The segments in which competition is possible and the segments of natural monopoly are all in the hands of the monopolies. Though new competitors have been introduced into the competitive segments, the original monopolists can put the competitors in a disadvantageous position in an unfair competition on the account of their exclusive monopolistic power. The government administrative departments do not have a sufficient and binding control over monopolies, nor are their ways of control soundly based on laws and regulations. The rational option to tackle these basic contradictions is to break administrative monopoly, open markets and let the market competition mechanism fully display its role in infrastructure.

II. Break administrative monopoly and promote separation of government functions from enterprise management, so as to create institutional conditions for fair competition in the infrastructure and public utilities sector.

The reform of the railways consists of four-tier separations. The first tier is to separate the networks from transportation, that is, to separate the infrastructure management of naturally monopolistic state railway networks from competitive railway transportation of passengers and goods, by organizing a unified state railway network corporation and a number of strong corporations for passenger and cargo transportation, and applying classified management. The second tier is to separate the trunk lines from the feeder lines. Individual comprehensive feeder management agencies should be set up, and those feeder lines with better conditions should be transformed into standard corporations. The third tier is to separate passenger transportation from cargo transportation. In passenger transportation, certain areas are not suitable for a total removal of control out of consideration for public good and should be compensated through the transfer payments, and the rest should be entirely open. The fourth tier is to separate general cargo transportation from container transportation, refrigerated transportation and special transportation.

In dividing the functions of the Ministry of Railways and advancing the reform of railway transport management system, it is necessary to segregate the function of managing the state property of railways from the Ministry of Railways, and to transfer it to the state property management organization. As a government functional department, the Ministry of Railways is mainly responsible for trade-wise administration of the railways throughout the country, supervision and management of railway state assets, management and control of railway transport markets and handling of certain social matters. The management of state assets, presently a function rested with the Ministry of Railways, should be turned over to the newly organized China Railway Construction Investment Corporation or to the railway transportation groups that are organized on the basis of economic regions and existing railway administrations, and in line with the modern enterprise system, which shall make decisions and manage their business in response to the transportation market independently as market players and legal entities. It is essential to clarify the nature of the railway transportation business and to define, in legal forms, the relations between the state and matters other than railway transportation, so as to create conditions for a market-oriented operation of the railway transportation business. I would suggest that the relationship between the commercialized operation of railway transportation and the nature of public products be defined in legal terms in connection of the revision of the Railways Law. When the railway transportation business suffers a loss in undertaking a state assignment, the state should compensate for the loss in accordance with the contract.

The reform in civil aviation should focus on dividing up the operations. First, profitable business should be separated from non-profit business. Non profit operations with small passenger flow in economically backward regions but having remarkable social benefits should be separated from aviation company operations, aviation fuel and materials business, airport operations with big passenger flows in economically advanced regions and other profitable operations, and should have different investment and operation modalities as well as different financial and tax policies. Second, naturally monopolistic business should be separated from competitive business. For airport services and other naturally monopolistic businesses, it is necessary to have control over such matters as business range, prices and service standards, while for non-naturally monopolistic operations, such as businesses of aviation companies, aviation fuel and materials business, it is necessary to break trade monopolies by introducing rational competition. Third, the service functions within the aviation industry should be separated in accordance with their specialities, that is, to have division of work in accordance with their specialization in passenger service, cargo transportation, general aviation, tourism, technical information, aviation catering, ground service and so on. Fourth, military aviation, civil aviation and aviation for general purposes should be separated from each other.

An approach of "severing first and reorganizing later" should be followed in advancing the reform of civil aviation management system. This reform should start with transforming the functions of the General Administration of Civil Administration and disbanding civil aviation administration agencies at the provincial level, and adopt a modality of national and regional vertical management, that is, to establish a streamlined and highly efficient two-level administration structure consisting of the General Administration of Civil Aviation and its regional administration agencies. The General Administration of Civil Aviation and its regional administration agencies should neatly sever official ties with enterprises under them, and their ways of administration should shift from the past simplistic practice of setting production plans and deciding on the examining and approving procedure to formulating and implementing the industry-wide overall strategic development plans. With regard to speeding up the reform of the airport management system, I would suggest that those airport assets owned by the central government should be, as soon as possible, transferred to local governments, and for the few airports that are still directly under the central government, airport companies should be established to operate them under the authorization of the State Council. The General Administration of Civil Aviation shall mainly perform the government function of administering industry-wide control over the airports, without getting directly involved in the management of airports. Reform of traditional air traffic control shall be based on international practices to re-divide military, civil and combined military/civil (mixed) aviation rights.

The telecommunications market should gradually be opened in total. First, the telecommunications infrastructure construction should be separated from telecommunication services. While telecommunications infrastructure construction is subject to certain restrictions, all restrictions on telecommunication services should be lifted. Second, the trunk networks in the telecommunication infrastructure should be separated from the local area networks giving access to terminal users, making it possible for competition between networks at the level of local areas. Third, general services should be guaranteed. The government must guarantee adequate supply of appropriate telecommunication services nationwide. If there is a shortage of general services, bidding should be called to select the lowest limit subsidy to guarantee the provision of general services. Fourth, through bidding or auction, a limited number of licenses should be issued to permit, as per respective license categories, the provision of voice phone service on communication lines, public lines or on the basis of self-operated telecommunication networks.

Breaking "the union between government and enterprises" will allow the Ministry of Information Industry to become a genuinely neutral control body. The establishment of the Ministry of Information Industry marked the arrival of the time for unified regulations concerning the information industry. Nevertheless, so long as the Ministry of Information Industry continues to take the responsibility for reforming the ownership system, internal administration and management and operations of the enterprises under China Telecom, the control policies that it has formulated cannot help being tendentious, thus making it difficult for the ministry to really perform its function as all-trade administration body. As a trade administration control body, the Ministry of Information Industry should represent the public good, that is, it should take a neutral stance and try to avoid interference from any interest groups in order to ensure the building of an effective competition mechanism within the telecommunications industry. Hence, a pressing task at the moment is to thoroughly disengage the Ministry of Information Industry from telecommunications enterprises in an effort to break "the union between government and enterprises," turning the Ministry of Information Industry into a genuinely neutral control body which will conduct fair control by treating all the market players and newcomers as equals.

III. The key to introducing adequate competition in China's infrastructure and public utilities sector is to form as quickly as possible a market-based price competition mechanism.

Competition is the most effective force for countering monopoly, as well as the single most effective means to protect the interests of consumers. In a competitive environment, the incentive mechanism for all enterprise managers is based on comparable merit standards designed to prompt them to reduce costs, increase production efficiency, and provide better products and services. Competition will also produce a lot of information that will help eliminate the information imbalance between owners and agents, and between the control body and the controlled, thus breaking the so-called information monopoly and forcing enterprises to set prices in accordance with marginal costs or average costs, so that distribution efficiency can be realized, which in turn will help increase the entire social efficiency. In a given period of time, competition is compatible for enterprises under different forms of ownership. In a competitive environment, both private and state-owned enterprises will increase their efficiency. But without competition, private enterprises under control would not necessarily have efficiency higher than that of SOEs, and possibly lower. The root cause of low efficiency of the SOEs in the infrastructure and public utilities sector lies in the lack of competition. Therefore, the top priority for reform in the infrastructure and public utilities sector is precisely to increase market competition, rather than to hastily set about to change the ownership pattern before competition is in place.

Price mechanism is the core of market mechanism. The work to build a price system that is sensitive in response, accurate in signals given, complete in functions and sound in operation is basic and key to the reform in the infrastructure and public utilities sector. For a long period of time in the infrastructure industries, instead of mainly following certain economic principles, China, to a great extent, took non-economic factors into account in setting controlling prices, which were largely a product of administrative decisions. Such pricing principles lacked incentives for enterprises to improve production efficiency, leaving them without a potential for self-development. Furthermore, many controlling prices were lower than marginal costs, which did not conform to the requirements of efficient allocation of social resources. Over the past few years, the government has relaxed price controls over some telecommunication and electric power products (services), resulting in an excessive capital entry into certain business areas of these infrastructure industries and disorderly competition. This represents a deviation from economic principles on pricing at the other extreme.

With the deepening of market-oriented reform, price control in the infrastructure and public utilities sector should mainly target at naturally monopolistic trades instead of non-naturally monopolistic general business areas. Owing to the competitive operations of a good number of enterprises, the competition mechanism will automatically regulate prices, and therefore it is necessary to gradually lift control over prices of competitive products in the infrastructure and public utilities sector, and let the market decide prices in response to the supply-demand relations. Only the prices resulting from free competition can reflect the relative shortage of resources, guide investors in the right direction for investment and bring about effective allocation of resources.

With respect to products and services of naturally monopolistic trades, their pricing methods should abide by the principle of "being fair, rational and truly feasible," and through negotiation and coordination among the government, enterprises and consumers to establish norms binding both sides of supply and demand on the market regarding market access, price and services. This will make it possible to maximize protection of the due interests of consumers while ensuring the enthusiasm of the producers for carrying on normal operations. It is also necessary to improve price control efficiency so as to prevent trades and enterprises from seeking excessively high profits by abusing their ability to monopolize the market, and fully display the role of the price mechanism in regulating resource allocations in a market economy.

The specific trades include: (1) Railways. I would propose that, under the premise of "separation between networks and transportation," the settlement prices between railway networks and transportation enterprises be set by the government, while controls on freight transportation prices should be lifted except for such special materials as those for agricultural and military purposes, and those on passenger transportation should be totally lifted. The traditional price system, which set a unified freight rate for the whole country should be replaced by product pricing of regional and specialized railway transport enterprises based on product value of individual transport enterprises and reflective of supply and demand in the market. (2) International experience in opening telecommunications markets has proved that the countries that have opened their telecommunications markets earlier have witnessed a faster development of the industry and lower prices for services. Therefore, telecommunications rates should be based on the public hearing system and be set by the market. (3) In the civil aviation industry, price controls should be relaxed. Except for naturally monopolistic infrastructure areas or infrastructure involving state security (air-space control and communication guidance facilities), where the state may continue with price controls, air transportation, airport service, air routes and other businesses of a competitive nature should sever their official ties with the General Administration of Civil Aviation and its branch agencies, and follow an air freight policy based on the supply-demand relations of the market. To meet the diversified demands of general consumers, flexibility in ticket pricing should be permitted with regard to different air routes, flights, types of aircraft, seasons and holidays, so as to gradually reduce the gap between domestic and international fares in response to the fiercer international competition following China's accession to the WTO.

IV. We should take appropriate measures in accordance with local conditions, and explore diverse ways to shape competition patterns in different industries.

Since different trades in the infrastructure and public utilities sector have different ways and means of introducing competition, it is necessary to actively explore an integrated reform program for each individual trade.

Reform of telecommunications industry: The general principle and direction should be unified planning, diversified sources of investment and open operations. To be specific: (1) Based on a thorough investigation and scientific research, the specialized organ established with authorization from the government will develop a unified plan for information infrastructure construction, the authority of which will be guaranteed by way of legislation. (2) For information infrastructure construction, unified standards and norms should be established to ensure that the telecommunications facilities are advanced and practical, and that various networks are connected with and communicable to one another. (3) With respect to investment, the stress on diversification of investment structure to ensure competition will not only increase channels for investment and quicken the pace of construction, it will also improve assets structure and management. (4) In managing and operating telecommunications infrastructure and services, it is necessary to break the monopoly by separating the operations between long distance and local calls, and between transmission networks and telecommunication business, to ensure the building of a competition mechanism within the telecommunications sector.

Reform of the electric power industry: Efforts should be made to further relax control, separate government functions from enterprise management, separate grids from plants, and encourage power supply to grids at competitive prices. To be more specific: (1) We should separate government functions from enterprise management. First, the State Power Corporation should position itself as an enterprise and transform itself into a corporation, instead of operating like just another specialized government department in charge of the electric power industry. Second, the central government should change its management mode that mixes the functions of the government and enterprises, and scientifically define the functions of the government, electric power enterprises and trade association, to reduce administrative interference in the electric power industry. (2) We should disengage power grids from power plants and encourage competitive power supply to grids. That is, in accordance with the principle of separating power generation from power transmission and distribution, the State Power Corporation will solely own and manage the national grid system, while the power generating corporation under the State Power Corporation should be broken up by region into a number of independent business entities before they turn into independent shareholding corporations. All power generating enterprises, whether SOEs, Chinese-foreign joint ventures or joint stock enterprises, must sell power to grids at a competitive price in an open, fair and equitable manner, so that electric power enterprises will be forced to improve management, reduce costs and reduce power rates. (3) We must further relax controls. It is important to further break monopoly and relax restrictions in the field of power generation. Restrictions on clients' choice of electric power enterprises should be gradually lifted. Major clients should be allowed to purchase electricity directly from power generating companies through grid systems, while power transmission and distribution enterprises should only charge a certain amount of "grid transmission fees," and stop engaging in sale of power.

Reform of the railways: The general direction is separation between infrastructure and transportation, and classified construction and classified operations and management. To be more specific: (1) Separate operation for infrastructure and transportation. That is, to do away with the all-in-one management system in the present railway transportation industry by separating railway infrastructure (railway networks) from the equipment running on the networks (passenger and cargo transportation). Network companies and transportation companies will be organized, with the latter to operate on a profit-oriented basis. (2) Classified construction. In the construction of railway lines and networks, it is necessary to make a distinction between projects for public good and for commercial purpose. Some railways are obviously meant for public good, such as for national land-use development, balancing economic development between regions, strengthening unity among ethnic groups, supporting economic development in border areas, or meeting military needs, and their construction must be financed by the state because they cannot reap normal size of profits or economic returns by operating on a profit-making basis. All other commercial railways have the conditions for market-oriented construction and operations and adequate commercial profits can be generated from building and managing such railways. For this type of railways, it is necessary to establish market-oriented diversified investment mechanisms, to encourage investment in railways from local sources and numerous non-governmental sources, with an aim to increase the funding channels for railway construction. (3) Classified operation and management. At present, railway transportation enterprises in China, apart from commercial operations, also undertake a great amount of transportation services for public good, such as rescuing operations and disaster relief, supporting agriculture, military transportation and special trains, at preferential prices or without any charges. The losses thus incurred have to be borne by the appropriate departments of the state.

Reform of civil aviation: Though civil aviation in China has witnessed a partial and initial separation of government functions from enterprise management as well as the breakup of enterprises, the control has not been fully lifted, which is manifested in incomplete competition. For the artificially propelled competitive market in civil aviation to survive, develop and grow stronger, the industry should continue with further reform. (1) It is necessary to further relax controls, encourage competition, and protect the effective progress of competition between enterprises. (2) When product competition develops to a certain extent, enterprises should be encouraged to merge with one another, moving the competition from the product market to capital market. (3) When controlled prices reach equilibrium, it is necessary to gradually relax control over prices, and let the competition mechanism restrain enterprises from raising prices and eliminate monopoly profits.

OPENING MARKETS AND ACCELERATING INDUSTRIAL REORGANIZATION IN THE INFRASTRUCTURE AND PUBLIC UTILITIES SECTOR

(*January 2002*)

Now, enterprise reform in China's monopolistic industries is basically carried out within the original state monopoly system. Likewise, the way to introduce competition is basically dividing and reorganizing of SOEs, and the new market players are also basically SOEs. Hence, in order to increase the efficiency and industrial competitiveness, a great amount of work should focus on deepening the reform of SOEs and transforming their operation mechanisms. With its accession to the WTO and in face of international competition, China should, on the one hand, further deepen the reform of SOEs, in which the joint-stock system is introduced in the infrastructure and public utilities sector and non-governmental investment is brought in to improve SOEs' property rights structure and transform their operation mechanisms; on the other hand, it should change those policies that are discriminatory to the access of non-state sectors of the economy, and introduce non-governmental operators, so as to bring about a situation in which SOEs, non-state sectors and foreign-invested operators compete with and promote one another in these industries. In the context of the accession to the WTO, the areas that China has committed to open to foreign investment should first be opened to domestic enterprises of all sectors of the economy. Through full competition among domestic enterprises within the transition period, the enterprises' competitiveness will be enhanced to keep up with the demands of international competition.

I. It is essential to advance the joint-stock system in the infrastructure and public utilities sector, as it is the basic form for the non-public economy to enter the sector.

In reforming the infrastructure and public utilities sector, it is necessary to press ahead with the joint-stock system so as to break the monopoly of the public sector. In this critical period for China's economic transition, accelerated introduction of the joint-stock system in telecommunications, civil aviation, railways, electric power and other trades of the infrastructure and public utilities sector will contribute to separate ownership from management rights and separate government functions from enterprise management, and help address investment shortage and increase operation efficiency. More importantly, the joint-stock system is the basic form for the non-public economy to enter into the infrastructure and public utilities sector. In history, it was the joint-stock system that had spurred the development of railways. We must adequately estimate the important role the introduction of the joint-stock system will play in promoting the access of non-public economy to the infrastructure and public utilities sector. We must also adopt practical reform measures and steps to advance the joint-stock system in an effort to end the situation featuring state control, trade monopoly and low efficiency. Practice shows that the traditional monopoly of the infrastructure by the state sector is the main reason for low efficiency in resource allocation and structural deviations that have bottlenecked China's economic development. In advancing the joint-stock system, we should gradually reduce the proportion of the state sector to make way for the non-state sector; and absorb large amounts of domestic and foreign capital to diversify investment and property rights in infrastructure. At present, there should be flexible arrangements for the proportion of state-owned equity rights in the sector in accordance with the unified national plan and in keeping with the new situation following

China's WTO accession. In fact, a smaller proportion of state-owned equity rights, if rationally planned, will be more favorable to promoting competition in the infrastructure and public utilities sector and its development.

It is necessary to expand the scope of the joint-stock system and develop market competitor in the infrastructure and public utilities sector. The estabishment of a competitive mechanism in this sector should go hand in hand with the transformation of the proprietary system. Only when an enterprise has clearly defined relations of property rights and a sound corporate governance structure can it become a competitor in the infrastructure, and the joint-stock system is the investment and enterprise organizational system best suited to the requirement to develop modern infrastructure under the condition of keeping diverse sources of investment. An important hallmark of modern corporate management system is the separation of capital owners and managers. The advantages of pushing through the joint-stock system are: a) ability to pool large amounts of funds within a comparatively short period of time, resulting in the socialized use of funds; b) enabling managers with specialized knowledge and managerial expertise to have the power to independently make operation decisions and improve economic returns; c) combining the responsibilities and rights of the investors and introducing the incentive mechanism with the result that losses and waste will be cut significantly, construction cycle shortened and construction efficiency and economic returns of an infrastructural project enhanced; d) helping the establishment of a government control system featuring separation of government functions from enterprise management; e) helping strong and core enterprises to form, through the capital market, modern enterprise groups, and improving the structure of market competition. It follows that the joint-stock system should be the main form of enterprise in the infrastructure and public utilities sector. In order to expand the scope of the joint-stock system in the infrastructure and public utilities sector, its introduction should be vigorously encouraged in the construction of profit-making projects in the basic industries and infrastructure, such as transportation, telecommunications and energy.

It is necessary to adopt a variety of effective forms to speed up the introduction of the joint-stock system. An accelerated introduction of the joint-stock system in the telecommunications, civil aviation, railways, electric power and other trades in the infrastructure and public utilities sector is an inevitable response to economic globalization and domestic requirements to adapt to the adjustment of the economic structure. For this reason, we should seize the opportunities and take a variety of forms to advance the joint-stock system in this sector. First, the joint-stock system should be gradually introduced into future profit-making projects in transportation, telecommunications, energy and other infrastructural trades, depending on the availability of conditions and bearing in mind the objective that it will eventually become a general practice. Second, those enterprises that can be transformed into standardized joint-stock companies should try to get listed as early as possible. Third, an enterprise that is not suitable for overall introduction of the joint-stock system may break down the whole into parts, and adopt a step-by-step approach. Fourth, an enterprise the conditions of which are not ripe for the introduction of the joint-stock system for the time being may start with the issuing of convertible bonds as the first step towards this goal. Fifth, when conditions are ripe, the scope of bonds issued to the general public should be expanded, so as to socialize investment in infrastructure through a variety of ways and create the conditions for the introduction of the joint-stock system in the infrastructure and public utilities sector.

A rigorous corporate governance system should be established in the course of introducing the joint-stock system into the infrastructure and public utilities sector. An important hallmark of the joint-stock system is the rigorous corporate governance structure based on the separation of capital owners from managers. This is the direction of the reform of the SOEs in general and in the state sector in the infrastructure trades in particular. In keeping with the requirements of the reform based on the joint-stock-system in the infrastructure and public utilities sector, the government should refrain from unnecessary administrative interventions in such enterprises or directly handling concrete matters related to personnel, management and finance in the capacity as an owner. The government should thoroughly change its scope of activity, modes of control and functions in the infrastructure and public utilities sector, bringing about a shift from direct management and control to indirect regulation and control.

II. It is necessary to give full play to the important role of China's non-state economic sectors and speed up the shift in sources of investment in the infrastructure and public utilities sector.

Making non-state economic sectors to participate in infrastructure construction is an important way to open the country's markets, break monopoly and accelerate reform in this area. For a long time in the past, the Chinese government had remained as the main investor in and operator of the infrastructure facilities and basic industries. The main source of funds was the government allocations and bonds, resulting in a unitary channel of funding and a serious shortage of funds. The main form of investment was direct investment, and a lack of risk-based mechanism restraining investors resulted in a widespread construction of redundant projects, poor management, low returns on investment and poor economic efficiency. Whether or not we can effectively solve the above problems to enable infrastructure construction to play its due role as the prop of the future economic and social development will depend on, first, whether or not we can effectively mobilize non-state and overseas capital to enter this sector, and second, whether or not we can improve the returns on investment by a big margin. The course of reform and opening up over the past two decades and more has shown that to break the monopoly of the state sector, open up the domestic market, introduce the competitive mechanism and promote the development of the non-state economic sectors are the most important experience in establishing a competitive market pattern in China's manufacturing industry. The monopolistic service trades and naturally monopolistic industries can make use of this experience in their reform. To open the markets, break monopoly and absorb the non-state economic sector for participation in the reform of the infrastructure area with the result that the non-state economic sector replaces the government as the main investor and operator in this sector — this is the main way to speed up the reform and development of China's infrastructure and public utilities sector.

An important task of the reform in this sector is to speed up the diversification of investment subjects. As far as investment and market-oriented reform in the sector are concerned, the government must not and cannot be the sole investment subject in this sector. Practice since 1998 has shown that sole and direct government investment is not the answer to the shortage of funds, still less to the backward state of this sector. Besides the non-governmental capital in its trillions of yuan government investment's contribution to the the GDP growth is limited and unsustainable. Only giving full play to the initiative of non-governmental capital and allowing it to enter the infrastructure and public utilities sector is the fundamental way to address this problem. Therefore, the gradual shift from the government to the non-state economic sectors as the main investment subjects is an important measure to speed up the development of the infrastructure and public utilities sector and the key to keeping its vitality. Speedy realization of such a shift is the fundamental way to resolve the most outstanding of the deep-rooted contradictions in the current reform of the infrastructure and public utilities sector in China and only thus can substantial progress be made in the reform.

At present, advancing the participation of the non-state sectors in the reform of the infrastructure and public utilities sector is of special importance. In the new century, accelerated development of the infrastructure and public utilities will be of vital importance to completing the strategic adjustment of its economic structure and achieving faster economic growth. Practice shows that the non-state economic sectors are equipped with a fairly strong incentive and restraint mechanism, and are the major players in the market economy. Their involvement in the reform of the infrastructure and public utilities sector will not only bring about the finding of new channels and room for their development, and provide China's basic industries with resources and motive forces for development, but will also be beneficial to breaking the long-term monopolies in the telecommunications, civil aviation, railways, electric power and other industries, bringing about an open and competitive situation, and prompting the basic industries to lower costs and improve services, efficiency and international competitiveness. Therefore, we should take the initiative to seize the opportunities and advance the reform in this sector.

III. Taking the initiative to seize the opportunities and advance the participation of the non-state economic sectors in the reform of the infrastructure public unities sector

Conditions are now ripening for China's non-state economic sectors to participate in the reform of the country's infrastructure and public utilities sector. Major progress has been made in the development of the non-state economic sectors over the past two decades and more, and they have come to be a main force in supporting the country's economic growth. With one third of the social resources, it turns out two thirds of the country's GDP, demonstrating considerable vigor. There has been a considerable accumulation of investment potential among the people, with private bank savings exceeding six trillion yuan, ready at any time to release a tremendous investment force. The Constitution of the People's Republic of China has already affirmed the non-state economic sectors as an important component part of the socialist market economy, and the document issued by the 15th CPC National Congress has also recognized its position and role. Such progress signifies that the conditions in terms of policies and institutions for its participation in the reform of the infrastructure and public utilities sector tend to mature. It is a pressing task to formulate specific policies and measures to encourage the non-state sectors to enter the infrastructure and public utilities sector.

Technological progress and institutional innovations have provided the technical conditions for the non-state sectors to participate in the development of the country's infrastructure and public utilities. In the past, the products and services of the infrastructure and public utilities sector used to be basically within the scope of public products. Moreover, the inseparability of the consumer utility of public products, the non-competitive nature of consumption and the non-exclusiveness of benefits made it impossible for the non-state sectors to effectively reap returns on the investment in the infrastructure facilities. That used to be an important root cause for the fact that the government had remained for a long time as the main subject of investment in infrastructure. In addition, the infrastructure and public utilities sector is characterized by natural monopoly in operation and is capital-intensive in terms of investment, which also had become a major barrier to the access of the non-state sectors. Technological innovations have made it possible to introduce a competitive mechanism into the monopolistic industries. Institutional innovations have also made the hitherto unrealizable collection of fees and compensation of benefits possible. Therefore, it is necessary to standardize the government regulations through institutional innovations, thus providing the opportunity and conditions for breaking administrative monopoly, and introduce non-governmental capital into the infrastructure and public utilities sector.

Reform should be accelerated in the infrastructure and putlic utilities sector to remove the institutional barriers hindering the access of the non-state sectors. At present, the main barrier to their access is administrative monopoly, especially the administrative barrier characterized by examination and approval over construction projects, which amounts to a veto power against enterprises intending to enter this sector. Second, the existing organizational system of the infrastructure and public utilities sector serves as an institutional barrier to their entry. Third, channels for financing are not accessible. Chinese banks lack specific divisions and channels for handling loans to non-state enterprises and, with respect to direct financing, there are excessive restrictions on the listing of such enterprises in the capital market. Funding has become one of the bottlenecks impeding the development of the non-state economic sectors. Therefore, it is essential to come up with legislation designed to provide a reliable protection for personal property. This will play a fundamental role in protecting property rights, removing industrial barriers and advancing the reform of the infrastructure and public utilities sector.

IV. It is necessary to adopt a variety of forms to expand the channels for the non-state economic sectors to enter the infrastructure and public utilities sector.

It is necessary to encourage non-governmental capital to enter the infrastructure and public utilities sector through conglomeration, consortiums, pooling of funds and buying shares. At the same time, it is necessary to lower the threshold for its entry by dividing up the projects. Unlike the garments, knitwear, plastics, low-voltage electrical appliances, catering and similar industries, where non-governmental capital can enter and operate on its own from the very start, infrastructure and public utility projects require a large amounts of investment, and present considerable industrial barriers. Moreover, non-governmental capital in China is small in size in most cases, and a single investor alone is not strong enough to enter this sector. Therefore, the form for the non-governmental capital to enter this sector can only be conglomeration, consortiums, pooling of funds and share purchase. Therefore, vigorous measures should be taken to encourage non-governmental capital to enter the infrastructure and public utilities sector by these means. For example, various forms of foundations can be set up to pool scattered non-governmental capital, which is then to be managed by professionals. This will reduce the risks of investment and help rouse the enthusiasm of non-governmental capital for investment. On the other hand, many projects that have both public good and commercial purposes can be divided for separate implementation. For example, railway transportation can be separated from railway construction, with the profit-making transportation part to be handed over to the market players.

Greater attention should be paid to the great role of the securities market in prompting the entry of non-governmental capital into the infrastructure and public utilities sector. The capitalization and marketization level of China's infrastructure facilities is very low. Take the power industry for example. China is the second-largest power supplier in the world, almost equalling the US in the total value of the industry's assets. Its installed generating capacity and output is 270,000 megawatts, four times the US figure. But the listed companies in the US power industry have a market value of 350 billion US dollars, and those of the British power industry, 120 billion US dollars. So far, there are only seven power companies listed in China and overseas, with a combined market value of about 7.2 billion US dollars. China is a "superpower" in terms of the total assets of its power industry, but belongs to the third world in terms of the overall capitalization level. A low capitalization level means an inadequate use of funds on the securities market, resulting in the long-term fixation and low efficiency of the assets in the infrastructure and public utilities sector, limiting its ability to adjust its industrial structure through the capital market.

At present, there are hundreds of listed companies in China, but only some 60 of them have their main lines of business in the infrastructure field. So there is still much room for the infrastructure and public utilities sector to develop by making use of securities. International experience shows that infrastructure has a high long-term investment value thanks to stable market demand, small risks, fairly stable returns and good profit prospects. Moreover, infrastructure enterprises, being large and not easily prone to manipulative stock trading, have a role to play in stabilizing the stock market. In order to combine the development of the securities market with the reform and structural adjustment of the infrastructure and public utilities sector, the government should give priority to the transportation, energy, telecommunications and other so-called "bottleneck" industries in raising funds through shares and bonds, injecting the good-quality assets of public utilities into the arena of listed companies, and building a bridge between the capital market and infrastructure and public utilities sector, so as to invigorate through the capital market the vast amount of existing state assets in the sector, and bring in funds to spur its development.

In terms of the modes of entry into the securities market, the infrastructure and public utilities sector may consider the following options: a) In large cities, the mode of holding controlling shares through investment. Large cities have fairly well developed infrastructure facilities, and a considerable amount of good-quality assets, which may be used as the basis for establishing stock companies; b) In small and medium-sized cities, local listed companies that have poor prospects for development but are eligible for issuing shares may be transformed by injecting into them local good-quality assets of public utilities and adjusting their business structure so that they become the main investors in local public utilities; c) Listed companies with an average prospect for development may be encouraged to invest or guided into investing in the public utilities and other infrastructure facilities that have relatively clear and stable returns on investment, so as to hedge against business risks and bring stable returns to the shareholders.

It is necessary to make full use of BOT (build, operate and transfer). This is an internationally accepted practice in infrastructure construction. With its WTO accession, China will enjoy very good prospect for using the form of BOT to attract foreign and non-governmental capital into its infrastructure construction. An infrastructure project with promising economic returns can attract the participation of non-governmental capital; a less-promising project may also improve its investment return expectancy through good institutional designs, and thus become more attractive to non-governmental capital. As the government employs various forms to improve the rate of return on investment, the key is to address the land requisitioning, project financing, compensation and other problems involved in BOT.

It is necessary to denationalize management right and let non-governmental capital run state capital. There are two ways for non-governmental capital to participate in the infrastructure: capital form and form of management right. The entry of non-governmental capital does not necessarily involve the transfer of state property rights; the denationalisation of management right itself is a very important indication of its participation. There are three alternative forms open to the denationalisation of management right in China's infrastructure and public utilities sector: looking for non-governmental operators and managers; recruiting non-governmental agents in marketing services and infrastructure products through bidding; and inviting bidders for providing logistical and technical support in the infrastructure field.

Different forms may be adopted to attract non-governmental capital in accordance with different types of the infrastructure facilities: a) telecommunications, railways, airports, harbors, urban public transportation and other infrastructure facilities that are both competitive and exclusive may be run with non-governmental capital holding partial shares, or controlling shares or even exclusive shares. Railways in the United States, the Wenzhou Airport in Zhejiang

Province and the Shihu Port at Shishi in Fujian Province were built with private investment; b) in the case of the infrastructure facilities that are not so competitive but strongly exclusive, if they are profitable and private enterprises are inclined to invest, the government should allow non-governmental capital to participate while giving guidance to it, but should not ban it with regard to investment. For example, with regard to toll expressways, bridges and tunnels, the government should restrict monopoly tolls to protect the interests of consumers while restricting vicious competition to ensure reasonable returns for the investors; and c) in the case of purely public products, for example, beacon towers and railways, participation by non-governmental capital is still possible if compulsory collection of fees from users is enforced.

A gradual approach to reform should be combined with the making of breakthroughs at focal links to bring about a fast expansion of the participation by non-governmental capital in infrastructure construction. By a gradual approach is meant gradual relaxation of the restrictions on additional assets in the infrastructure and public utilities sector and attraction of non-governmental investment in the sector as a way to gradually reduce the relative proportion of the state-owned assets and promote the shift in the operators in the sector. By making breakthroughs at focal links is meant reduction of state assets at focal links to make way for non-governmental capital in the case of the existing assets in the infrastructure and public utilities sector. There are three specific ways of doing this: a) selling a portion of state assets through property rights substitution and transfer with the proceeds from sales to be handed to the state treasury; b) distributing a portion of state assets in forms of shares and bonds among employees of SOEs in accordance with their years of service in exchange for their consent to give up their status as employees of SOEs and as compensation for the low wage system that was the practice in the past. This is done by combining the reform of the proprietary system with that of the labor system and the social security system, so as to thoroughly do away with the "iron rice bowl" practice (i.e, lifetime employment); c) commissioning a portion of the existing state assets for authorized management. Authorized management of assets is different from contractual management or leasing, but a "revolution in management right" in the sense that management right is denationalized by transferring it to the market. At present, it is necessary to combine the gradual approach to reform with the making of breakthroughs at focal links, that is, combining the reform in the case of additional assets with invigorating and reorganizing the existing assets in an organic way, in an effort to effect a fast expansion of the participation by non-governmental capital in infrastructure construction.

RECONSTRUCTING THE GOVERNMENT REGULATORY AND SUPERVISORY SYSTEM SO THAT IT PROPERLY MATCHES AN OPEN ECONOMY

(January 2002)

Effective government regulation and supervision is the precondition and basis for ensuring effective competition in the infrastructure and public utilities sector. In a given sense, a new-type government regulatory and supervisory system that properly matches the socialist market economy, an open economy, is an important indicator of a mature socialist market economy. Judging by the reform so far in the telecommunications, electric power, civil aviation and other industries, the reform of the infrastructure and public utilities sector in China still focuses on the separation of government functions from enterprise management, as well as other basic issues, such as creating a competitive situation by ending the original state monopolies through break-ups and reorganization. Once competition is introduced, how to maintain the competitive environment and standardize competition in accordance with the law, how to adjust the functions and methods of the government regulatory and supervisory agencies in keeping with the needs of a competitive market, and how to regulate the naturally monopolistic links in accordance with the law in order to prevent an abuse of market power — these issues all call for further in-depth discussion.

I. Government regulation should aim at protecting effective competition.

China has made major progress by introducing competition into some sectors which used to be regarded as being naturally monopolistic. The outstanding contradiction remaining to be resolved is limited competition in some business operations of certain industries that are naturally monopolistic. Because of their obvious economy of scale, direct and excessive competition will lead to waste, low efficiency and other negative consequences. Included are power grids, information networks, water supply networks, railway networks and other physical network economies. But this does not mean that competition cannot be introduced into these fields. Competition introduced into them is competition for share of markets. Once the main producer is selected through an auctioning mechanism, competition pressure from potential entrants into the market and the strong restraining mechanism over the behavior of the current market supplier will propel the current producer/supplier to improve his/its performance, the reputation of the enterprise and competitiveness.

Government regulation and supervision are the precondition and basis for ensuring effective competition in the naturally monopolistic economic sectors. When the government decides to carry out market-oriented reforms in those SOEs that have a very strong capacity for monopolizing the market and introduce a competitive mechanism, the conflict between the interests of the enterprises and the society as a whole is very obvious. In order to protect the interests of consumers and prevent the monopolies from making use of their monopolistic power to obtain market power from other sectors, the government should design an appropriate regulatory and supervisory mechanism, and adopt proper policies to hold in check the monopolistic force of these enterprises. For example, it is necessary to reinforce the existing and potential forces for competition by eliminating barriers or adjusting the structure of the monopolistic market; and break the monopoly of information by enterprises, obtain information on cost reduction potential and enforce price controls.

II. It is necessary to define the basic regulatory and supervisory functions of the government in the infrastructure and public utilities sector under the market economy.

Under the government regulatory and supervisory system, featuring the separation of government functions and enterprise management, the enterprises take the maximization of profits as their business objectives. However, since many lines of business in the infrastructure and public utilities sector are natural monopolies, these enterprises are thus able to set monopoly prices and provide below-standard services. This requires the government to take necessary regulatory measures to standardize the market behavior of the enterprises. Within the government regulatory and supervisory mechanism with government functions separated from enterprise management, the regulatory and supervisory functions of the government mainly cover the following aspects:

1. The formulation of government rules and regulations on the subject. The government should formulate rules and regulations concerning the establishment of government regulatory and supervisory agencies, division of their functions and powers, and major adjustments to the market structure, in accordance with the technical and economic features of specific trades in the infrastructure and public utilities sector. Such rules and regulations should be drafted by the legislative affairs office of the government and fix a basic framework for the new government regulatory and supervisory system, constituting in fact a program for reforming the government regulatory and supervisory system.

2. Issuing and revising enterprise business licences. The specialized government regulatory and supervisory agencies for various infrastructure trades may be authorized to issue and revise enterprise business licences, which should contain details specifying the obligations of the enterprises concerned and business standards with regard

to prices, services and fair trade. At the same time, the government regulatory and supervisory agencies should make partial revisions to the business licences in response to the developments of individual trades and changes in supply and demand.

3. Controlling prices and supervising over their implementation. Price control over infrastructure trades is an important part of the government regulation and supervision tasks. The government should set controlling price ceilings in view of costs, technological progress and potential for improving production efficiency in specific infrastructure industries, and make periodic adjustments, so as to spur enterprises to improving production efficiency.

4. Exercising control over market access. An important objective of reforming the government regulatory and supervisory system in the infrastructure and public utilities sector is the promotion of competition and bringing the competitive mechanism into play, which requires permission for new enterprises to enter the sector. On the other hand, the infrastructure trades have fairly obvious economies of scale or scope, which necessitates control over the number of enterprises entering these industries, in order to avoid excessive competition. This requires the government to exercise control over market access. Such control is in essence control of the number of licences to be issued and the spacing of their issuance.

III. Early establishment of independent and specialized regulatory and supervisory agencies is the precondition for maintaining the mechanism for fair competition among equals in the infrastructure and public utilities sector.

As administrative enforcement agencies, administrative regulatory and supervisory organizations should represent the public interest, that is, take an impartial stand, as free as possible from interference by any interest group. Any public policy they formulate must reflect the interests of all relevant interest groups as far as possible. In order to ensure their impartiality, it is essential to establish independent and specialized regulatory and supervisory agencies to perform the new government regulatory and supervisory functions in the electric power, telecommunications, gas, aviation and other infrastructure trades while abolishing the government regulatory and supervisory system that integrated government functions with enterprise management. Only thus will it be able to truly ensure a separation of government functions and enterprise management in the government regulatory and supervisory system in the infrastructure and public utilities sector.

IV. It is necessary to advance the reform of the regulatory and supervisory system in China's infrastructure and public utilities sector, taking the establishment of independent regulatory and supervisory agencies as the objective.

The government should reform the original control mode in which ministries and commissions exercised regulatory functions, and establish independent regulatory and supervisory agencies at an early date, in order to address the mixing of government functions with enterprise management or government-enterprise alliance in China's control system in the infrastructure and public utilities sector. Due to the fact that the infrastructure trades are highly specialized, China should establish leanly-staffed but highly efficient specialized control agencies separately in these trades. In view of the fact that new control agencies need extra staff while the original ministries and commissions under the State Council will have surplus staff because of fewer functions, the new, independent agencies may recruit personnel who have both technical knowledge and managerial expertise from the administrative departments of the infrastructure sector. At the same time, as government control invariably involves economic, political, technological and legal issues, it follows that the government should recruit an appropriate number of experts from non-governmental quarters to participate in government control, so that specialized control agencies are made up of managerial experts from the industries concerned, technological experts, economists and jurists. The following lines of thinking are suggested for the establishment of the regulatory and supervisory agencies in particular trades in view of the progress that various infrastructure trades have made in the ownership transformation:

1. It is proposed that in the telecommunications industry a telecommunications control bureau be formed, which enjoys legal status, is made up of technological and managerial experts in the telecommunications industry, economists and jurists, and placed directly under the State Council. The original control agencies in cities and counties will, after the separation of government functions from enterprise management, form part of the national vertical control network under the telecommunications control bureau, which should exercise fair and efficient control over telecommunications across the land. And as conditions become ripe, the Ministry of Information Industry shall be gradually abolished.

2. Effective control over the power industry also necessitates the establishment of an independent control agency separate from the government. It may be called the Electric Power Control Bureau, as a public institution enjoying the status of a legal entity. It can be established by the State Council, and be subject to state supervision.

3. The railways industry at present has not truly separated government functions from enterprise management, making it difficult to exercise effective control, so there is a *de facto* absence of a regulator. Therefore, it is proposed that an independent control agency — the State Railways Regulatory and Supervisory Bureau — be established to exercise the regulatory functions.

4. The civil aviation industry has initially separated government

functions from enterprise management, with the General Administration of Civil Aviation and local bureaus in fact discharging the functions of regulators of the industry. The key tasks at present are: a) to determine the legal status of the civil aviation bureaus as regulators of the industry; b) to reform the existing civil aviation management system by drawing on the experience of independent control agencies in other countries, with the aim of becoming truly independent civil aviation regulatory and supervisory agencies that have achieved complete separation of government functions and enterprise management.

V. It is necessary to prevent the regulators from forming a government-enterprise alliance in reforming the government regulatory and supervisory system that mixed government functions and enterprise management.

The core content of the government regulatory and supervisory system is the relationship between the government and enterprises. Therefore, the key to reforming the system is to adjust this relationship. China's infrastructure trades traditionally practiced a regulatory and supervisory system that was typical of the integration of government functions and enterprise management. Since the reform and opening up, some trades have begun to implement a regulatory and supervisory system reform featuring the separation of government functions and enterprise management, in order to introduce competition. In this process, the former government administrative departments (various ministries and commissions) have gone through a gradual transition from being owners, regulators and managers to being market regulators charged with the functions of trade regulation and market access management. What was most conspicuous about the past practice of ministries and commissions serving as regulators was the fact that the administrative regulators were competent government departments administering relevant industries or even original proprietors of enterprises. Owing to the lack of a market for supervising regulators in China, the selection of regulators is divorced from an open voting mechanism, so that the regulators need not go after the maximization of votes, but pursue almost an identical objective as that of the enterprises, that is, maximization of departmental interests. Therefore, when they formulate policies, they are prone to lean toward the enterprise groups they used to administer. Such a natural alliance of interests on the basis of the father-son relationship between the regulators and enterprises has a negative impact of fatal proportions on the establishment of government control and its effects. First, a regulator that is both an administrative department and administrator of the industry concerned cannot possibly take an impartial stand by treating all market participants as equals, and newcomers to the market and non-state enterprises are highly vulnerable to discrimination. Second, once such a government-enterprise alliance is formed, it is entirely possible that the consumer interest groups and the enterprise groups that have just gained access to the market are cold-shouldered, and their legitimate rights and interests disregarded in the course of enacting and enforcing laws. Third, since the current political and legal system is not yet in a position to break such an alliance, the regulators, in misusing their administrative powers, will also reduce the efficiency of resource allocation in the trades under their control.

VI. We must bring the initiative of both the central and local authorities into play within a rational plan.

An important part of the effort to apportion the functions and limits of powers is to strictly apportion investment rights. As China's market economy becomes daily mature and the fundamental role of the market in resource allocation takes on an increasingly bigger share, there is an objective demand for dividing the areas of government investment from those to be determined by market forces. However, the reality now is that, on the one hand, there is no scientific and legal division of scope for investment by the central and local authorities; and on the other, the decision-making and management powers of the central and local authorities with regard to investment are not bound by rigorous legal responsibility either. For a long time, a growing diversity of sources of investment has resulted in a complexity of investment management and, in particular, multi-channel, scattered government management of investment, which is an important factor behind redundant construction projects. At the same time, time-consuming examination and approval procedures for infrastructure construction projects, low efficiency, loss of markets and missing of opportunities as a result of poorly defined functions and powers are all problems that should not be overlooked. It must be fully recognized that intensified investment is an important government fiscal action, and also the investment action of enterprises and society in general, bearing on the development and expansion of the investment and factors of production markets. Here government action has an important exemplary role. The shift from a unitary government investor to multiple investors in government, enterprises and other quarters of society in no circumstances means a relaxation of efforts to study and define the limits of government powers to invest. Along with the progress in the reform of the financing system, investment policies covering investment by the state, localities, various parts of society and foreign investment have gradually been put into practice, and many large projects have been constructed which would have been impossible or could not have been done well in the past. This provides the task of clearly defining functions and powers in view of new historical conditions, and a broader and more profound background.

The state can exercise effective indirect control over infrastructure enterprises by holding controlling shares or non-controlling shares. It should consider formulating a special law or decree on the state (including the central and local governments) holding controlling and non-controlling shares, in accordance with which the government holds shares in management organizations, influencing infrastructure enterprises mainly through the operations of the supervisory boards and examination of enterprises' long-term plans. At the same time, auditing departments should also have a part in the supervisory indirect management of the infrastructure enterprises in which the government holds shares. In Germany, the government treats enterprises with government investment differently in accordance with their different tasks, participating in the management of the freely competitive infrastructure enterprises in accordance with the ratio of government shares in them. All large infrastructure enterprises with government investment are profit-oriented, and their boards of directors wield a considerable decision-making power. In addition, the German federal government applies regulatory and preferential measures to infrastructure enterprises that have special tasks. Such enterprises generally make up a big proportion of the infrastructure enterprises, and their charters and business rules take the fulfilment of the state tasks as their objective; they can go after profits only within the limits permitted by the objective. If losses are incurred from discharging federal tasks, the government must bear them in accordance with the law. In order to reduce the burdens resulting from such tasks, the law also provides that enterprises in this category are eligible for certain preferential tax treatment.

It is necessary to use "golden shares" in a correct way. In a system featuring the separation of government functions and enterprise management, infrastructure enterprises will have decision-making power in production and management, taking the maximization of their interests as the objective. At the same time, many infrastructure trades and business areas are naturally monopolistic, allowing only one or a tiny number of enterprises to operate. This gives rise to the possibility of distorting social distribution efficiency, that is, it makes it possible for these enterprises to use their market monopoly to seek monopoly profits by setting monopoly prices and lowering standards of services. This requires the government to take necessary control measures to standardize their actions. The main British practices in this respect are: a) to formulate relevant laws and regulations; b) to issue and revise enterprise business licences; c) to draw up price control policies and supervise their implementation; and d) to control market access and exit by enterprises. From this it can be seen that after the establishment of a government control system featuring the separation of government functions and enterprise management in the infrastructure sector, the government does not practice a laisser-faire policy toward these enterprises, but exercises indirect control over the main business activities of them through redefining the new control functions of the government. At the same time, the British, French and other governments in practice use "golden shares" to exercise effective control over infrastructure enterprises to safeguard the national interest. By "golden shares," it is not meant physical shares but mainly the government's veto power over the major decisions of these enterprises. France instituted the "golden shares" mechanism in the course of privatizing its state-owned infrastructure enterprises with a view to protecting the national interest, and retained the relevant stipulations on this mechanism in its privatization act of 1993. Thanks to its high degree of caution, this practice of protecting the national interest through the use of "golden shares" as the "veto power" can ensure that enterprises in the infrastructure and basic industries can be transformed into corporations in a standardized way in circumstances under which state-owned infrastructure enterprises make up a heavy proportion and their structure is complicated.

It is necessary to make overall plans. As the successful experience of developed market economy countries shows, expansion of investment in the infrastructure calls for making unified plans. Take the transportation industry for example. National or interregional railway trunk lines, main national highway routes, major national ports, major inland waterways, national gateway airports and air traffic control systems and equipment should be funded mainly by the central government or, when necessary, jointly with local authorities. Sea coasts and air space are national resources, and projects for constructing harbors of 10,000t-ton-class ships or above and thus using areas of coastline should be approved by both the central and provincial (autonomous regions and municipalities directly under the central government) governments, and the use of air space in the construction of civil airports should be approved by the central government. In accordance with overall national plans, departments, industries and localities are to be encouraged to invest in the construction of railways, highways and docks; foreign businesses are to be encouraged to invest in the production of railway transportation facilities, highway and harbor machinery and equipment or, in joint ventures, cooperation and other forms, to participate in the construction and operation of local railways and their auxiliary facilities, highways, independent bridges and tunnels, harbor facilities and civil airports. Under the prerequisite that the state controls the overall transportation price level, transportation enterprises are to be allowed to set differential and floating transportation prices in accordance with standards of service, seasonal changes, and changes in the market demand.

VII. It is necessary to build and improve a legal system concerning competition and control, and enhance the standards and efficiency of government control on the basis of such a legal system.

As the experience of developed countries in reforming government control of the infrastructure industries shows, this reform should be led by legislation and carried out in accordance with legal procedures, and government control is exercised on the basis of the legal system. The reform of the government control system in China's infrastructure and public utilities sector has followed the tradition of "reform first and legislation later." Due to a serious delay in the administrative control legal system, although some results have been achieved in the reform of certain areas, such as civil aviation and telecommunications, many problems have cropped up in the absence of an overall legal framework, such as the mixing up of government functions with enterprise management, wrangling among departments, chaos in the market, redundant construction projects, low economic returns of projects and serious losses and waste. Even if laws on relevant industries were published, they had been drawn up by the competent departments administering these industries and therefore have limitations. More importantly, the laws and regulations that have been in force do not provide for the establishment of specialized law enforcement agencies that are clearly defined, unified and authoritative for implementing these laws and regulations, but instead have handed the unified law enforcement over to some existing state administrative departments, which, to make matters even worse, have overlapping functions, thus inevitably leading to poorly defined responsibilities and powers among management departments, inconsistency in enforcement, shirking of responsibilities among departments and laxness in law enforcement.

China should speed up legislation concerning the infrastructure and public utilities sector in order to adapt to the needs of the socialist market economy, address the problems existing in the current reform in this sector and improve control efficiency. High on the legislative agenda should be the "Telecommunications Law of China" and the "Civil Aviation Law of China." At the same time, the "Electric Power Law" and the "Railway Law" should be revised. These laws should be formulated or revised by the National People's Congress jointly with the relevant departments in accordance with the different technical and economic features of the different infrastructure trades in combination with the current government control system and its reform objectives, before they are promulgated by the National People's Congress for implementation. The main content of the laws and regulations on government control over the infrastructure and public utilities sector should include setting the objectives and procedures of reform, designating specialized law enforcement agencies with clearly defined functions and powers, defining the specific content of enterprise licences, and the responsibilities, rights and interests of enterprises, major policies concerning prices, standards of services, terms of market access, and other issues.

In order to maintain the integrity of the independent law enforcement agencies and respond to public opinion, it is advisable to consider establishing organizations like consumers' associations in the related infrastructure trades. The framework of government control over the infrastructure and public utilities sector should be legislation on government control, the specialized and independent regulatory and supervisory agencies that are established in accordance with the law should enforce the relevant laws and regulations in accordance with law, and consumers' associations for their part should exercise social supervision over the regulatory and supervisory agencies.

It should be noted that the enactment and enforcement of the "Anti-Monopoly Law" after China's accession to the WTO will be of exceptionally important significance. The main thrust of the current anti-monopoly reform in the infrastructure and public utilities sector is to break state monopoly and introduce market competition. In the reform and reorganization of the monopolies, market monopoly forces (such as China Telecom in the telecommunications industry) may come into being, and it is necessary to avoid the replacement of the original state monopoly by market monopoly. With China's WTO accession, the entry of transnational corporations and their competition from a position of strength may also lead to new market monopoly. Market monopoly can be overcome only by making relevant laws. On the other hand, with China's WTO accession and the deepening of reform, changes will take place in the ownership structure, and the entry of foreign investment and the observation of WTO rules will make it highly necessary and urgent to formulate laws that are compatible with international rules and aim to standardize the order of competition. The making of the "Anti-Monopoly Law" and other related laws should take such circumstances into full consideration and be speeded up.

THE ENTREPRENEURSHIP SYSTEM AND ESOP IN THE NEW STAGE OF REFORM

THE ENTREPRENEURSHIP SYSTEM AND ESOP IN THE NEW STAGE OF REFORM

CHINA'S WTO ACCESSION AND INNOVATIONS IN THE ENTERPRISE SYSTEM

(February 2002)

From a long-term and overall point of view, China's WTO accession is in essence a matter of reform and innovation. Two years ago, I termed it as signifying the country's second round of reform and opening up, and as ushering in a situation in which the opening up promotes reform.

First, the WTO accession will bring changes to the process of the market-oriented reform. In accordance with the country's original schedule, China was to have built a fairly rounded socialist market economy by around 2010. Judging by the actual developments surrounding the WTO accession, this time frame will be shortened. In other words, China will take a more substantial step within the next five years in building a socialist market economy. There are two basic assessments: One is that, as described in the "Tenth Five-Year Plan," China has initially built a socialist market economy; the other is that China has initially built the basic framework of the socialist market economy. In my view, the use of the "basic framework" is more objective and more accurate, because reform has not yet made substantial progress in many aspects, and in some aspects stagnation has set in. In such circumstances, we will meet far greater difficulties than in the past now that we are to fulfil within five years what had been planned for ten years.

Second, the WTO accession will bring a change to the motive

force for the reform. The reform so far has been proceeding in keeping with the country's plan based on the domestic needs. From now on it will derive its main motive force from the opening up. It will become far more transparent and its criteria will be dovetailed to internationally accepted practices and the WTO rules. China's socialist market economy will link up with the modern global market economy. Therefore, the motive force for the reform is not only internal but also external.

Third, the WTO accession will bring new features to the reform. Reform in the next stage will show the features of structural reform. Two years ago, I called for "shifting from basic reforms to structural reforms." For example, the focus of the rural reform in the new century is on the relations between town and country. If urban and rural reforms are not coordinated, rural reform will, to a great extent, find it difficult to move forward. Another example is the lack of coordination between enterprise reform and government reform, and between the reforms at the micro and macro levels, which is the root cause for the failure to separate government functions from enterprise management despite efforts over many years. Therefore, viewed from whatever angle, future reforms are not reforms of any individual systems but an institutional issue, a structural readjustment coupled with structural reform. Such a structural reform will become a very important hallmark of reform in the future.

To enterprises, the WTO accession means competition in terms of products and trades. But it should also be seen, from a long-term and overall point of view, that it also means an issue involving reform.

I. Reform of the Property Rights System and Innovation of the Enterprise System

1. Socialization of the subjects of property rights. The most important foundation of the socialist market economy is the realization of the socialization of property rights subjects. What was wrong with China's traditional planned economy was the unitary subject of property rights resulting from the serious shortage of property rights subjects. While shortage of goods was the main manifestation of the planned economy, the unitary proprietary system and the shortage of property rights were the institutional causes of this manifestation. Reform over the past two decades and more has resulted in a certain progress in socialising owners of property rights. However, the limited progress in SOE reform over the past few years has, in most cases, been directly linked to the lagging behind of the reform in property rights, because the reform of the proprietary system is closely linked with innovation in the enterprise system.

First, against the background of China's WTO entry, enterprises need to handle their relations with the government in an appropriate manner. How to display the role of the government while preventing it from overstepping its powers or failing to perform its functions — the fundamental issue is how to address the relations of property rights. Overstepping of powers or assumption of wrong roles on the part of the government can hardly be avoided if the unitary state ownership and the practice of the state holding absolute control of shares linger on in some competitive trades for a long time to come. Second, with an irrational structure of property rights, an effective corporate governance structure can hardly take shape.

2. The reform of the property rights system and scientific and effective government administration of state assets. In recent years the government has stepped up the management of state assets only to show a tendency of adding more levels of management, so much so that it has interfered with the decision-making power of enterprises by acting as their real controller. If this problem is not properly resolved it will lead to a situation in which the government will keep expanding its scope of management, issuing more and more arbitrary orders, while the decision-making power of enterprises will be more and more severely restricted. In such circumstances, enterprises will encounter numerous obstacles if they wish to develop through competition in the fast-changing markets. In fact, the state assets management system calls for reform, first by changing from the one-level ownership by the State Council to multi-level ownership, and second, to authorize enterprises or entrepreneurs to manage state assets. The state assets management agencies should cease to meddle in the specific management of assets by enterprises.

3. Reform of the property rights system and development of medium and small SOEs. Medium-sized and small SOEs have developed faster in some areas than in others in recent years, due to the reversals in the reform of the property rights system. Reform in this respect has been criticized as privatization or a drain on state assets. Despite many discussions on this subject in recent years, such efforts have become very difficult whenever the reform of the property rights system was brought up. Some authorities would rather see enterprises lose money than allow them to carry out reform in this respect. Therefore, the delayed reform of medium-sized and small SOEs in some places and trades is directly related to the delay in the reform of the property rights system.

II. Realization of the Valuc of Entrepreneurs and Institutional Innovation of SOEs

1. Entrepreneurs becoming real owners of enterprises is a general trend of development of the modern enterprise system. Discussions on corporate governance structure and the practice of the developed countries in particular have brought up the issue of insider control stemming from the separation of ownership from management power. This issue was first raised in the US during the 1970s and 1980s. The separation of ownership from management power led to the emergence of agents and insider control, hence the need for a corporate governance structure. However, in the 1990s the CEO gradually became owner of a portion of an enterprise's property rights. Some people have described this as a return to the state of classical enterprises, while others have called it an expression of post-modern enterprises. An entrepreneur has become an owner of an enterprise not because he is an entrepreneur but more because he is playing an ever more important role in the development of the enterprise, and its development needs have required him to become one of its owners. This has given rise to changes in the corporate governance structure, with the main responsibility of the board of directors being to select a proper CEO for the enterprise, and turn him into one of its owners. When the entrepreneur becomes an owner, a great change takes place in the corporate governance structure, which is no longer based on the separation of ownership and management power, but practises a combination of the two in him under the prerequisite of recognizing his role. Some people have referred to such an enterprise as a post-modern enterprise.

I have said that an entrepreneur without property rights is not a modern entrepreneur, nor is an entrepreneur without full decision-making power in management an entrepreneur in the true sense. This is a very important issue. Entrepreneurs becoming owners of enterprises is a requirement for developing enterprises and a general trend of development of modern enterprises.

2. How are we to appraise pioneering entrepreneurs? Entrepreneurs of a pioneering type are those who have made major contributions to the survival and growth of their enterprises at their start-up and take-off stages. A group of commendable pioneering entrepreneurs have emerged from the reform and opening-up process over the past two decades and more. I issued an appeal to "save the pioneering entrepreneurs" at a seminar on the value of Chinese entrepreneurs held in August last year in the Great Hall of the People, in Beijing. My address at the seminar dealt with the following points:

First, these entrepreneurs are valuable assets of enterprises for development, linked as they are to their very survival and development, the corporate culture and governance structure. They have a bearing on the image, development and reputation of their enterprises.

Second, there is a general failure in real life to build a community of interests between these pioneering entrepreneurs and their enterprises. The "Chu Shijian case" is a typical case. (Chu, as board chairman and president, had built a small local SOE into a nationally known tobacco company in Yunnan Province, but was later sentenced to life imprisonment for embezzling a large amount of money. One view emerging from the discussions surrounding his case is that had he been adequately rewarded for his contributions to the enterprise under a rational entrepreneurship system, he might not have been tempted to steal from the company.) His downfall is attributable to personal reasons, but is also a tragedy caused by an institutional flaw. The modern enterprise system cannot allow more entrepreneurs to repeat Chu Shijian's tragic case. I have met with many pioneering entrepreneurs, one of whom is Wang Guangxing, president of the Yeshu Group in Hainan Province. Without him, the group could not have grown from a workshop with net capital of less than 20,000 yuan into a big company worth several hundred million yuan. He identifies his worth and ambition with the group. He attempted to weave himself, his employees and the senior managerial staff of the enterprise into a community of interests by changing the enterprise's property rights, in the hope of laying an institutional foundation for long-term, sustained development. The reason why it has lagged behind in its competition with the Wahaha Group and the Robust Group in recent years is its unitary state ownership.

Third, it is essential to recognize and realize the value of pioneering entrepreneurs. Last year, the Workers Congress of the Shuangxing Group in Shandong Province made two decisions concerning Wang Hai, president of the group, demonstrating the employees' care and consideration for a pioneering entrepreneur like him. An auditor commissioned to determine Wang Hai's contributions found that they were worth one billion yuan.

In a modern market economy, the role of entrepreneurs has become ever more important, and for them to become owners of enterprises is an inevitable trend of development and an important foundation of the modern corporate governance structure. This issue is crying out to be studied by relevant government departments.

3. Giving incentives to pioneering entrepreneurs in the form of shares will play a very good exemplary role in the interest of enterprise development and the emergence of more outstanding entrepreneurs.

III. Reform of the Enterprise Income Distribution System and Renovation of the Enterprise System

1. The income distribution reform has a growing role in renovating the enterprise system. The development of modern enterprises has shifted its focus from seeking ordinary capital to seeking human capital. Especially against the WTO background, this issue has grown in gravity and urgency.

2. An enterprise's community of interests is closely linked with its income distribution system.

3. Corporate culture is inseparable from interest distribution mechanism. Only a good and effective interest distribution mechanism can nurture a good and cohesive corporate culture, and turn corporate culture into part of the enterprise system, so that there are both soft and rigid restraints. Microsoft's Bill Gates has declared that he has never doubted his employees' loyalty to his company. At least 80 percent of Microsoft employees hold shares in the company in proportion to their contributions, shaping up a distinctive Microsoft corporate culture based on the company's employee stock ownership plan (ESOP).

In 1994 I set forth my views on property rights of labor power and ESOP. This was something quite new in China at that time. In the socialist market economy, do the employees have the right to distribute the surplus profits of an enterprise beyond their wages and bonuses? In 1952, China's state assets, converted from confiscated bureaucrat capital, stood at 20 billion yuan. Now they have reached several trillion yuan. Farmers have contributed part of the growth through the "scissors prices," but most has come from contributions made by the employees of the SOEs. Now people have pooled money for ESOP but have still been dismissed in the course of "privatisation." In contrast, France has provided that an enterprise hiring more than 100 employees is obliged to practice what is called a shared economy, with a set proportion of surplus product to be distributed among them. In the United States, 11 percent of enterprises practice ESOP by which employees do not have to pay any money, while the enterprises apply for low-interest bank loans. At the same time, ESOP is free from interest tax. In Britain, a shared economy has existed for several dozen years. In China, under the socialist market economy, employees of SOEs start ESOP by buying a portion of shares with their own money, while another portion of shares is distributed free. Yet this is still condemned as a drain on state assets — does this not call for deep thought?

Therefore, reform of the enterprise income distribution system is manifold, the most important aspect being the reform of the property rights system. Last year, I advanced the term "people's market economy." The essence of the socialist market economy is a combination of the general public as the beneficiaries of interests with the market competition mechanism. Without a successful solution to the relations of property rights, our market economy may not be necessarily a good market economy. What distinguishes a good from a bad market economy is who the beneficiary of interests is. A good market economy with vitality and sustainability is one that can organically combine the general public as the beneficiaries of interests with the market mechanism.

Reform of the enterprise property rights system has developed to the extent where such a structural reform based on the reform of the property rights system will inevitably and inextricably involve macroeconomic reform and reform of the government system. Only thus will it be able to find good ways to address the series of contradictions and difficulties following China's WTO accession and form a good institutional foundation for economic and social development.

Therefore, in discussing the competitiveness of enterprises against the WTO background, what is most important is to address the issue of institutional innovation, identify the general trend and special features of China's reform against this background, and willingly and with initiative tackle various contradictions and problems. Only by following this guiding principle can we find a way out suited to the development of enterprises.

INNOVATIONS IN THE ENTREPRENEURSHIP SYSTEM IN THE NEW STAGE OF CHINA'S REFORM

(January 2003)

In discussing innovations in the entrepreneurship system it is important to start off by making two basic assessments: First, are there entrepreneurs in China? It should be said that the reform and opening up over the past two decades and more have given rise to quite a few entrepreneurs, especially of the pioneering type, who have made great contributions to the reform and development of their enterprises. Second, has an entrepreneurship system been established in the country? It should be said that so far there is not yet an entrepreneurship system suited to the market economy. That is a major flaw in the reform and opening up over the past two decades and more. There are entrepreneurs, but there is no entrepreneurship system — this is a sharp contrast. Two conclusions can be drawn from this: (1) Due to a lack of an institutional environment as a guarantee, the formation of Chinese entrepreneurs as a group has been slow, and they are limited in number; (2) the environment in which entrepreneurs are nurtured is complicated and in an unstable state. In such special circumstances, the innovation of the entrepreneurship system that we are urging refers mainly to a shift from the cadre management system of enterprises in the traditional planned economy to a modern entrepreneurship system. This institutional shift is closely related to the new stage of the reform.

The WTO accession is an important indicator marking the entry of China's reform into a new stage. This new stage has three salient features: (1) Reform by opening up. A dual motive force for the reform — international and domestic — is already in place. Just as the report to the 16th CPC National Congress said, "We should... accelerate reform and development by opening up." (2) Government reform as the focal point. To make and implement rules and link up with the world economy is first of all the business of the government. The aim of taking the government reform as the focal point is to separate it strictly from the enterprises, so that it takes care of its own business. (3) Structural reform as the main difficulty in the new stage of the reform. China has initially completed the reform in the basic areas over the past 20 years and more, such as allocation of resources through the market. However, various structural reforms focusing on readjusting basic relations of interests are far from being complete, and some of them have not yet carried out in depth. This involves the question of pushing forward the economic restructuring as a whole, the contradiction between the economic restructuring and macroeconomic policies, and the relations between the economic and political restructuring. It should be seen that, while the reform has made major progress in the past two decades and more, it has seriously lagged behind in three areas: the reform of the property rights system, the reform of the income distribution system, and political restructuring.

At present, the reform has entered the stage to tackle the hard issues characterized by readjusting the major relations of interests. The new stage of reform can create an institutional and social environment favorable to the establishment of the entrepreneurship system and materialization of the value of entrepreneurs. The report to the 16th CPC National Congress put forth many new and important viewpoints, which will serve as important guidelines for the reform in the new stage. Take the materialization of the value of entrepreneurs for example. The report called for "unleashing all the vitality contained in work, knowledge, technology, management and capital, and giving full play to all sources of social wealth for the benefit of the people." It went on to lay down the principle that work, capital, technology, managerial expertise and other factors of production should participate in the distribution of income. This important principle marks a historic breakthrough as far as its significance for the materialization of the value of entrepreneurs is concerned.

I. The Pressing Situation Regarding the Innovation of the Entrepreneurship System in the New Stage of Reform

The pioneering entrepreneurs who have come to the fore since the reform and opening-up program began are outstanding representatives of Chinese entrepreneurs. Practice shows that they are the chief representatives of the common interests of their enterprises, promoters of enterprise system innovations and cultivators of corporate culture. Their own practice has proved their value as entrepreneurs. However, due to the lack of institutional guarantees for entrepreneurs, something has gone wrong with a number of pioneering entrepreneurs one after another, even widely influential ones. We have seen the "Chu Shijian case" of the Hongta Group in Yunnan a few years ago and the "Lao Derong case" of the Shenzhen Energy Co., and the "Li Jingwei case" of the Jianlibao Group of Guangdong Province a few months ago. Ms. Lao Derong was among the first national selection of 33 pioneering entrepreneurs announced at a get-together held in Guangzhou last year for entrepreneurs across the country. The audience was deeply touched as she related the difficulties she had encountered at the meeting. Then half a year later I learned of her removal from her post as head of the group. The "Li Jingwei case" also happened at about the same time. The "Chu Shijian case" jolted entrepreneurs nationwide a few years ago, triggering discussions and whisperings of all sorts. Such instances have increased steadily. What does this show?

I do not deny that there are irregularities of all kinds or even illegal practices in specific operations involving apportioning shares to managers. I think the real intention of most entrepreneurs in experimenting with the system of enterprise managers holding shares was to explore and establish a standardized entrepreneurship system. Its essence is how to enable entrepreneurs to form a long-term and direct community of interests with their enterprises in the course of the enterprises' growth so that the entrepreneurs will have their value materialized and become real representatives of the common interests of their enterprises, innovators of the enterprise system and cultivators of corporate culture. Now, many of them are making every effort to win understanding and support from the government and society at large. In the case of Wang Hai, president of the Shuangxing Group of Qingdao, although some assessors have given a very high appraisal of his contributions to his enterprise, and the Workers' Congress has decided to make him its lifetime president, I think what he really wants is the establishment of the entrepreneurship system so that his value as an entrepreneur can be materialized. These examples show us how important and urgent it is to establish the entrepreneurship system looming behind the so-called "age-59 phenomenon" (referring to the occurrence of embezzlement cases among some SOE managers nearing retirement age presumably because they have not been adequately paid in the absence of an entrepreneurship system).

On November 18 last year, the China Federation of Enterprises and the Japanese Economic Federation jointly held a seminar on industry in China and Japan in Suzhou, attended by the board chairmen of Toyota and Matsushita of Japan. Toyota chairman Mr. Hiroshi Okuda is the head of the Japan Federation, and nicknamed the "emperor" of Japanese industry. His success story from being an ordinary Toyota employee 40 years ago to being its boss today and other similar international cases merit our attention. Since the reform and opening-up program was launched in China more than 20 years ago, Chinese pioneering entrepreneurs have worked hard for their enterprises for a dozen or even two dozen years, yet cases of "age-59 phenomenon" have kept surfacing from their midst. Leaving aside their personal factors, such phenomena cannot but testify to the serious delay in the establishment of the entrepreneurship system in the country. At present, enterprise reform and development need more entrepreneurs. It is a fact that they are a rare asset that China lacks. But without an early innovation of the entrepreneurship system, it will be very difficult to form and expand the ranks of entrepreneurs, who will, in the course of innovating the entrepreneurship system, face some problems at the policy, institutional and legal levels.

At present, a grim and urgent reality is that if the establishment of the entrepreneurship system is not resolved quickly, then the consequences will be: (1) it will be difficult to advance the reform of the SOEs. In order to really solve the problems of the SOEs, one of the solutions, to say the least, is to materialize the value of entrepreneurs. (2) After China accedes to the WTO, enterprises will hardly be able to retain managerial professionals. This will be even truer of the SOEs and those enterprises where the state holds controlling shares. (3) Efforts to sustain economic growth will be adversely affected. China will have to keep an annual GDP growth rate of at least 7.08 percent in the next 18 years in order to meet the target of building a well-off society in an all-round way. The realization of this goal cannot be separated from the role of entrepreneurs as a group. (4) It will be very difficult to solve the employment problem well. Their efforts will be needed even more in order to turn a portion of people in the low-income group into members of the middle-income group. The realities of China's economic and social development have already placed rather urgent demands on the establishment of such a system. Therefore, it is essential to advance the efforts to innovate the entrepreneurship system and expeditiously address the issue of materializing the value of those scarce entrepreneurs of the pioneering type who have come to the fore since the beginning of the reform and opening-up drive. A satisfactory solution to this issue will provide a good institutional foundation and policy environment for the solution of a series of other issues such as managers and employees holding shares.

II. Major Problems Facing the Innovation of the Entrepreneurship System in the New Stage of Reform

1. The mechanism for the nurturing of entrepreneurs. An entrepreneur is the epitome of abilities and qualities, which include mainly the ability to discern risks, the courage to take them and the capacity for innovation. Such abilities and qualities are the result of choice through the market, and cannot be made through administrative appointments. Whether the entrepreneurs-owners are non-public or private ones, or professional entrepreneurs, they have all come to the fore through the market. Therefore, the administrative system of appointing managers of SOEs and enterprises in which the state holds the controlling shares should be changed as quickly as possible to pave the way for a mechanism to nurture entrepreneurs mainly through the market. At the same time, the government should step up its efforts to develop the market for enterprise managers, set up a database on them, promote their rational flow by removing the sectoral and geographical restrictions on such a flow, and promote professionalism and socialization among them. It is necessary to set up a scientific training system which offers them systematic training in political theory and practice, moral ethics and corporate culture.

2. Enterprise founder mechanism. In the enterprise system of the West, a founder enjoys certain special prestige. A founder is the starter, representative and foundation-layer of an enterprise. China's enterprise system has not yet had an express stipulation on this point, nor is the value of a founder recognized in real life, still less materialized. Experience over the past two decades and more has shown that Chinese pioneering entrepreneurs have played the founders' role, either as those who started from scratch or as those who rejuvenated their enterprises. As the first group of entrepreneurs coming to the fore in the course of reform and opening up, they are trail blazers in developing their enterprises; they have made outstanding contributions in increasing the wealth of their enterprises by a big margin and played the chief role in promoting institutional innovation and corporate culture. The recognition of founders and the realization of their value will play an immeasurable role in enterprise growth and expansion of the ranks of entrepreneurs.

3. Risks taken by entrepreneurs and innovation mechanism. The courage to take risks and the capacity for innovation are the essential hallmarks of an entrepreneur. To expand their ranks, it is necessary to set up a risk and innovation mechanism, encouraging them to blaze new trails and make decisions boldly. It is necessary to shape an environment for innovative and pioneering managers to come forward.

4. Controlling power mechanism for entrepreneurs. In the modern market economy there are two important changes in enterprise institutional arrangements: (1) an enterprise shifts from being one run by the original unitary monetary owners to a community of interests comprising monetary owners, entrepreneurs and other interested parties. An enterprise is no longer one possessed by unitary monetary investors, but by common interested parties, including human capital as represented by entrepreneurs; (2) dominance of the enterprise by monetary owners has shifted to the enterprise governance structure with entrepreneurs playing a leading role. The modern enterprise system emphasizes the leading role of entrepreneurs in corporate governance structure. Only within this institutional arrangement, and coupled with other mechanisms, will it be possible to solve the problem of further development of the enterprise. The main problem we face now is that the leading role of entrepreneurs in the corporate governance structure has not been brought into full play. In such circumstances, an all-round introduction of the independent director system can hardly achieve the desired results of the policy designers.

5. Incentive mechanism for entrepreneurs. The incentive mechanism for entrepreneurs that we emphasize is not a simple type with salary plus bonuses, but one mainly based on property rights. Such an institutional arrangement has two effects: (1) what entrepreneurs want is an incentive mechanism based mainly on property rights as a demand of the risk mechanism on the incentive mechanism; (2) an incentive mechanism based mainly on property rights is an institutional foundation for bringing the initiative of entrepreneurs into play, and thus ties them closely to their enterprises for a long time.

6. Market assessment mechanism for entrepreneurs. The value of entrepreneurs is assessed in the market and materialized through competition in the market economy. At present, vigorous efforts should be made to develop and standardize intermediary organizations for assessing the value of entrepreneurs. To this end, regulations for assessors should be formulated, and so should regulations on fixing the value of their human capital and converting it into shares, as well as on details regarding the participation of managerial expertise in income distribution.

7. Entrepreneur credit mechanism. An entrepreneur alone is a symbol of credit. A person with poor credit cannot be an entrepreneur in the modern market economy. Since the building of a credit system in China faces a grim situation, entrepreneurs have a major responsibility in this endeavor. Therefore, it is necessary to establish and improve the credit appraisal and restraining mechanism for them.

8. Supervisory and restraining mechanism for entrepreneurs. Within the modern corporate governance structure in which entrepreneurs play a leading role, it is all the more necessary to tighten the internal and external supervision over and restraint on them. In building a corporate governance structure, China should draw on the CEO system of the US, as well as the supervisory board system of Germany and the employee participation programs of Japan.

9. Social security mechanism for entrepreneurs. This involves two major problems: (1) protection of their property; and (2) protection of their safety. China is at critical juncture of economic transition at the moment, and the right of entrepreneurs to own private property and enjoy social security is an important part of the effort to innovate the entrepreneurship system. A good solution to the above two problems will bring about a social environment enabling them to run their businesses without worries, and to succeed.

III. Policy Environment for Innovating the Entrepreneurship System in the New Stage of Reform

1. Quantification of state-owned assets. The establishment of an incentive mechanism for entrepreneurs, especially the one featuring rewards in property rights and purchase of property rights in SOEs and enterprises in which the state holds controlling shares cannot bypass the question of quantifying state-owned assets in actual operations. That is to say, since entrepreneurs, especially the pioneering ones, have led their enterprises in increasing the state assets by several billion, several dozen billion or even several hundred billion yuan over a period of 10 or 20 years, are they entitled to rewards in property rights out of a small portion of the net increase in state assets set aside for that purpose in recognition of their tremendous historical contributions? Facts show that such a practice will be beneficial to enterprise development, the increase of state-owned assets and the establishment of the entrepreneurship system. Therefore, such quantification should be recognized, encouraged and standardized. The problem is that there are not yet such policies or institutional arrangements. Moreover, some existing policies do not permit this. Some one-sided tendencies and thinking in terms of absolutes seem to have staked out this issue as a "forbidden area." People are exploring ways to directly combine entrepreneurs with the interests of enterprises in the course of developing a mixed-ownership economy. In my view, quantification of state-owned assets should not be rejected in a simplistic manner; what should be rejected is the use of illegitimate means to unconditionally quantify state-owned assets as rewards for those who have not contributed to the increased value of state-owned assets. We should permit the practice of compensating entrepreneurs who have made historical contributions out of a portion of the assets set aside from what they have contributed. Therefore, we should make a concrete analysis of the issue concerning the quantification of state-owned assets rather than reject it altogether.

2. The principle of "he who invests owns." This is a principle of the market economy. What needs to be pointed out here is that we should not interpret the word "investment" in a traditional, one-sided way. In the modern market economy, "investment" includes investment not only in money, but also in human capital and other factors of production, and, moreover, investment in human resources is playing an ever greater role. So far, some of our policies still equate "investment" with monetary investment. For example, a document issued in the early 1990s by relevant ministries and commissions of the State Council stated explicitly that the principle of "he who invests owns and gets the benefits" should be applied in accordance with the start-up investment of an enterprise. It also stated that the property belonging to collectives, individuals, or foreign governments and corporations but having no legal basis due to some historical or other reason should be defined as state-owned assets in accordance with the principle of special protection under state ownership. Such stipulations ignored the role of managerial expertise, work, technology and other factors of production in increasing the value of assets, have done much harm to the establishment of the entrepreneurship system and did not accord with the basic principles of the market economy. I suggest that major revisions be made to such policies in accordance with the guidelines of the report to the 16th CPC National Congress.

3. On the implementation of the principle that managerial expertise, as an important factor of production, participates in income distribution. The 15th CPC National Congress put forward the principle that managerial expertise, technology, capital and other factors of production were encouraged to participate in income distribution. What encouragements have we seen? More than five years have passed, yet we have not seen the relevant policy documents. Some localities and enterprises have instead been wrongly criticized for making experiments in accordance with the guidelines of the 15th CPC National Congress, and some entrepreneurs have got into trouble for doing this. The report to the 16th CPC National Congress once again stated explicitly that it was essential to establish the principle that work, capital, technology, managerial expertise and other factors of production participate in the distribution of income. It represented a big step further than the report to the previous congress, going beyond "encouragement" to call for establishing the principle that managerial expertise and other factors of production participate in income distribution. We earnestly hope that the competent government departments will soon come up with relevant policies and regulations in accordance with the guidelines of the 16th CPC National Congress, and at the same time allow the localities and enterprises to make explorations in the reform in accordance with these guidelines.

4. On financing policies related to entrepreneurs holding shares. In the US, ESOP (including managers holding shares) does not require managers or employees to pay a single cent; it is up to the enterprises to provide guarantees for bank loans, to be paid back by instalments with money from annual dividends on property rights. Under the loan terms, managers in most cases are required to hold no fewer than 10 percent of the total shares held by the employees, and relevant laws provide that such loans are exempt from interest tax. In China, relevant laws and regulations do not allow enterprises to provide guarantees for bank loans borrowed to finance the scheme of managers and employees holding shares. In some cases, managers and employees have been criticized for purchasing shares from their enterprises with their own money. It should be made clear that in China, managers and employees holding shares is a kind of risk investment and designed to form a community of interests between managers and employees on the one hand and their enterprise on the other. Therefore, it is necessary to create conditions in many ways for establishing a property rights incentive system for entrepreneurs, especially relevant policies and regulations on financing. Pending a proper solution to this question, it is unavoidable that various distorted methods or even erroneous practices should crop up in the course of finding sources of funds.

5. On revising the Company Law. Since China's Company Law is essentially based on the system of paid cash money, some stipulations are not entirely reasonable; whether on the paid capital system or company guarantees, they have a major impact on the innovation of the entrepreneurship system. I suggest making some major revisions to the Company Law in light of the actual conditions with regard to the development of the market economy, and in accordance with the guidelines of the 16th CPC National Congress. In addition, laws and regulations on securities, taxation and banking should be revised with a view to providing a legal guarantee and a good policy environment for materializing the value of entrepreneurs.

DEFINITION OF THE VALUE OF CHINA'S PIONEERING ENTREPRENEURS

(April 2002)

The growth of entrepreneurs is one of the hallmarks of the market economy in China. After more than 20 years of reform and opening up, China has initially brought into being a group of entrepreneurs with Chinese characteristics worthy of being called pioneering entrepreneurs. They are most valuable assets. They share something in common: (1) they are bold in innovation, adept at tackling problems, and dare to run risks; (2) they have a sharp eye for market opportunities, and are good at grasping them; (3) they are strong leaders; (4) they are far-sighted, credit-conscious and decisive, and show strong will; and (5) they have made exceptional achievements in enterprise management.

It is of considerable urgency to recognize and realize the value of pioneering entrepreneurs. (1) They are lowly paid and at least half of them are faced with a dilemma as regards the "age-59 phenomenon." (2) Since the enterprises they lead are generally leaders in their own industries, the question of realizing their value will not only have a direct bearing on the survival and development of their own enterprises, but also have a certain impact on the competitiveness of an entire industry.

The acute shortage of entrepreneurs is a serious problem confronting China, now a member of the WTO. Pioneering entrepreneurs are outstanding representatives of Chinese entrepreneurs and role models for the latter. An early recognition and realization of their value will generate a favorable impact on the formation of a contingent of Chinese entrepreneurs.

I. Two Major Roles of Pioneering Entrepreneurs in Chinese Enterprises

To recognize the value of pioneering entrepreneurs, it is necessary first of all to recognize their great role in their enterprises. They have proved by their examples that they have made outstanding contributions to the significant growth of their enterprises, advanced the innovations of the enterprise system, and nurtured corporate culture. They have played a major role in upgrading China's industries and improving their competitiveness, and at the same time performed meritorious services in adjusting the country's ownership structure.

1. Pioneering entrepreneurs are the chief representatives of enterprise communities of interests. They consciously represent the interests of their enterprises and shoulder the responsibilities of organizing resources, and running and expanding enterprises on behalf of the owners, closely linking their lot with the success or failure and rise or fall of their enterprises, and maximizing the common interests of the enterprises' beneficiaries while pursuing their career development. To realize their full value, it is necessary to make them shoulder greater responsibilities as owners of enterprise property rights, and play a full role as the "chief representatives" of the communities of enterprise interests.

2. Pioneering entrepreneurs are those who are both advocates and doers in the innovation of the enterprise system. In the course of the market-oriented reform, especially in the reform of the SOEs, an effective corporate governance structure is what entrepreneurs work on and achieve in their innovative activities. Pioneering entrepreneurs consciously act as representatives of enterprise owners and, with a deep understanding of the need for enterprise development for a standardized corporate governance structure, vigorously advance the formation of such a structure, and cultivate corporate culture. A standard corporate governance structure and a special corporate culture in turn provide the entrepreneurs with a highly efficient management platform.

II. Two Shifts in Modern Enterprise Institutional Arrangements

Success stories of pioneering Chinese entrepreneurs have shown that the value of entrepreneurs is closely related to their positions and roles in their enterprises. An important reason why modern enterprise institutional arrangements emphasize and give prominence to their role is the swiftly rising role of human capital with entrepreneurs as the main group. Especially with the fast growth of the knowledge-based economy since the 1990s, the position of entrepreneurs in the corporate governance structure has risen markedly, as reflected in the following two shifts:

1. The shift from the traditional enterprise system which mainly emphasised the core role of monetary capital in the enterprise to the modern enterprise system under which monetary capital, human capital (with entrepreneurs as the core) and other beneficiaries of enterprise interests act together. In the traditional enterprise system, human capital and other non-monetary capital factors were basically not entitled to the distribution of surplus of the enterprise, while under the modern enterprise system, human capital, with entrepreneurs as the main body, has not only acquired the right to participate in the distribution of the surplus of the enterprise, but enjoys an ever more important position in the structure of enterprise property rights. This is especially obvious in hi-tech enterprises.

2. The shift from the investor-centered corporate governance structure to the entrepreneur-led governance structure. Within the traditional corporate governance structure, the core of the power to run an enterprise was the board of directors, representing its owners, while the entrepreneurs were so-called "senior employees" hired by the owners, and had very limited management power. In the modern enterprise system, agency cost as a result of information asymmetry has received growing attention, and entrepreneurs have acquired increasingly greater actual control of enterprise management, and become the core of the corporate governance structure.

III. Two Types of Values for Pioneering Entrepreneurs

The two major roles of pioneering entrepreneurs in enterprises show that an entrepreneur without property rights is not a modern entrepreneur in the real sense, nor is an entrepreneur without full decision-making management powers a true entrepreneur.

1. Pioneering entrepreneurs should become owners of enterprise property rights. This has two meanings. First, an entrepreneur is an important creator of the enterprise's wealth, and to form a community of interests between him and the enterprise by converting his human capital into shares is the main form of materializing his value and the most important content of the incentive mechanism for entrepreneurs. Second, entrepreneurs' actually holding a portion of enterprise property rights is an important condition for them to fully exercise the decision-making power in management. The reform of the SOEs in China is in a critical period, and making entrepreneurs, especially pioneering ones, into partial owners of enterprise property rights through the reform of property rights system will have a many-sided positive impact on the development of the enterprises.

2. Pioneering entrepreneurs should become leaders in the corporate governance structure. The role of entrepreneurs is reflected not only in the materialization of their own interests, which has a direct bearing on the development of their enterprises, but also in their leadership of enterprise management. Entrepreneurs of the pioneering type have shown, by their successful examples, that enterprises in which entrepreneurs have bigger decision-making powers in management have shown more effective management and faster development than the others, and are more favorable to the establishment of an effective corporate governance structure. In the modern market economy, the first and foremost aim of our effort to urge and emphasize the establishment of a standard modern corporate government structure is to enable entrepreneurs to display their role more fully.

IV. Two Forms of Realizing Enterprise Equity Rights for Pioneering Entrepreneurs

The issue of entrepreneurs holding shares has caught growing attention. The holding of equity rights for entrepreneurs of the pioneering type is different in some ways from that for those of the general type, because the former aims not only to set up an incentive mechanism for entrepreneurs, but more importantly to solve the question of recognizing the great contributions of pioneering entrepreneurs as well as their special position and role in the enterprises, and compensating them. Therefore, equity rights for pioneering entrepreneurs should be realized by following the principle of combining purchase and free distribution of shares with due consideration to both incentives and distribution, and to both the past and the future.

1. Give incentives in equity rights to pioneering entrepreneurs. Pioneering entrepreneurs are important contributors to enterprise wealth. To make them partial owners of enterprise equity rights is a materialization of their value, and meets the need to establish a community of enterprise interests. In view of this and proceeding from the actual conditions in China, it is essential to give incentives in equity rights to pioneering entrepreneurs, that is, relevant government departments or the authorized state assets management agencies they designate shall convert a portion of the net increase of state (or collective) assets into equity rights as rewards for pioneering entrepreneurs in accordance with their actual contributions to their enterprises, in recognition of and as compensation for their value.

2. Pioneering entrepreneurs should be allowed to buy, out of their own money, a limited portion of equity rights at set prices. When they buy enterprise equity rights, they will be better able to share risks with other owners of the enterprises and achieve an identity of interests with the enterprises in the latter's development.

In actual practice, different types of enterprises should be allowed to adopt different designs of incentives in equity rights and the buying of equity rights in light of concrete conditions. Various factors should be balanced in setting the amount and percentage of equity rights that will go to pioneering entrepreneurs as incentives and be sold to them, with the ratio between incentives and sales roughly balanced, say at a ratio of one to one. Different types of pioneering entrepreneurs (for example, those who have started from scratch, those who have rejuvenated their enterprises, and those who have distinguished themselves in the reform of the SOEs) should be differentiated in the amount of the equity rights they are entitled to and the ratio between those to be awarded as incentives and those to be sold to them.

V. Two Ways to Ensure Full Decision-making Powers in Management to Pioneering Entrepreneurs

1. Practicing the CEO system by drawing on the experience of foreign corporate governance structure, and gradually institutionalising it. The emergence of the CEO system has reflected the general trend in the evolution of the modern enterprise system. The board of directors vests greater power and responsibilities in the CEO, and at the same time grants him the corresponding right to share the enterprise surplus and benefit from the enterprise's increased assets (such as options). In China, pioneering entrepreneurs have been playing the *de facto* role of CEOs, assuming much greater responsibilities than those of enterprise managers in general. Hence, they have been able to show a good record of achievements. Their CEO role is mainly a result of personal prestige and charisma rather than institutionalization. I suggest that the CEO system be introduced to enterprises with better conditions, and institutionalized.

2. Making a breakthrough in the reform of the state assets management system by placing the responsibilities of state-owned equity rights on pioneering entrepreneurs. Practice shows that authorized management of state capital by pioneering entrepreneurs is an effective method of state-owned property rights management. Because of the special affinity they have formed with their enterprises, they regard the enterprises as their own lot or even what they stand for, so they can consciously play the role as the representative of the owners. By so doing, the responsibility of management can be ensured to the fullest in the interests of the effort to keep and increase the value of state assets.

VI. Two Proposals Concerning the Recognition and Materialization of the Value of Pioneering Entrepreneurs

The materialization of the value of pioneering entrepreneurs involves two aspects — past and future. The main form of materializing their future value is to ensure their right to participate in the distribution of the surplus of the enterprise through institutional innovations; the materialization of their past value is policy sensitive, for it involves the adjustment of the stock of assets.

1. It is essential to make, in light of the actual progress in the reform of SOEs, a concrete analysis of the question concerning the quantification of state-owned assets, apply different practices to different situations and, in the spirit of advancing with the

times, make timely adjustments and breakthroughs. Those SOEs whose pioneering entrepreneurs have really made outstanding contributions to the increase of their net assets should set aside a portion of the increased assets as rewards for the entrepreneurs on the basis of objective assessment. This should not be regarded as a drain on state assets, but rather as recompense for their labor, and a full recognition and affirmation of their contributions. It will serve to provide greater incentives to entrepreneurs and be beneficial to the stable development of the SOEs, and to maintaining and increasing the value of state assets.

Of course, an unconditional quantification of state assets for those entrepreneurs who have not contributed to the maintaining and increasing of the value of state assets should be resolutely opposed. Supervisory efforts should be intensified, with the aim of preventing such moves as to quantify for selfish purposes and encroach on state assets.

2. It is necessary to give a new and all-sided interpretation to the principle of "he who invests owns." A modern enterprise's process of investing in production is in fact a process of joint input of non-human capital and human capital, and their joint working to create wealth. Under the new economic and technological conditions, the role of human capital has become ever more prominent. In the process of economic transition, it is not an all-sided approach to emphasize only the control power and residual claim of the investors in material capital without recognizing the usufruct of the investors in human capital. The human capital of pioneering entrepreneurs is pivotal to the formation and increase of enterprise assets in the process of their development and their investment in a form of human capital should be entitled to reasonable returns.

The principle set forward at the Fourth Plenary Session of the 15th CPC Central Committee that the distribution in accordance with work and the distribution in accordance with factors of production should be combined and its guideline that technology, managerial expertise and other factors of production should be allowed and encouraged to participate in the distribution of enterprise profits have in principle provided the basis for entrepreneurs to participate in the distribution of enterprise profits. Active and bold experiments with ways for their human capital to participate in the distribution should be allowed.

VII. Two Guarantees for Realizing the Value of Pioneering Entrepreneurs

In China's current social, legal and institutional environment, the government has an especially important role to play in bringing about an environment favorable to the existence and development of entrepreneurs. To recognize and realize the value of pioneering entrepreneurs, it is necessary to solve in the course of actual work a series of contradictions and problems, among which the provision of effective protection for their private property right and the formation of a market mechanism for recruiting managers are the most important institutional guarantees.

1. The establishment of a market mechanism for recruiting and administering entrepreneurs is the most important institutional guarantee for realizing the value of pioneering entrepreneurs and forming a contingent of entrepreneurs. The work involved includes doing away with administrative ranks for managers of the SOEs, and the administrative procedure of appointing and removing them; introducing in an all-round way the professional manager system of modern enterprises by which managers are recruited through the market and appointed by the board of directors; accelerate the reform of the proprietary system in the SOEs so as to turn the SOEs into true players in the market economy; abandoning the practice of administering, encouraging and restraining entrepreneurs through administrative means, and establishing a market-oriented incentive and distribution system in keeping with enterprise management and future development; and assessing, supervising and restraining them through institutional, legal and economic means. At the same time, it is necessary to develop qualified intermediaries and legal service providers for assessing the value of entrepreneurs.

2. To provide legal protection to private property rights of entrepreneurs. Private property rights of entrepreneurs including the property as a result of their legal business and honest work, the rights that pioneering entrepreneurs have obtained as a reward to their outstanding contributions to enterprise development and the right of entrepreneurs to participate in the distribution of the surplus of the enterprises on account of their investment in the form of human capital should all be approved at the policy level, and placed under strict legal protection.

THE PRACTICE OF ESOP IN CHINA NEEDS TO BE STANDARDIZED

(*August Issue of* Reform in China, *2001*)

Experimentation with ESOP has been going on in China for several years, but on the whole it is still at the exploratory stage. However, as China practices the market economy, and the current-stage reform to tackle the hard issues focuses on the tasks of readjusting interest relations and balancing interest groups, more and more Chinese enterprises are taking the initiative in adopting ESOP.

Now, Chinese enterprises are adopting ESOP extensively and in an all-round way; not only medium-sized and small SOEs in their multitudes but also some large SOEs and non-state owned ones are experimenting with it. In such circumstances, we suggest that relevant government departments standardize the work by institutionalizing it, and take the initiative in advancing its sound development.

I. ESOP in Chinese enterprises should move from the extensive experimental stage to the stage of standardized development.

1. Along with the deepening of SOE reform and advance of the proprietary system reform, ESOP is already widely adopted in China.

At present, an increasing number of enterprises have adopted

ESOP through various forms in the course of enterprise reform, gradually shaping a general trend in the reform of the proprietary system.

(1) There has been a considerable number of enterprises that have adopted ESOP, and more will follow suit. In terms of trades, it has spread from enterprises in the foreign trade and economic cooperation sector that were among the earliest to experiment with standardized ESOP to virtually all enterprises in competitive areas and some monopolistic trades. In geographical terms, in addition to Shenzhen, Beijing, Shanghai, Jiangsu and other coastal provinces and municipalities, pilot projects have been conducted in central and western provinces such as Yunnan, Guizhou and Gansu and the Ningxia Hui Autonomous Region. In terms of enterprise scale, in addition to medium-sized and small SOEs, which have generally adopted ESOP, some large SOEs have introduced it in the course of transforming their ownership system, or are actively planning to do so. In terms of enterprise type, it has been introduced into not only non-listed SOEs, but also into some non-SOEs and listed companies.

(2) Close to 30 provinces and municipalities directly under the central government have come up with relevant regulations concerning ESOP, in order to standardize and advance the work in their own localities. However, such regulations vary greatly from place to place, since some provinces and municipalities have issued them in the name of the government while others in the name of functional government departments. In some provinces, the trade union federations have drawn up the regulations and are charged with the responsibility to implement them, while in other cases, the economic restructuring departments of the government have done the job. In some provinces, such regulations have been issued not only at the provincial level, but also at the prefectural level or even county level. This has led to a variety of practices and modes of ESOP, for example, the Beijing mode, featuring ESOP societies as independent social legal entities, the Shanghai mode, which relies on trade unions of enterprises to carry out such activities, the Shenzhen mode, featuring industrial and

commercial registration of ESOP societies with trade unions as their basis, and the Jiangsu mode, by which employees hold stocks either directly or through ESOP societies.

(3) Some provinces and municipalities have listed legislation on ESOP in their near-term legislation plans. Standing committees of the people's congresses of these provinces and municipalities have listed such legislation in their legislation plans for the coming years in order to avoid various problems in the course of experimentation and extension of ESOP, and provide a stable institutional environment for the work. Such local efforts will provide useful experience for the subsequent formulation of national norms.

(4) A number of intermediaries and agencies have come into being to provide consultancy services concerning ESOP, in keeping with the extensive spreading of the practice. But some intermediaries are professional, while others are not; some are independent consultancy firms or law offices having legal person status, while others are affiliated to research institutes and do not have the status of an independent legal person. Some have already worked out standard and sound operational procedures, and are staffed with qualified professionals. A case in point is the foreign trade and economic cooperation sector, which has brought about a lawyer-based standard ESOP consultancy system by training leading coordination lawyers and putting in place a qualification verification system. In contrast, some are poorly staffed, and have got involved in the field just to make money. This augurs ill for their client enterprises.

2. The early formulation of nationwide norms is an issue that cannot be bypassed, since the ownership transformation of SOEs involves the reduction of state-owned shares, protection of the rights and interests of state-owned shares, and especially compensation for employees of SOEs.

From the perspective of establishing a modern enterprise system, the introduction of ESOP is beneficial to changing the unitary property rights structure of the SOEs and practicing diverse ownership, and is an important way for the withdrawal of state capital from general competitive fields and reduction of state-owned shares. Introduction of ESOP, combined with cash input and substitution of existing assets to bring in non-governmental capital, is yet another effective way to withdraw state capital to make way for non-governmental capital. There are numerous practical problems yet to be tackled regarding how to strike a balance between protecting the rights and interests of state-owned assets and giving compensation to employees of the SOEs who have made contributions to their enterprises, in the course of assessing and confirming the value of the assets of the original enterprises, and setting up and issuing employee stocks. In the face of limited access to direct financing, many enterprises have offered preferential treatment in ESOP by giving some benefits to employees in order to pool funds for enterprise development and win employee endorsement for the transformation of enterprise ownership. Various localities have also paid some compensation to SOE employees in proportion to their historical contributions when the latter are asked to sever their ties with the SOEs, and have come up with a series of preferential policies regarding ESOP. The purpose is to shape an environment favorable to the reform of the proprietary system of the SOEs. But different localities differ widely in standards for paying compensation to employees, in the proportion of shares to be distributed and in the margin of preferential treatment to those employees who were paid their shares in one lump sum. There is also a lack of rigorous procedures for confirming and assessing state assets, or whatever procedure there is cannot be strictly followed. Failure to address these problems at an early date will bring many adverse effects on the ownership transformation of the SOEs and the work of reducing state-owned shares. The need to standardize the work of reducing state-owned shares, prevent a drain on them, and protect the rights and interests of state assets urgently requires unified stipulations concerning the qualifications of agencies for assessing state assets in the course of enterprise ownership reform, as well as in paying compensation to SOE employees.

3. As ESOP is increasingly linked with income distribution among employees, an early establishment of unified norms will be of important significance to rationalizing relations of income distribution, and adjusting relations of interest in the current stage.

To a certain extent, the process of reform is one of readjusting the original relations of interest. The reform of the SOEs is in essence aimed at rationally readjusting the interest relations between the state and enterprises, between an enterprise and its employees and between employees at different levels within the same enterprise, constructing a community of interest between an enterprise and its employees and maximizing the interests of various beneficiaries. Due to the differences in the industries in which specific enterprises are operating, uneven progress in ownership transformation and the changes in the country's overall pattern of income distribution, ESOP has become increasingly linked with employees' income distribution. This has been conspicuously manifested in the fact that most SOEs have adopted the method of singling out the best assets from the main body, and turning them into the joint-stock system first, with the result that the employees of the remaining enterprise earn less than those of the joint-stock enterprises who hold enterprise stocks; numerous laid-off workers of SOEs who live off existence allowances with the historical compensation still eluding them have much lower incomes than the employees of many strong enterprises who hold enterprise shares; and with the incentive and restraint mechanism in place in many SOEs, the income gap between principal managerial and professional staff and employees in general keeps widening. These outstanding contradictions and problems are important factors impeding the process of transforming the ownership of the SOEs, as well as practical problems adversely affecting social stability. To consider and advance the standardization of ESOP at a higher level will have an important and lasting impact on the rationalization of the income distribution order and the adjustment of the interest relations, because this institutional change will bear on the vital interests of the masses of employees as China's transition process picks up speed.

II. Expediting the Formulation of Unified Norms to Facilitate Sound and Orderly Development of ESOP

1. The aim of expediting the formulation of unified norms should be to promote the sound and orderly development of ESOP.

The fundamental institutional changes stemming from the economic restructuring over the past two decades and more have changed China's economic structure and the environment for enterprise operations in many ways, generating a tremendous impact on the internal proprietary structure and operating mechanism of enterprises. This is the background against which ESOP has come to the fore in China. In the knowledge-based economy or new economy, human capital is the most important element of the core competitiveness of an enterprise. Facing the WTO and economic globalization, how to construct an enterprise incentive and restraining mechanism compatible with the requirements of international market competition so as to attract and keep high-level managerial and professional personnel for improved competitiveness is a pressing task for Chinese enterprises of various types, especially the SOEs. It is a general practice in the market economy for enterprises to act upon the theories of modern enterprises, practice the system of managers holding shares and ESOP in a variety of forms, fully develop human resources, establish the critical role of human capital in the development of modern enterprises, and standardize and improve the corporate governance structure. The introduction of

ESOP is of immediate significance in addressing the "age-59 phenomenon" widely prevalent in the course of enterprise reform and development, preventing the drain on the best brain of enterprises, and encouraging the SOEs to shift their mechanisms. It is also linked with the reform of the income distribution system, and improvement of the social security system. Practice shows that ESOP as an innovation of the proprietary system has lasting vitality in the period of economic transition. Therefore, standardizing the ways for Chinese enterprises to introduce ESOP will have a far-reaching influence on China's social and economic development during the period of economic transition.

2. The core of the effort to formulate unified norms should be to create conditions and provide support for an orderly advance of ESOP in many ways.

Proceeding from the actual conditions in the country, and drawing on international experience, various localities have given some policy support and preferential treatment to employees in the course of introducing ESOP. The preferential treatment includes preferential terms for asset transfers to employees and those for payment in a single lump sum; preferential treatment in tax on dividends; and preferential treatment for those dividends that are reinvested directly. Such policy support and preferential treatment have created favorable conditions for smooth enterprise ownership transformation. The introduction of ESOP, by turning a portion of state assets into stocks for sale to employees in a change of proprietary rights, is beneficial to ensuring maintaining and increasing the value of state assets, promoting a thoroughgoing change in the operating mechanism of the SOEs, and achieving a strategic reorganization and structural adjustment of the state economic sector. At the same time, by transferring state-owned property rights, the government also transfers risks in the management of state assets while increasing risk responsibilities of enterprise managers and employees. The enterprise managers and employees will be subject to considerably greater risks and pressures after their enterprises have introduced the joint-stock system. The employees in such enterprises will no longer keep their original status as employees of the SOEs, and, except for social security, their income and benefits will depend entirely on how their enterprises fare in the market competition. In such circumstances, the government should give support to ESOP in banking, taxation and other related areas by drawing on international experience and in reference to the policies related to the ownership transformation of small SOEs, for that will be of positive significance in advancing ESOP. In addition, in the situation featuring economic transition, the employees should be allowed to pay for shares in the form of human capital. This will greatly help them, because they often do not have enough money to buy shares, while constituting a form of turning knowledge or human capital into shares. At present, the pooling of human capital for shares is faced with difficulties, which, among other things, are expressed in technicalities in legislation. Therefore, it is necessary to seriously study and specify guidelines and methods of assessing human capital to pave the way for those employees who need to buy shares with human capital.

3. The focal point in establishing the unified norms is to work out an early solution to the problems extensively encountered in the introduction of ESOP.

Despite the differences among various localities in their specific regulations concerning ESOP, they have encountered many common problems in practice. The problems that call for close examination include:

First, the scope of applicability of ESOP. As current practice shows, the arrangement for the applicability of ESOP has been made roughly from the following three angles: First, restrictions in terms of types of enterprises. For example, some places have stipulated that ESOP is limited to enterprises with sole state investment and those in which the state holds controlling shares; some have stipulated that it applies only to limited-liability companies and share-holding cooperative enterprises; and others have included the listed companies. Second, restrictions in terms of industries in which the enterprises operate. For example, some places have excluded state monopolies, and some other special trades and enterprises; and others have stipulated that only enterprises with good economic returns are eligible. Third, restrictions in terms of nature of enterprise. For example, restrictions are placed on the applicability of ESOP in relation to the different nature of enterprises, namely, SOEs, collective enterprises and Sino-foreign joint ventures. In our view, ESOP is widely applicable in this special period of economic and social transition in China, and enterprises with better conditions should be allowed and encouraged to decide on their own to introduce ESOP under the precondition of following the unified norms.

Second, establishment of ESOP and the source of shares. The source of shares is the first problem that an enterprise will encounter in introducing ESOP. As far as the forms to obtain equity rights are concerned, the regulations of various localities fall mainly into three categories: a) issuing additional shares; b) combining the issuing of additional shares with sale of existing assets and transfer of equity rights; and c) launching of ESOP.

In actual practice, the form of issuing additional shares for the introduction of ESOP is more readily accepted by the original investors of an enterprise (mainly state investors). Transfer of equity rights for ESOP is still quite controversial at present. The most important problems are: a) Determining the scope of the asset transfer. Some provinces and municipalities have stipulated that assets for transfer in the ownership transformation of the SOEs generally refer to those profit-oriented assets whose property rights have been determined and whose value has been assessed, while the way to treat the non-profit-oriented assets is generally to separate them completely and, after equity right determination and value assessment, hand them over to organizations authorized by the state assets management agencies for management. However, some localities did not specify the scope of assets for transfer, so some enterprises have transferred non-profit-oriented assets in the course of ownership transformation. Views are seriously divergent on whether it is right to transfer non-profit-oriented assets together with profit-oriented ones, and what should be the principles and standards for such transfers. b) On the handling of invisible assets. The documents of many localities do not contain express stipulations on the value assessment and handling of invisible assets of enterprises. Nevertheless, it is a problem that enterprises cannot bypass in ownership transformation.

Third, proportions of shares for employees. Most localities do not specify the proportions of shares to be held by the employees. Some places do have restrictions on the proportions, but vary in actual figures. For example, some localities have graded proportions in accordance with the total capital stock of the enterprises — the smaller the total capital stock an enterprise has, the higher the proportion of shares to be held by the employees of that enterprise. Some have placed a ceiling on the proportion, while others have set the lowest proportion. We are of the opinion that since enterprises differ in the localities and trades they operate, nature, type and scale, it would be inappropriate to set unified proportions of shares, but should leave it to the enterprises to decide at shareholders' meetings.

Fourth, source of funds for ESOP. To sum up, actual operations involve the following methods: employees' cash payment; bank loans; lending to employees from enterprise public welfare funds; bonuses for net increases of enterprise assets; conversion of patents and technological know-how into shares; conversion of enterprises' surplus wages and bonuses into shares; and shares resulting from other lawful means. Pilot projects show that employees' cash payment is the main form, but diverse forms are developing. This reflects to a certain extent the historical nature and adaptability of ESOP during China's economic transition. But, so far, many key issues related to the source of funds for ESOP remain to be clarified, such as the legal basis for converting human capital into shares and assessment, and provision of loans by banks and other banking institutions.

Fifth, ratios of shares among employees. The localities differ greatly in the ratio of shares between the managers of an enterprise and the employees in general. For example, some localities have set a ceiling; others have graded the highest proportions in accordance with the scale of enterprise assets; and still others have set the threshold and the lowest proportions in an effort to encourage managers to become big shareholders. The scale of equity rights involved in the ownership transformation of medium-sized and small enterprises is not big, and the gap among employees in the amount of shares held is not big either. But in the case of enterprises having a big scale of assets or offering a large amount of shares for employees, there should be institutional standardization and clarification on what exactly is the proportion for ESOP, what should be the proper limits of the gap among employees in the amount of shares held and how to balance fairness and efficiency in the introduction of ESOP.

Sixth, forms of ESOP. Should the employees hold shares directly or indirectly through intermediaries? Should such intermediaries be established inside enterprises or should outside intermediaries be commissioned? These questions are bones of contention for various localities in introducing ESOP, and also key links in advancing it. In actual practice, most provinces have provided that employees should hold shares by establishing ESOP societies or similar organizations. For example, Beijing, Shanghai, Tianjin, Nanjing, Shaanxi, Ningxia and other places have enacted express stipulations to that effect. Some provinces and municipalities allow employees to hold shares directly or indirectly through ESOP societies. We suggest that China, by following international practice and also taking into consideration its concrete conditions, should operate ESOP under institutional management as far as possible.

Seventh, the organization and nature of ESOP. Many localities provide that employees should hold shares by establishing ESOP societies. Generally speaking, an ESOP society is a legal entity exercising the shareholders' rights on behalf of all shareholding employees in a unified way, yet its legal status has not yet been confirmed in a unified way, which is an outstanding problem. At present, there are several different stipulations concerning the organization and nature of ESOP societies. In some places they are defined as social bodies having legal entity status and need to register with local civil affairs departments. In other places they are established with trade union organizations as the support and operate in the capacity of trade unions as legal entities. And in still other places, they are established with trade union organizations as the support and need to register with local industrial and commercial administration departments. In addition, some places are experimenting with appointing common trustees, who can be employees of the same enterprise or natural or legal persons outside the enterprise. These stipulations lack a definite legal basis, are filled with various institutional flaws and need to be unified and standardized.

Eighth, management of employees' equity rights. Stipulations on the management of employees' equity rights involve the rights and interests of the employees in question. In China, most provinces and municipalities have a "no-transfer" clause in their provisional rules or trial regulations on ESOP. As China's economy is in a special period of transition and the enterprises face complex circumstances, whether or not to allow employees to transfer and inherit their shares under certain conditions is a question yet to be studied. Our view is that the employees usually receive support from the state and enterprises in raising funds to buy shares, and if they were allowed to transfer shares without any restrictions, this would not only lead to the disintegration of ESOP but also negatively affect the securities market, thus touching off a series of social problems. Therefore, we suggest that withdrawal, transfer and inheritance of employees' shares should be prohibited in principle, and that only when they retire or leave their enterprises on death, transfer elsewhere, resign or are laid off should they be allowed to transfer the shares they actually hold to other employees in accordance with the law or the ESOP societies may buy back the shares they actually hold within the legally set deadlines.

III. Promoting Unification and Standardization of ESOP in a Stage-by-Stage, Flexible and Practical Manner

1. Separate regulations or guidelines on ESOP should be issued as soon as possible by the State Council or with its approval.

Considering the fact that the introduction of ESOP involves a number of functional departments of the government, the State Council should formulate and publicize separate regulations or relevant stipulations on ESOP at an early date under the prerequisite of overall planning, in an effort to unify and standardize the practices concerning ESOP. Or competent functional departments could study and formulate relevant guidelines to be issued with the approval of the State Council.

2. Standardizing in accordance with classification, by which various ministries and commissions come up with guidelines concerning their own fields of work.

The unification and standardization of ESOP practices may also involve the method of standardizing in accordance with classification, by which the competent ministries and commissions formulate norms for different types of enterprises. For example, first, the China Securities Regulatory Commission, in cooperation with other agencies, comes up with regulations on ESOP for listed companies, which will be of immediate significance for improving the management of ESOP of the listed companies and existing internal employees' shares. Second, the State Economic and Trade Commission takes the lead in formulating regulations on ESOP for large and medium-sized SOEs in cooperation with other departments. Third, various specialized functional ministries and commissions formulate regulations on ESOP for special trades and enterprises.

3. From the long-term point of view, it is necessary to eliminate restrictive articles or add relevant ones when revising the Company Law, to leave room for ESOP.

Considering the need for consistency with the existing laws and the close relations between ESOP and the Company Law, we suggest that relevant articles be added in connection with the revision of the Company Law, which is being contemplated, making corresponding adjustments and necessary stipulations on important contents concerning ESOP.

4. Revising the relevant articles in the banking, taxation and other laws and regulations, to create the environment and conditions favorable to ESOP.

Banks should be allowed to provide credit services for ESOP on preferential terms. To this end, it is necessary, first of all, to relax relevant legal restrictions on banks and other banking institutions to provide low-interest loans for ESOP. Second, it is necessary to relax policies on mortgage loans to allow employees to mortgage securities and immovable property for loans to buy shares. Third, other shareholders of an enterprise should be allowed to guarantee the enterprise's borrowing of money from banks on behalf of the employees who buy shares, with the capital and interest to be paid back out of the dividends from the employees' shares. Fourth, enterprises introducing ESOP should be entitled to preferential treatment in credit services.

Full use of the lever of taxation should be made to support the introduction of ESOP. The government's provision of incentives in taxation to the interest parties is the main factor behind the success of ESOP in other countries. Government preferential treatment in taxation includes: 1) a tax holiday of 3-5 years, during which the income of banks and other banking institutions from interest on the loans in support of ESOP are exempt from taxes in accordance with a fixed percentage; b) the part of the dividends from ESOP that has been used to pay back bank loans is exempt from personal income tax; c) the dividends that are not cashed for direct consumption but reinvested in the enterprise should be exempt from personal income tax; and d) when enterprise wage funds are converted into shares, they should enjoy preferential treatment in taxation.

5. The localities and enterprises should be allowed and encouraged to actively experiment under the prerequisite of unified norms.

The enterprises differ widely from one locality to another, and their institutional conditions are not entirely the same. Under the prerequisite of unified norms and along with further progress in the development of ESOP, the government should adopt an open and flexible attitude by allowing places with better conditions to explore a variety of ways for standardization.

6. Including legislation on ESOP in the legislation plan for the next 3-5 years in order to provide a solid legal guarantee for ESOP.

The market economy is in essence an economy based on a legal system. The process to speed up the standardization of the ESOP work is also one of gradually providing a legal basis for it. At present, administrative regulations and relevant policies on the subject are only transitional measures. For the ultimate standardization in this respect, institutional construction has yet to be placed on the legislative agenda. Only legislation will be able to provide the appropriate stable and solid institutional guarantee for ESOP.

图书在版编目（CIP）数据

中国：改革进入新阶段 / 迟福林 著.
—北京：外文出版社，2004.1
ISBN 7–119–03484–7
Ⅰ. 中... Ⅱ. 迟... Ⅲ. 经济体制改革－研究－中国－英文
Ⅳ. F121
中国版本图书馆 CIP 数据核字（2003）第 094286 号

英文翻译	王宗引
英文审定	李振国
责任编辑	胡开敏
装帧设计	蔡 荣
印刷监制	张国祥

中国：改革进入新阶段

迟福林 著

*

©外文出版社
外文出版社出版
（中国北京百万庄大街 24 号）
邮政编码 100037
外文出版社网址 http://www.flp.com.cn
外文出版社电子信箱: info@flp.com.cn
sales@flp.com.cn

三河市汇鑫印务有限公司印刷
中国国际图书贸易总公司发行
（中国北京车公庄西路 35 号）
北京邮政信箱第 399 号 邮政编码 100044
2004 年（小 16 开）第 1 版
2004 年 1 月第 1 版第 1 次印刷
（英）
ISBN 7–119–03484–7/Z·682（外）
08600
17–E–3591P